For the memory of

Ann Brightmore-Armour, one of many
Ricardians who sadly passed away while
I was writing and recording my songs
about Richard III and

the Wars of the Roses.

SONGS ABOUT RICHARD III
(2022 revised edition)

by
Ian Churchward

Introduction by Kathy E Martin

Little boosts a fiction writer's confidence more than the knowledge that their work has made a lasting impact on a reader. A glowing review on Amazon is wonderful, as is a complimentary letter sent to the author care of their publisher. Knowing that a stranger has been sufficiently moved by one's literary endeavours to express their appreciation in writing is heart-warming and extremely encouraging. But what if that stranger is also a creative type, a song writer perhaps, who finds himself so inspired by one's novel that he decides to write a song about it? That's exactly what happened to me when Ian Churchward read my debut historical novel, *The Woodville Connection*, and then sat down to write a song called 'Francis Cranley' after the book's chief protagonist. When Ian contacted me to tell me about the song, I can honestly say that it was one of the proudest moments of a writing career that spans almost three decades.

Of course, once I'd listened to the song (which is excellent but does contain plot spoilers so don't listen too closely to the lyrics if you haven't yet read the book) I was eager to know more about Ian and his band, The Legendary Ten Seconds. I soon discovered that, like me, Ian has a keen interest in the life and times of Richard III although he and I came to the Ricardian fold by different paths. I was an impressionable thirteen year old when I picked up my mother's copy of *We Speak No Treason*, the late Rosemary Hawley Jarman's impassioned defence of Richard III disguised as a brilliant novel. The book left me eager to learn more, so I saved up to buy Paul Murray Kendall's seminal biography of Richard. After that the die was cast; I had no doubt where my sympathies lay in the York/Lancaster/Tudor debate.

Ian Churchward came to the Ricardian cause somewhat later in life but I suspect his loyalty is no less binding than mine. A dedicated musician whose preferred leisure activity is composing songs on his guitar, Ian had to be coaxed by his wife from his musical lair to watch a documentary about the discovery of Richard III's remains. As he cheerfully admits, his intention had been to stay for a few minutes before escaping back to his music. Instead he found himself watching, spellbound, to the end of the programme. The Ricardian magic had worked again, a fact for which those of us who enjoy folk music with a historical bias should be heartily thankful. Since 'discovering' Richard, Ian and his band have produced some fantastic songs on themes familiar to all Ricardians. In fact, the track titles on The Legendary Ten Seconds' CDs read like a guide to some of the key places in Richard III's story or to the people that mattered most to him: 'Ambion Hill'; 'Sheriff Hutton'; 'The Battle of Barnet Song'; 'The Road to Middleham'; 'The Lady Anne Neville'; 'Richard of York'; 'A Warwick'; 'Lord Lovell's Lament', to name just a handful. And whether mournful and thought-provoking or jaunty and spirit-lifting, Ian's songs always offer a satisfying marriage of the medieval and the modern.

I believe I owe a debt of thanks to Elaine, Ian's wife, because if she hadn't persuaded him to leave his studio in order to watch that particular documentary, it's likely that I would never have experienced the unique pleasure of listening to a song about Francis Cranley. I'm tempted to go even further and say that it's a debt shared by all who combine a love of music with a keen interest in Richard III. So to Ian, Elaine and to all the members of the marvellous Legendary Ten Seconds, I say thank you for the music.

K E Martin
May 2016

Kathy Martin signing a copy of one of her books at York House in Stony Stratford, February 2016.

Chapter One
Before Richard III

My first band was called Chapter 29. I loved the Syd Barrett version of Pink Floyd and especially the album, 'Piper at the Gates of Dawn' so I wanted the name of my band to be Chapter 24. I have a vague recollection that back in about 1981, one of my friends suggested that this particular Pink Floyd song from their first album might be a good name. Another friend, Jerry Brimicombe, with whom the band was formed, had wanted to call it Palm Trees 99, which I thought was terrible because it gave me visions of funk rock music which I don't like. We reached the compromise, largely in my favour, of Chapter 29 and Mike Peakman, later to become Lord Zarquon, arranged our first gig at a venue called The Casino in Paignton. It was probably our worst performance ever, but we gradually improved after that January 1982 debut.

I was into 1960's music in a big way and still am, because I love the music of The Velvet Underground, The Beatles, The Doors, Jefferson Airplane and The Shadows. Punk music inspired me to try to learn to play the guitar, especially Joe Strummer of The Clash. In the late 1970s, as far as I was concerned, punk music was very new and exciting. Some of my school friends formed a punk rock band called Das Schnitz and even released a single which made a big impression on me. The lead singer of Das Schnitz was Tim Dodge and he had let me borrow the first two albums by The Clash. A few years before that he had also introduced me to the wonderful recordings of Eddie Cochran. For a long time I wasn't much of a guitar player, and because I couldn't play other people's songs I immediately started to make up my own. My early attempts weren't very good but every so often I came up with some I considered to be reasonable. I tended to try to write my songs in a 1960's beat

music style. I took my inspiration from bands like the Yardbirds and
the Brian Jones era Rolling Stones. Eventually I learnt how to play
some of the sixties songs that I liked, for instance 'Arnold Layne' by
Pink Floyd, 'Midnight Hour' by Wilson Pickett, 'Pride of Man' by
Quicksilver Messenger Service, 'Heart Full of Soul' by The Yardbirds
and 'Ticket to Ride' by The Beatles.

Chapter 29 had various line ups, playing my songs and others written
by various band members. The June 1982 to August 1983 line up
was my favourite, with Phil Andrews, David Clifford, Jeremy
Brimicombe, Liz Honeywill, Shelley James and I. With Phil, Dave
and Jerry I would later form another band called The Morrisons.

As Chapter 29 we rehearsed and recorded most of the songs we
wrote at a rather dilapidated studio in what was probably once a
warehouse in Swan Street, Torquay. This was where Das Schnitz had
recorded the songs for their record. It was really a health and safety
nightmare. When it rained, water would start coming through the
roof, sometimes next to the electric light bulb in the ceiling. The
building next to it fell down one day! To get to the rehearsal room
you had to walk up lots of stairs and it was very dark and dingy. It
had a toilet which must have been really filthy but you couldn't tell
because it was too dark to see. The girls in the band were too scared
to go to the toilet on their own because it was rather creepy. If there
had ever been a fire at the bottom of the stairs while we had been
rehearsing then we would have been trapped. There was no other way
out unless you would have been prepared to jump out of a window
(with no glass in it) which was a long distance from the road below!
There was an eight-track recording facility on the top floor, and
below that a rehearsal room where we recorded our songs. The guy
who ran the place was called Steve Norris. Our friend Mike Peakman
called him Steve "do-it-for-a-fiver" Norris, because if you asked Steve
how much it would cost to use the rehearsal room, he would always
say, "I'll do it for a fiver."

We recorded lots of our original songs at the studio in Swan Street and put them onto cassette albums. The first was called 'Playing in the Rooms of Twilight' (1982), and the second one 'A Bizarre Joy' (1983). The cover of the first album had a photo of a recorder being held by Dave Clifford, who was the bass player in the band. He is an amazing bass player and the best one with whom I've ever played. The second album cover had a flying saucer space ship, which had been etched in some way by Jerry Brimicombe, the keyboard player. Both cassettes had quite good reviews in a national music newspaper called Sounds. The title of the second cassette album originated from a review of the first album in Sounds when our music was described as being a bizarre joy. Actually there was even a third cassette album made up of live recordings from some of our gigs in Torbay, which I recall was given away with a Torbay fanzine called *Swim*. The fanzine mainly covered the local music scene, and was edited by a friend of the band, called Neil Rider. *Swim* was an acronym for South West Independent Music. Our band was part of a music co-operative called Popular Obscurities. The "obscurities" bit was very appropriate and was mainly held together by our friends Mike Peakman and Simon Larkin. John Peel, the Radio One DJ, actually came along to a gig organised by the co-operative at a pub called The Skipper in Brixham. I couldn't attend this event but I was able to listen to it being broadcast live on Radio One which was quite exciting.

After the cassette album phase, we recorded a couple of demo tapes at Swan Street, and I would send cassettes of our songs off to various record companies, gradually building up a substantial collection of rejection slips and letters. It was often a struggle to get gigs because we didn't play any well-known songs. Out of desperation we played at some unsuitable venues. When we played at a pub called The Palk Arms, the landlord complained that the sound of the bass guitar was making his beer glasses rattle. "There was no bass on that cassette of your songs that you gave me!" he complained.

I kept a diary of my musical adventures from 31st August 1980 until 5th August 1991. Halfway through writing this chapter I suddenly remembered the diary, and on finding it was surprised to discover I had kept it going for so long. I thought it had been abandoned after my first band split up. The earliest entries cover the period when I was trying to form a band. The very first reads as follows:-

"Hi there all you non-existent fans. Well, here I am on Sunday morning, slightly the worse for last night, when I had too much to drink and got home to find I'd forgotten my key. It was two in the morning and, not wishing to wake my parents, I had to sleep in my Dad's car. Oh yes, I did also make an unsuccessful attempt to climb through my bedroom window."

Presumably my Dad had not locked his car and maybe we didn't worry too much about locking our cars in those days? I do remember this incident although before I read about it in the diary, my recollection was that I had got stuck trying to climb through the window and in a drunken stupor, trying to be quiet, managed to do the exact opposite and woke my parents. But that must have been another night.

Not all of the diary was written by me. I used to lend it to various band members, who would sometimes write sections about gigs, rehearsals, arguments at rehearsals, recording sessions, getting drunk at the pub and new song ideas.

After Chapter 29 split up in 1986, I played in a band called The Morrisons. We actually had a record played on The John Peel Show in 1987. It was a flexi disc with the label artwork created by my friend Graham Moores. John Peel played our song called 'Listen to Your Heart' twice on his Radio One show and he also read out the Torquay address of Phil Andrews. Over the space of a few weeks we received a deluge of mail from people throughout the UK asking for a copy of our flexi disc. The needle stuck the second time John Peel played it, which was really funny and John blamed the Radio One equipment for damaging our disc.

I got the idea for our disc from a band called The Chesterfields who had previously had their flexi disc played on the same radio show. I knew their bass player quite well, I think he had shown me the artwork for it and then it had been played by John Peel. I said to myself, " Well it worked for Simon Barber's band, The Chesterfields, so perhaps it will work for my new band." I can still remember Phil Andrews excitedly knocking on my door one evening after he had heard our song being played on the radio. I had recently moved out of my parent's house and had just bought my own place but I hadn't been able to afford to have a telephone installed. So that was why Phil had to come over to share the news and of course back then we didn't have mobile phones or the internet.

I used to listen to the John Peel show quite a lot, mainly in the late 1970's and early 1980's. I discovered loads of great music listening to his show and it was mainly obscure stuff. The best band that I discovered listening to his show was The Misunderstood who recorded five brilliant tracks in 1967 which included the songs 'My Mind' and 'Find a Hidden Door.' Sometimes John Peel could be quite hilarious, especially when he accidentally played a record at the wrong speed, for instance playing it at 45 rpm for the entire song by mistake and then announcing that it should have been 33 rpm! I heard this sort of thing happen more than once. I think there was one track by Public Image that he played at the incorrect rpm that actually sounded better at that wrong speed!

Most of The Morrisons' songs were composed by Phil Andrews. I went through a phase where I didn't compose much, but was content to help arrange those he had written. I think the chorus of 'Listen to Your Heart' was my idea. My guitar-playing had improved, and I was able to work out simple guitar solos for some of the songs. After the flexi disc we had a twelve-inch four-track EP released on Playroom Discs. Graham Moores created the artwork of a guitar with a broken string for the EP cover. It was a drawing of the guitar of Brendan Holden, a band member of The Chesterfields. I can remember being at one of the first gigs of The Chesterfields watching and listening to Brendan playing that guitar.

Playroom Discs was an independent record label run by a nice couple called Karen and Gordon who lived in Brighton. Phil and myself went to stay with Karen and Gordon at their place in Brighton. One evening in Brighton at a disco we danced to somebody playing the records of 'Have You Seen Her Face' by The Byrds and 'She's Got Everything' by The Kinks (probably my favourite songs by those two bands). In the Brighton Lanes I purchased the two issues of an old music magazine called Zigzag which included the story of Quicksilver Messenger Service as recounted by John Cipollina their lead guitar player. I had my usual spell of suffering from hay fever allergy symptons while we stayed in Brighton and spent the best part of a day reading those Zigzag magazines confined to bed with itchy eyes and a runny nose. So many times when I went away on holiday I would be ill with what I thought was a heavy cold but now I think I was probably suffering from a type of allergic reaction to my new surroundings.

In 1987 I developed the obsession of supporting my local football team. Jerry Brimicombe had been a big fan of Torquay United since about 1977. I think the first game he went to see was a victory over Burnley. He told me that Torquay were in the Guinness book of records for scoring the fastest ever own goal in a football match. We were in a shop that had a copy of the latest edition of that book and he showed me the details of it with Pat Kruse scoring the own goal. What it didn't tell you and I later learned was that Torquay actually scored all four goals in the match which was a 2-2 draw at home to Cambridge United. Jerry hadn't been at the game but an old school chum called Chris Donovan had been there to witness it in January 1977. Dave Clifford was also a supporter of Torquay United. The first time he went to Plainmoor was in 1972, he thinks that Torquay were playing Hereford United. Jerry and Dave persuaded me to go to a game in 1987. I had been to a game earlier in the 1980's with Jerry and had found it quite boring but after going to a few games in 1987 I caught the football supporting bug. We got so into the football that The Morrisons ended up sponsoring part of the football kit of one of the Torquay United players. These were the boots of Sean Haslegrave in the 1987 to 1988 season with the London Inn at Shaldon sponsoring the rest of his kit. It was quite an exciting time with the Gulls just missing out on promotion and losing to Swansea City in the play-offs. Supporting Torquay United can be quite stressful if I am perfectly honest. In all of my time supporting them I think there have only been about two mid table seasons, with quite a few promotion chasing ones, but usually out weighed by far more relegation battles.

Now this reminds me of Gary Monk who once played at Torquay United. He lived next door to us and I can remember him as a young boy playing football with his brother in their garden. It reminded me of when I used to do the same when I was their age and every so often my football would accidentally get kicked over the garden fence into the neighbour's house. This was owned by Mrs Page-Thomas who lived in the property prior to Mr and Mrs Monk. She was a rather grumpy old lady who would refuse to give the ball back. One day when Gary and his brother were playing football in their garden, the ball came flying over the wall by our driveway. It had been raining earlier in the day and the football landed in the wet grass next to where my Dad was painting the outside wall of his bungalow. It splashed mud all over the wet paint on the wall and my Dad was really cross. When my Mum told me about this I reminded Dad of the arguments he used to have with the former neighbour when she wouldn't give me back my football. Gary Monk would eventually go on to play for Swansea City and was their captain when they gained promotion to the Premier league. Later he was also their manager. The Morrisons split up in 1988 and Jerry and myself formed a new band called Just a Shadow with some other friends, Andy and Bridget England, whom I'd met in the early 1980's at a venue called Tapps in Milborne Port. I remember thinking it was rather strange to have a port that wasn't near the sea! Andy and Bridget were playing in band called India at Tapps, and they performed a version of 'White Horses', a song I hadn't heard since I was a child. I loved it. This song was the theme tune for a children's TV programme I used to enjoy. In fact, I watched it mainly *because* of the 'White Horses' tune!

With Just a Shadow I started to write songs again, and also met my wife-to-be, Elaine, when she joined the band. After a couple of years, when Andy England had to move to a new job in another part of the country, Just a Shadow split up. I then took part in a few short-lived music ventures, which included Elaine, step children and brother-in-law.

The last entry in my diary is dated 5th August 1991. By this time I had moved to my house, called Rock Lee, where I have my home recording studio set up in the basement. I moved there in January 1991 and because I found moving house so stressful I am still living there.

"Writing this in the basement of the house, listening to the demo we recorded with Simon Larkin a few months ago. We recorded 'Since You've Gone Away', 'Just Like the Day Before', 'Rebecca's Leaving', and 'Walk in the Sun'. Unfortunately the vocals came out rather distorted, so we're going to redo them in a few weeks' time. I've recently purchased an eight-track portastudio, so we are able to record our own demo tapes from now on. Actually, we've already started recording on my new machine. My first attempts were rather basic versions of 'Beautiful One'

and 'Since You've Gone Away'. They were rather rough and ready as the backing tracks were taken from a recent rehearsal."

During this period we played very few gigs and concentrated on recording songs on the portastudio mentioned in my diary. This used cassettes. Writing and recording songs came to an end for a couple of years when my son Tom was born and I lost interest in playing the guitar. Partly I was too busy being a father. For about two years in the mid-1990's I didn't play. I remember picking up the guitar, noticing the strings were very rusty, then starting to strum a few chords. An idea came for a song, but I didn't go on. What was the point of composing a new song? No one was ever going to hear it.

Towards the end of the 1990's I started playing guitar for a ceilidh band based in Exeter. This was my introduction to English folk music. I was asked by Nigel Howells to stand in at short notice, for his band called Storm Force Ten. I had to learn their set list in two weeks and I hadn't played the guitar for about two years! I was given a tape recording of all of the songs played by Nigel Howells on his melodeon. I tried playing along and it was hopeless until my stepson, Guy Bolt, came to the rescue showing me that there were lots of quick the chord changes. I'd never tried to play folk songs on my guitar before so I hadn't appreciated that the chord changes might be so swift. Guy is a very talented musician, he can play the drums, piano, guitar, harmonica and has a really good singing voice. When he was in his early teens, after he had just learnt how to play the drums, I showed him how to play some simple chords on the guitar. Within two weeks he was a much better guitar player than me!

Shortly after I started playing with Storm Force Ten I also played in a band with my wife Elaine, stepson Guy Bolt, and David Clifford. This band was called Shady Grove (inspired by the title of the third album of Quicksilver Messenger Service) and we played a mixture of covers and our own material. Some of the covers were very obscure for instance 'Too Long' by Quicksilver Messenger Service. Other songs such as 'I Fought the Law', written by Sonny Curtis and recorded by Bobby Fuller, also by The Clash, are quite well known. As a band, Shady Grove lasted for a couple of years from around 1999 until sometime in 2002.

I played in the ceilidh band for nearly ten years. It was originally called Storm Force Ten, and later became Phoenix (rising from the ashes of Storm Force Ten!). The band played instrumentals of tunes such as 'A Hundred Pipers'. This became a major influence on my attempts at writing songs. I started to use folk music chord changes in my song writing. Another big influence was an album I borrowed from Nigel Howells. This album was 'The Bones of All Men.' It consisted of medieval and Tudor sounding instrumentals with catchy tunes, played with a mixture of modern and older traditional instruments. I was in heaven listening to it. I remember there was a song called 'How Does it Feel' that I had come across in about 1982, by a relatively unknown band called Grim Noel (this was Graham Moores' band), which had a medieval feel to it. I instinctively wanted to hear lots more such songs, but had never heard any others apart from 'Greensleeves.' I Probably hadn't tried very hard, but then again there was no internet in those days and it wasn't so easy to find some types of music. Now you can find just about anything and everything quite easily from the world wide web. What joy to have finally discovered a whole album with catchy medieval/Tudor sounding tunes. I felt inspired to try to compose my own similar instrumentals. The first one was called 'Medieval Garage,' because my friend Andy England said it sounded like medieval garage music. The next one that I composed I decided to call 'The Field of Cloth of Gold', because I read in a history book by Roy Strong about the real Field of Cloth of Gold of June 1520, during the reign of Henry VIII. I continued to play gigs with the ceilidh band on a regular basis, while at home I was recording a few songs every so often, now using an eight track mini disc recorder. The mini disc recorder was much better than the cassette portastudio and improved the quality of the sound. It allowed you to have much more flexibility with over-dubs. One of the problems I found with the cassette-based recorder was that after a while there was a tendency for the cassette tape to stretch slightly, which could make the recorded music sound a bit 'wonky' on playback. One of the first songs that I recorded on the mini disc recorder was 'Remember My Name', which concerned the First World War. I had never composed a history-based song before. Previously my songs had usually been about love and the usual angst-ridden failure of being rejected by the opposite sex. What I also hadn't realised, until I got my stepson to play drums on the recording, was that it was the first time I had written a song that wasn't in a 4/4 time signature. The influence of the tunes I had been playing in the ceilidh band was now becoming more and more apparent.

I decided to ask Andy England if I could release some of my solo artist recordings on his record label which was called Golden Pathway Records. This independent record label was originally set up by Graham Moores and then Andy took over running it. Andy was happy with my request and I decided to call myself The Legendary Ten Seconds. You might be tempted to think that this relates to my attention span during a conversation, or perhaps the length of time my patience will last while trying to phone a call centre.

It was in 1983, I think, that I took my cassette recorder along to a local gig in Torbay, at a venue called the 400 Club, by Torquay harbour. I made a short recording of a local punk band. The recording is rather short because I didn't find the music very tuneful. I listened to the recording the next morning and it sounded absolutely hilarious to my ears. You hear lots of noise as the band start to play the introduction of their song, then the lead singer shouts out a swear word, and the cacophony of the band gets louder and louder. Suddenly, in the middle of it all, Phil Andrews, obviously sitting next to the cassette recorder, shouts out, "My God what an awful row!" This is followed by some feedback and the lead singer ranting out in time to the noise of his band. I played it to some of my best friends later that day and they loved it! I made them some copies of the recording and Dave Clifford took his copy to Brentford in London where he was at university. He played it to his flat mate, Carl Hutson who also thought it was a wonderful recording and Carl called it 'the legendary ten seconds'! Thereafter the recording would be played for many years to come by myself and my close friends and fondly remembered as 'the legendary ten seconds', even though the length of the recording is actually about twenty seconds. As far as I am aware this is the only live recording in existence of that local punk band. I have now got the recording on a memory stick which I usually listen to in shuffle mode whilst driving. Oh, the wonders of modern technology. This plays the songs in random fashion, and you never know what you're going to be listening to next. Every so often 'the legendary ten seconds' will be selected and it still makes me laugh out loud when I hear it.

I recorded one EP and three albums as The Legendary Ten Seconds, for the Golden Pathway record label. Graham Moores created the artwork for the EP and two of the album covers. The artwork for 'Podtastic' was painted by my wife and this was the third album. I gave it that title because it contained various jingles that I had recorded for radio stations and podshows. I seem to go through phases with my music and that was my radio jingles phase. I think my best jingle was the one that I wrote for the podshow of Ed Ovett in the USA called Ed's Mixed Bag. The highlight of his show was when he recorded and played a version of the jingle with his singing on it.

The first Legendary Ten Seconds CD released by Golden Pathway records contained four songs, one was the instrumental Medieval Garage and another was the one about the First World War. I suppose that when you look at the lyrics it isn't obviously about that war. In my mind's eye it was about someone on the eve of the war in the summer of 1914, and then, many years later, looking back. There is a painting in my dining room of three Edwardian ladies walking through the English countryside on a summer day. It reminds me of my grandmother, who told me she saw a Zeppelin flying over London when she was a girl. Inspired by that painting, I wrote the song in the same room. When I started recording songs about Richard III, this song was revisited and I rewrote the lyrics, recording it as a song about an archer. Here are the lyrics for the First World War version.

'REMEMBER MY NAME'

Country lanes and gentle pastures
Sunny skies and fields of hay
But war clouds have gathered
And I must leave you

So if I never see you again
Please don't forget me
and remember my name

Tower blocks and concrete
Motorways and fields of graves
The war clouds that gathered
Have now blown away

Our lives once so happy
Now shattered and torn
Some call it progress

But others will mourn

Another source of inspiration came from reading a book about the unofficial Christmas truce in 1914 during the First World War. During the ceasefire period some of the German and British soilders in the trenches played football in no man's land. My uncle Eric (one of Dad's brothers) lived with my grandfather in a flat overlooking part of the remains of the medieval wall in Exeter. With my Dad and my sister we would often visit their flat and as a boy I used to enjoy looking at my grandfather's First World War medals that were kept in a tin.

In between all the songs on my first Legendary Ten Seconds' album I inserted silly jokes and phrases spoken by two of my friends, Steve Honeywill and Nigel Howells. On the next album titled 'Woeful Wonders and Stupendous Blunders,' I did something similar but yhis time using the voice of Nigel. There is a Tudor-sounding instrumental called 'Fanfare for the King' and also there is my song called 'Senlac Ridge' which is about the battle of Hastings. This was a battle which had fascinated me since my childhood. As a young boy I would recreate the battle on my bedroom floor using a large set of marbles and lego bricks. In my imagination each marble represented a Saxon warrior and each lego brick a Norman. At the end of the battle of Hastings song I recorded my friend Nigel Howells speaking in his very pretend posh voice, "I say chaps we'd better watch out, one of those French idiots will have someone's eye out in a minute!" I also inserted short joke songs in between the proper songs on the album. This was my silly joke song phase. For instance I wrote one about insurance called 'Exclusion Clauses' to the tune of 'Champion the Wonder Horse.' Another silly one was 'Hairloss 2000' about a fake hair gel product.

'EXCLUSION CLAUSES'

If you need insurance for your home
You'll get the swiftest quote you've ever known
See the speed with which we answer the phone
You'll hear about us everywhere you go
The time will come when everyone
will know the name of
Exclusion Clauses Friendly PLC
We'll decline your claim but we're very friendly!

The idea for this type of thing came from one of my favourite album by The Who called 'The Who Sell Out'. Their song about spot cream is a classic. The album has radio jingles and adverts in between the songs. I probably inherited the ability to make up silly words for well-known songs from my father. I remember when I was in my early years at grammar school, that my Dad, who was a maths teacher, used to sing "Mathematics Hard to Do" to the tune of 'Breaking Up is Hard to Do' by Neil Sedaka. This was in the early 1970s when David Cassidy was singing the song in the Partridge family TV series. Dad was a lecturer at South Devon Technical College, which was next to my school and we'd go home together after he'd finsihed teaching for the day. When we got home, out would come the biscuit tin and on would go the TV. My Mum would come home next and cook the evening meal, by which time I'd had too many biscuits and usually didn't feel like eating much of what she'd cooked.

Somewhere in all this (probably about 2006) I recorded enough songs for an album with Graham Moores. For these sessions we used Graham's Apple Mac computer which had Logic music software. I played bass and sang on the recordings whilst Graham played guitar and Guy Bolt played the drums. The only exception to this was a small piece of slide guitar playing that I did on an instrumental called 'The Witch Outstrips the Wolf'. The tunes were virtually all written by Graham and eventually made it onto an album called 'Wonderclock' which was released on Richard the Third Records in 2016. The songs were originally going to be released on Golden Pathway as an album by The Psycho Daisies, but that never quite happened.

Having mentioned the album 'Wonderclock', I have recently discovered some interesting information about one of the songs, which is called 'Bloody Meadows'. A lady in the USA emailed me to ask if the song was about the battle of Tewkesbury, and I realised I didn't know, because I wasn't the composer, and I had never thought to ask Graham. I had always imagined it was about the English Civil War in the 1600's. I emailed Graham to ask him, and he sent me this interesting information, which I think is worthwhile including here: *"'Bloody Meadows' is a bit of a mash-up really. There is an area of the Wars of the Roses in Tewkesbury, a 1471 battlefield site still called Bloody Meadow. There was also an English Civil War battle near Chagford, Dartmoor that I think was called Bloody Meadow, 1643. I actually wrote it after going to an English Civil War re-enactment at Witney, Oxford in 1994.*

"It was a really dry, hot and breezy day and the re-enactment was taking place in a field of stubble. A gun crew set the stubble on fire and the breeze fanned the flames - soon it was a firestorm and it was moving towards us in the crowd and the car park. We all panicked and ran. Some were able to get to their cars and drive off. Others just had to run away.

"About 50 cars were completely engulfed in flames - a couple of petrol tanks exploded. Probably the most frightening thing I've ever seen. I was really lucky that I was late that day and was last in the car park. The fire started just as I arrived and I was able to drive out. I parked up some distance away and went back on foot - by that time the firemen were stopping all access to the site.

"Interestingly it seems to be called the Battle of Wind rush Valley - didn't know that."

Graham also sent me details of the article from The Independent about the fire (which happened on a Bank Holiday in August) that inspired the words for his song. The article describes the incident in great detail, with at least twenty people being injured. It required fifty firemen to fight the blaze, which was fanned by strong winds.

Back to my story . . . I was very impressed with the Logic music software and decided to buy a second hand Apple Mac which I then started to use rather than my mini disc recorder. I could never have worked out how to use the software without Guy's help, and I remember it took us two days to work out how to find the reverb setting using the music software on the computer. It didn't help that the Logic music manual appeared to contain no information about this vital effect that is used in the recording process.

The Legendary Ten Seconds' third Golden Pathway album features another one of my fake or pseudo Tudor instrumentals called 'Tudor Tune' and a song called 'Dorchester Fair'. The words for the song were written by my wife. The idea for the lyrics came from reading a book by Bernard Cornwell about an archer at the battle of Crécy, where the banners of the English army made the archer think of a fair he had been to at Dorchester. I suggested to Elaine that it might make a nice idea for a song. These are her words

'DORCHESTER FAIR'

The day that I took you to Dorchester fair
The sunshine the laughter we hadn't a care
The flags and the bunting the stalls and the carts
The cries of the hawkers all gladdened our hearts

We marched along gladly lads out on a spree

I carried the favour you'd given to me
The ribbon you'd worn to tie up your hair
The day that I took you to Dorchester fair

We formed up in lines, stared out across the field
And the sun glanced and glimmered on helmets and shields
The banners flew gayly and the shouts on the air
All carried me back to Dorchester fair

For a moment I stood there bewildered and still
Then an order was given we rushed for the hill
The cries and the fury the pain and the fear
Would I ever again see Dorchester dear

Now the stunned and the weary limp home to find rest
And I finger the ribbon tucked close to my chest
Will the clamour, the scene, the stench ever fade
Will I find my way back to my Dorchester maid

Come a day when the sun shines on bonnets not helms
When we walk arm in arm under Dorchester's elms
When with pleasure I buy you new ribbons to wear
Come a day when I take you to Dorchester fair

In the winter of 2008 I was ill with Bell's palsy. I may also have had
shingles at the same time. If so, this would have been for the second
time as I had previously been ill with this in 1982 (my stepson,
stepdaughter, mother and my grandmother have also had shingles).
I had recently started a new job which had involved quite a bit
of travelling and I was feeling a bit stressed at the time. Having
said that, I was just starting to become comfortable with my new

job when I became ill. I had mild ear ache on a Thursday, then on the Friday evening I had trouble speaking. I went to bed, and on waking up couldn't shut my right eye. Also, that side of my face was suddenly quite lopsided. I thought it was a stroke, but Elaine, who worked at Torbay hospital, was certain that it was Bell's palsy. This was confirmed by my doctor. For about a month I couldn't read without the aid of a magnifying glass, and I couldn't speak properly for about two months. I was off work for one month, and during this time I was at home feeling very sorry for myself as I sat in front of the television, watching episode after episode of Time Team repeats. It took me half a year to recover, and even now I have a weakness on the right side of my face. You can see it in photos if I'm trying to smile. At the time I was really worried that I wouldn't be able to sing again. Having mentioned time team I remember a few years ago while I was painting the front wall of my house having a conversation with my neighbour who had recently moved to Torquay from Brighton. He now works as a self employed landscape gardener and he told me that he used to have a catering business and for a few seasons he did the catering for Time Team. Apparently he had sometimes been able to have the team of archaeologists singing football songs in the evening back at an hotel. I also found out that my neighbour supports Leicester football club and the year we had our conversation was the season (2015-2016) that Leicester came top of the Premier League.

About the same time that my first songs appeared on Golden Pathway records, my old band called The Morrisons reformed. The catalyst for reforming the Morrisons was Firestation records in Germany. This independent record company released a compilation album which included one of the songs that my band had recorded in the 1980's. This was followed by another album called 'Songs from the South of England' which contained most of The Morrisons' recordings from the late 1980's.

From 2006, the second (reformed) version of The Morrisons recorded and released one EP and three LP albums on the Golden Pathway record label. This was followed by one EP and two albums on Pastime records. Guy Bolt played drums on all the albums, except the last one. Here is the press release for The Morrisons' final album which makes the band sound much more well known than it really is:-

PRESS RELEASE *July 2013 MORRISONS BREW NEW CD ALBUM FROM VETERAN C86 INDIE BAND THE MORRISONS*

Not to be confused with the superstore or the plethora of Doors and Jim Morrison tribute bands, original C86 indie band The Morrisons have released their new album 'Morrisons Brew' on the local Exeter label, Pastime Records .

In 1987 John Peel played their debut flexi single 'Listen To Your Heart' on his acclaimed Radio One show, and their 'Rainy Day EP' which was their first release on Pastime records, received a 5 star review in Artrocker magazine. Ric Rawlins described it as 'magically delicious'.

Since arriving onto the music scene all those years ago, The Morrisons haven't looked back and despite a long break from music in the 1990s are still going strong after first forming in 1986. Their new CD shows them sounding as fresh as ever, with their melodic brand of Byrds-inspired jangly guitar pop as relevant today as it was when indie music first announced itself back in the mid-Eighties.

The present band members are Phil Andrews, lead vocals and guitar; David Clifford, bass; Adrian Maxwell, percussion; Ian Churchward, guitar and vocals, and Elaine Churchward, backing vocals

'Morrisons Brew' is the 26th release by Exeter indie label Pastime Records, set up to promote and support indie acts recording and performing in the Exeter and Devon area.

For further information, photographs and review copies of 'Morrisons Brew' by The Morrisons contact: Pastime Records, C/O Andy Botterill,

Copies of the new CD are available at £5 + p&p
All songs were recorded, engineered and mixed in Ian's basement by The Morrisons.

The songs are generally written in a basic format with lyrics by Phil and then developed and changed by all the band members as they move towards completion so they are very much a "sum of the parts" rather than an individual's own. There are no pre-conceived ideas or styles and basically all band members write their own parts around the basic structure and the song ends up where it ends up!

I very much enjoyed the recording sessions for all of the albums, and was particularly pleased with the harmony vocal I worked out for a song called 'Waiting for a Train', which was on the last Golden Pathway album called 'Listen to The Morrisons'. I was also very pleased with the vocal harmonies Elaine and I performed on the version of 'Arrow in Your Heart', which is on the 'Morrisons Brew' album.

The second version of The Morrisons ended for the same reason as the first; Phil Andrews decided to leave. Phil had gone through a very difficult period in 2012 when his father had died, and I also expect he had grown tired of the band and the very minimal number of album sales. Whatever we tried seemed to make no difference to our lack of success. We had the internet to market our music, but there is so much music available that we found it virtually impossible to generate any sales. To me music on the internet is a bit like a tune by an unsigned band being a drop in the ocean that gets lost in the sea. Another thing that didn't help was the name of the band. Anyone searching on the internet for our band would more than likely have struggled to find us and would probably instead have found links to Jim Morrison of The Doors, Van Morrison and Morrisons supermarket! So in that respect our name was a poor choice. That was one of the reasons that I decided to call my solo music project The Legendary Ten Seconds. The name is so unusual

and it is now fairly easy to find my music on the internet with this
name.

Artwork for the last album of The Morrisons which was created by Graham Moores. This includes the image of Brendan's guitar (of The Chesterfields) which was drawn by Graham for the Playroom Discs EP that was released in the late 1980's.

THE MORRISONS PROUDLY PRESENT....

MORRISON'S BREW

A COMPACT DISC RECORDING

PASTIME RECORDS Nº TWENTY SIX

Chapter Two
Loyaulté me Lie

So The Legendary Ten Seconds started off as a solo project and then sometime in 2012 I made some recordings of my songs with Lord Zarquon. This was shortly before Phil left The Morrisons. At this time I never thought that Lord Zarquon and myself would get on so well musically. I was very disappointed when Phil left The Morrisons (this band had been my main focus for many years) and when he did the rest of the group and I decided to carry on as a new band called Session 75 with my son Tom joining on vocals and playing guitar. At about the same time Lord Zarquon had decided to quit his band called Strange Red Earth when he had gone through a very difficult time trying to look after his father who was in very poor health. His mother was also suffering badly from dementia and was in a nursing home. Sadly both his parents died shortly after he and I started recording songs together.

The first songs I recorded with Lord Zarquon are included on an album called 'Good Fortune' and contain the usual standard pop-song-type lyrics. Little did we know that the subject matter of my songs was due for a very dramatic change. It was at the beginning of the year in 2013 that Lord Zarquon came over to my basement recording studio with his keyboard and played me a nice melody line he had worked out. It was a very lovely folky sounding melody which he played using a Mark II Mellotron flute sound on his Nord keyboard. I worked out the chords to go with the melody and so we had the music for an introduction and verse for a new song idea. Yet we had no idea for any lyrics and we also required a chorus. The hardest thing that I used to find about trying to write a song was usually trying to think of an interesting idea for the lyrics. Love is the most obvious one but I had grown tired of using that theme.

A few days later I was in my basement and had just started to play the guitar when my wife called down to me from our kitchen. "Ian, there's a programme on TV about Richard III. Do you want to come up and watch it?" Well, to be honest, I wasn't sure that I *did* want to watch it because I was enjoying strumming my guitar and I don't watch much TV. However I *am* interested in history, so—thank the heavens above—I put my guitar down and went upstairs, imagining I'd watch for a few minutes and then go back to the guitar. Instead, I sat down to watch the most amazing documentary I had ever seen, and within a few minutes any thought of going back to my guitar was abandoned until the programme had finished.

The things that I remember most from the documentary was the information relating to the Richard III Society, the first revealing of the skeleton in the car park and at the end when the reconstructed model of the head of Richard III was shown. You could see the emotion in Philippa Langley's face when she saw the curvature of the spine in the uncovered grave. It was one of the most exciting moments I have ever seen. So there was truth in the Tudor myth that Richard had been a hunchback! That was my immediate thought. Maybe this was what Philippa had been thinking at that moment as well? Later in the documentary we learnt that Richard wasn't a hunchback, i.e. suffered from kyphosis, instead he had a sideways curvature of the spine. This was a condition called scoliosis, of which I had not heard before.

That there was a Richard III Society I had been vaguely aware, and thought it rather strange, although at the same time I had long been curious about Richard III without investigating further. One of my favourite childhood reads was my Ladybird book about Warwick the Kingmaker. The Wars of the Roses are a confusing period of English history that I had never fully understood, but at the same time I could easily recite the list of the medieval Kings of England, in the correct historical order, from Edward the Confessor through to Henry VIII. I always thought that the style of armour in the late 15th century looked superb. Anything earlier seemed half formed, anything later looked too modern. I always considered the Tudor fashions to look rather ridiculous, but those of the fifteenth century were quite full of style. Just think of the most famous portrait of Richard III in his doublet which is in the national portrait gallery. His hat, with its jewelled brooch, is truly wonderful.

When I was a young boy I must have read that Ladybird book about Warwick the Kingmaker countless times. I had not realised that Richard, as Duke of Gloucester, had been at the same battle that resulted in the death of Warwick. For some reason my sympathy had always lain with the House of York. I have a tendency to feel sorry for the loser. For instance I felt it was a shame that Harold had lost the Battle of Hastings and it feels a bit like the English national football squad being beaten by the French. I felt sorry that Richard III lost the Battle of Bosworth, and could never understand why Northumberland and the Stanleys didn't help him to defeat Henry Tudor and his band of French mercenaries. What was the matter with them for goodness' sake? Although the House of York won the important battles of Towton, Barnet and Tewkesbury it all came to a tragic end for the Plantagenet House of York at Bosworth.

As far back as I can remember I seem to have always been interested in History. I can clearly remember my Dad finding his old stamp album in the garage and showing me the page of Bosnia and Herzegovinia with the stamps of the Archduke Ferdinand and his wife. From this I learnt that their assassination had led to the start of the First World War. This also led to one of my first hobbies which was collecting postage stamps, and this encouraged my interest in History and gave me a decent knowledge of basic geography.

History was my favourite subject at school. Maths was one of my weakest subjects which must have been a disappointment to my father who taught this. He used to make a joke of it by saying that

I had inherited my mother's side of the family, the stupid side! I got a grade A at foreign history A level and I now wish I had gone to university and maybe I could have become an archaeologist. If I think back to when I was 18 years old then I remember that I was completely fed up with studying and exams. By the time I left school I was tired of history and interested in music. It took me several years to become interested in history again.

So I didn't go to University and I didn't become an archaeologist or an historian. Instead I drifted into a job working as a bank clerk with Barclays Bank. In the evenings and at weekends my main all consuming hobby was trying to play guitar in various bands. Most of the work at a bank is rather boring but I have fortunately worked with lots of people who always had a good sense of humour. I could tell you about many funny moments. One of the comical highlights of my 27 years working for Barclays Bank was probably the day that the business banker of the office in Paignton, a certain Mark Bowey, put cellotape over the mouth piece of my phone. So throughout that day nobody could hear me properly via my telephone. It was only with my last telephone conversation at the end of the day that one of the girls on another floor of the office said "Ian you are ever so quiet, I can hardly hear you, has Bowey put cellotape over the mouthpiece of your phone?" Looking back, the first 10 years of working for Barclays were actually really good but I didn't realise it at the time until they introduced sales targets. Every year after that seemed to become increasingly difficult as far as I was concerned. I have felt vindicated by my reluctance to sell a certain loan protection policy for many years in light of the compensation that has now been paid to consumers due to the miss selling of this type of payment protection insurance.

Due to centralisation I was eventually made redundant by Barclays which was actually something I was happy about as I received a very good redundancy package. I was very lucky to quickly find new employment working for a very good Swedish bank which was opening new offices in the United Kingdom. As I am writing this we are in the middle of the outbreak of the Corona virus which is causing huge problems all over the world. In the United Kingdom many businesses are presently shut down, the football season has been suspended, theatres and shops are closed. But vital services are being maintained and I now feel quite proud that as a bank clerk I am considered to be a key worker because I am employed in a sector that provides an essential service.

In my study were two history books covering English history. One was *The Lives of the Kings and Queens of England* by Antonia Fraser, and the other *The Story of Britain* by Roy Strong. While waiting for my computer to start up, which with time seemed to take longer and longer, I would always turn to the sections about Richard III in those books. I lost track of the number of times I consumed those passages. Roy Strong is particularly harsh about Richard. Stating that Richard III had taken the throne via a pathway soaked with the blood of his victims. At the time I believed every word of it, but for some reason I had wished it were not true. Despite what the history books said I felt sorry for Richard and still wished he had won the battle of Bosworth!

In about 1995 my family had enjoyed a very memorable holiday in Yorkshire and we had visited Middleham. There was an English Heritage shop at the castle and I had been tempted to buy a novel about Richard III. I could always recall the opening paragraph of the novel, about Richard becoming scared as darkness fell, because he was lost in a forest. I decided not to buy the book because I didn't want to read a novel about him murdering the Princes in the Tower of London. This is how he has been consistently portrayed in most of the older history books; that of the evil hunchback uncle murdering his young nephews.

But I must go back to the amazing inspiration aroused after watching that documentary about Richard. I now realised that the new song idea could be a song about him. Back I went to those two history books, to re-read those sections about Richard III and I quickly came up with the words for the verse sections of a song. Now all I needed was a chorus. A few days later, while ironing some shirts, a chorus tune with the words came to me. I called the song 'The House of York,' and recorded myself singing the lyrics and playing the tune on my acoustic guitar. Then I gave the recording to Lord Zarquon. The next time he came over to my house I listened to what he had done to my very basic recording. He'd added keyboard sounds, including that wonderful Mellotron flute melody line on the introduction, an amazing church organ sound and drums. In my humble opinion he had produced a masterpiece.

For a while, Lord Zarquon called the song 'Richard of York,' which was incorrect, but that was the title used on the story behind the song which featured in the August 2013 edition of Folkcast. It was said to be the tale of King Richard III and Henry Tudor, with a spoken narrative by Babba. Folkcast is a podcast based in the UK, covering folk, folk-rock, singer-songwriter and roots-based music. A podcast is a bit like a radio show, only you listen to it via the internet. Here are the words for the song about the demise of the Plantagenet dynasty.

'THE HOUSE OF YORK'

It was at Bosworth Field that a king was slain
Despite it all Lord Stanley felt no shame
The mayor of York he did mourn
For his loyalty to Richard he had sworn

Long gone to his death

Long gone his dying breath
Long gone the house of York
Of treachery there is much talk

For the death of the princes he carries the blame
And their mother she would curse his name
For the Woodvilles he did despise
But was he the victim of Tudor lies

Long gone to his death
Long gone his dying breath
Long gone the house of York
Of treachery there is much talk

How they would mock his crooked spine
Shakespeare too with the passage of time
Buried at Greyfriars church
Now a car park is where she searched

Long gone to his death
Long gone his dying breath
Long gone the house of York
Of treachery there is much talk

After listening to what I considered to be a rather fabulous
recording, I suggested to Lord Zarquon that perhaps we could
consider producing a concept album about Richard III. Lord
Zarquon is a huge fan of concept albums and in some ways our music
has a similar style to the late 1960's concept albums of The Moody
Blues, which are probably his favourites. He uses the Mellotronics
MTron Pro and the Nord Viking mellotron samples, which can

produce truly ethereal organic sounds and are very similar to those found on the recordings of The Moody Blues.

I decided to have a look on the internet to see if there were any books I could buy about Richard III, and immediately discovered that there seem to be more books about this much maligned monarch than anyone else. Not just history books but also novels. My initial dilemma was trying to decide which books to buy out of such a huge choice. It began to dawn on me that if there was a Richard III Society and so many books about this king, then a whole album of songs about him, once finished, might prove to be quite popular and fairly easy to sell. At last I could find a larger audience who might be interested in my songs. After all there seemed to be lots of people interested in Richard III, but not that many songs about him.

After spending several hours of research on the internet I decided that *The Daughter of Time* by Josephine Tey looked like a good book to start with. It was the first and best book I read that was solely about Richard III (until I read that book I had only encountered history books containing a single chapter about him at the most). To me, the most exciting part is where you learn that Bishop Stillington told Richard III that the marriage of Edward IV to Elizabeth Woodville was invalid. This is because of a previously secret contract of marriage that Edward IV entered into with Lady Eleanor Talbot and at which the elderly Bishop had officiated as a priest. By marrying Elizabeth Woodville Edward had committed bigamy.

The Daughter of Time is one of the most unusual and entertaining books I have ever come upon. Elaine read it a few days after me, then her best friend Debby Helmore, and then I let my Mum read it. Debby's husband, Phil Helmore told me that he had once enjoyed listening to it as an audio book. We all felt the same way about *The Daughter of Time*. *The Maligned King* by Annette Carson came next and the initial chapter about the possibility that Lord Anthony Woodville may have been involved in poisoning Edward IV gave

me the inspiration for the words for this next song. The music was
written with the help of Lord Zarquon.

'LORD ANTHONY WOODVILLE'

Lord Anthony you look down with disdain
You've seen misery you've seen pain
Could you have poisoned a king
I doubt that we could suspect such a thing

Lord Anthony Woodville were you right
In the joust you took such delight
Lord Anthony Woodville you weren't wrong
In the house of York you did not belong

Lord Anthony when you walked through the door
My heart fell down to the floor
Lord Anthony when you left the hall
I could relax at the devil's call

Lord Anthony Woodville were you right
In the joust you took such delight
Lord Anthony Woodville you weren't wrong
In the house of York you did not belong

Anthony Woodville was a famous jouster during the reign of Edward
IV which I feel would be the medieval equivalent of the present day
most well-known Premier League football players.
In Annette Carson's book I also found out that Richard III's best
known motto was *Loyaulté me Lie*, which is old French for *Loyalty
Binds Me*. After reading the page in the book that covered this, I

immediately had an idea for a new song. I picked up my guitar and wrote 'Loyalty Binds Me'. I have to admit it has got the most obvious rhyme for a song set in the Middle Ages, which is 'Lord' and 'sword'! It's the medieval equivalent of 'you' and 'blue' in a modern pop love song! It didn't take me that long to write it but for some reason I couldn't decide if it was in a 4/4, 3/4 or 6/8 time signature. I quite often use a metronome for when I record my songs to try to keep myself in time. For the recording of 'Loyalty Binds Me' I managed to somehow play a 3/4 or a 6/8 rhythm to a 4/4 metronome time signature. It did make it rather difficult to record the guitar for the song. One warm summer evening, Lord Zarquon and I drove over to Berry Pomeroy castle and he filmed me singing the song outside the castle walls. I remember the first time that I ever visited this castle. My father took me when I was about 10 years old. It has a very impressive gatehouse and I think it is fantastic to have such a wonderful castle just a few miles from my home.

'LOYALTY BINDS ME'

Loyalty binds me to my brother the king
In victory we will rejoice and sing
At Barnet and Tewkesbury we won the day
Loyalty binds me with my faith on display

Loyalty binds me to King Edward my lord
Who reclaimed the throne with his mighty sword
Defeated Lord Warwick his life he did lose
Loyalty binds me to the friends that I choose

Loyalty binds me to King Edward the Fourth
For he has made me the lord of the north
At Middleham castle I now reside

Loyalty binds me with Anne as my bride
Yes loyalty binds me to Anne at my side

I then decided to call the new album idea 'Loyaulté Me Lie' and I checked on the internet on how to type the letter e with an acute accent. It's alt + 0233 = é. With the title of the album chosen, I now needed to write some more songs, and felt confident in my ability to do so. I thought about the Richard III Society and the song called 'Village Green Preservation Society' by the Kinks, and so I wrote a song called 'Fellowship of the White Boar.' Just as Ray Davis bemoaned office blocks and skyscrapers in a song, while praising little shops, I could criticise the Tudors and praise the alternative beliefs of the Richard III Society. I do recall that for some reason when I was recording this song, I couldn't seem to remember if the gentleman who founded the Fellowship of the White Boar, later to become the Richard III Society, was a Saxon or a Saxton Barton. I got it right in the end. Also, when I first wrote the lyrics, I used the word 'countries', but then changed it to 'counties' in the last verse. I was rather pleased with the guitar solo that I worked out on my Fender Telecaster guitar. It has a Bigsby tremolo arm to give it some extra wang-twang. Just like the one that John Cipollina had on his Gibson SG in the 1960s.

'THE FELLOWSHIP OF THE WHITE BOAR'

We were founded by Saxon Barton
As the fellowship of the white boar
Named after King Richards' standard
And the badge that his knights often wore

We do not accept Tudor slander
It really is quite absurd

All the lies, rumours and falsehoods
Told about Richard the Third

Walpole spoke out for King Richard
And we feel we must do the same
We heartily recommend that you should read
Any books that defend his name

We do not accept Tudor stories
They really are quite absurd
All their lies, rumours and falsehoods
Of the life of Richard the Third

We're a historical society
The Richard the Third Society
A historical society
We're the Richard the Third Society

We have branches in so many counties
You'll find us on Facebook as well
We publish a once yearly journal
The truth about Richard we tell

We do not acept Tudor doctrine
It really is quite absurd
Tudor lies, rumours and falsehoods
Of the life of Richard the Third

I can't recall where the inspiration came for 'The Battle of Barnet Song.' It might have been while reading *'The Sunne in Splendour'* by Sharon Penman. Her book contains a very vivid and exciting account of the battle. This was the next book I read about Richard III. Although I couldn't remember the title of the book I had seen in the English Heritage shop in Middleham back in the early 1990's, I had a very strong feeling that it was going to be the same one. As soon as the book arrived, I saw the opening paragraph was just as I had remembered it. Isn't it strange that I could remember that paragraph from a book I had only briefly glanced at in a shop from many years ago, yet I wouldn't be able to tell you anything of the opening paragraphs of more recent books I have read?

When I started to write the 'Battle of Barnet Song' it was meant to have serious lyrics. It soon turned into a comedy song about a knight and his men arriving late for the battle, and having some wine and ale to give them enough courage to join the fight. Instead of joining the battle they drink too much, fall asleep and wake up to find the battle is all over. This time I've rhymed 'Lords' with 'Swords' so I have a slight variation using the plural of the words compared to the singular in 'Loyalty Binds Me.' So I said to myself, "Now I must be careful not to use that rather obvious and not so original rhyme in another song!"

Lord Zarquon helped me write some of the music. My son Tom and my best friend Phil Helmore joined in with the singing on the chorus when we did the recording. I play the main lead instrumentation on a mandolin and slide guitar. At the end of the song I recorded Phil Helmore saying "My head hurts. We'll have extra duties for a month for this one. I wonder who won?!" All rather ridiculous I know but it makes me laugh.

'THE BATTLE OF BARNET SONG'

My men I think you can hear
That the battle of Barnet is near
Though late for the fight we might be

Let's rest for a while by this tree

The three sons of York are our lords
For them we do raise our swords
To the battle of Barnet we ride
The white rose of York is our pride

The noise of the battle is great
For shame we've arrived far too late
I'm thirsty so let's have some wine
For a quick drink I'm sure we've got time

The three sons of York are our lords
For them we do raise our swords
To the battle of Barnet we ride
The white rose of York is our pride

A drink of ale would be good
Then no more am I understood
Alright one more drink I agree
Then the battle we will surely see

The three sons of York are our lords
For them we do raise our swords
To the battle of Barnet we ride
The white rose of York is our pride

But my courage it has surely gone
And the wine it was rather strong
The ale has gone to my head
We don't fight we sleep instead

The three sons of York are our lords
For them we do raise our swords
To the battle of Barnet we ride
The white rose of York is our pride

I think we drank far too much ale
In valor we did rather fail
Like a mist the battle has gone
But my hangover does linger on

A few years on from recording that humorous song I recorded myself singing a new version of the last chorus.

The three sons of York are our lords
We're too drunk to raise our swords
To the battle of Barnet we crawl
In a drunken heap see us fall

After reading *The Sunne in Splendour*, I read *The White Queen, The Red Queen* and *The Kingmakers Daughter* by Philippa Gregory. During this period I was also watching the 'White Queen' TV series which was in June 2013. I found it quite exciting to see Richard III portrayed as a very handsome young man with many good qualities. I watched most of the episodes several times via BBC iPlayer, although the historical inaccuracies annoyed me. There was no Lord Hastings and Anthony Woodville seemed to be portrayed as a combination of those two people. The battle of Bosworth with snow on the ground was a complete joke. I wonder how Philippa Gregory felt about this? She couldn't have been happy. I thought it was very interesting how she described the same scenes in the different novels from the viewpoints of different characters.

In the summer of that year I had an operation on my left wrist to cure carpal tunnel syndrome. It had got to the stage where it was becoming quite uncomfortable to play the guitar. I suspect the years of playing that instrument had resulted in the problem. Both my mother and her sister had the same wrist problem and operation. Both worked as secretaries in the days of manual typewriters. Although it was a very sad occasion at my aunt's funeral, in the eulogy for my Mum's sister, my auntie Betty, I heard a funny story. When my auntie Betty was working as a secretary she had made a mistake in a letter that had been dictated to her, by accidentally typing the letter 's' rather than a 'w' for a letter addressed to a Mr Whitehouse.

For several weeks after my wrist operation I couldn't play the guitar so I tried to learn to play keyboards using just my right hand. Somehow I managed to compose some songs in this fashion and you can even hear me playing keyboards on the recording of 'The Mystery of the Princes.' My keyboard part sounds a bit like a harpsichord. The keyboard solo is played by Lord Zarquon, using his Minimoog. This is a monophonic analogue synthesiser so that only one note can be played at a time. My wife wrote the words to this song. All the best lyrics were written by her, although I now think I should have changed the line 'When Richard of York came into power'. Richard III was *never* Richard of York, although I suppose he was from the House of York, but Richard of York was really the younger of the Princes in the Tower. Not to be confused with Richard, Duke of York, who was the father of Richard III. Damn, too many Richards! There are too many Edwards as well. Quite often I have become confused by some of the books about the Wars of the Roses as to which Richard, Henry or Edward the author is referring. I expect I am not the only one to get confused.

I wonder if the mystery of the missing princes will ever be solved? It is surely the main reason why so many of us are particularly interested in Richard III. Obviously there is the possibility that Richard may have been responsible for having them done to death but I often think that there is a very strong likelihood that they were moved from the tower of London and that Perkin Warbeck was in fact the younger prince.

'THE MYSTERY OF THE PRINCES'

A mystery whispers it's way through the years
Murder or mercy, bloodshed or tears
What was the fate of the boys in the tower
When the Duke of Gloucester came into power

Did Richard recall his own childhood flight
Out of the danger, away from the fright
Or could it be true against justice and sense
He gave out the order despatching them hence

Could he have sent them to safety abroad
To his sister Margaret away from dischord
A good man maligned or a murder concealed
Was the truth hacked to death at old Bosworth Field

Although I had finished reading it several months ago, I recalled that near the end of *The Maligned King* by Annette Carson there is mentioned the reminiscence of Jean di Meglio of the army of Henry Tudor marching through the wheat fields on the way to Bosworth, and this gave me the idea for the song called 'Wheat in the Field'. This was another song that I composed playing the keyboards very badly with just my right hand. When my wrist had recovered from the operation I was then able to play my 12-string Rickenbacker for the lead guitar part on the recording of the song. This guitar was a 40th birthday present from my wife, and my friend Dave Clifford drove me up to Brentford in his car to help me buy it. This was during the period when we were both playing in our Shady Grove band. I always loved the 12 string guitar sounds of the Byrds and I hoped that I might be able to recreate the sound in Shady Grove. But I never seemed to get my Rickenbacker to sound quite right. I think that my lead guitar playing on 'Wheat in the Field' was the closest I ever got to sounding like a Byrds 12 string electric guitar sound.

'WHEAT IN THE FIELD'

The wheat in the field soon ready for harvest
The year of fourteen eighty five
The ripening wheat in the fields in august
Ruined when Tudor did arrive

The men of Henry Tudor's army
Trampling through the wheat fields
The men of Henry Tudor's army
Marching off to Bosworth Field

The wheat in the field never reached the millstone
Henry Tudor didn't seem to care
His men at arms caused such destruction
With little chance of quick repair

The men of Henry Tudor's army
Trampling through the wheat fields
The men of Henry Tudor's army
Marching off to Bosworth Field

The wheat in the field crushed by an army
Oh the damage they did cause
And many poor folk did go hungry
The new King Henry they did abhor

The wheat in the fields
Then dust beneath the heels
Scattered like memories
And fading in the breeze

Perhaps I am being unfair about Henry VII, for in a book about Bosworth by Chris Skidmore, which I read sometime after writing 'Wheat in the Field', there are some details of the reimbursements made for the crops that had been damaged by Henry's army. Annette Carson mentions this as well in her book but she says that apart from Merevale Abbey and a handful of villages around Atherstone no compensation was paid. Perhaps there was other compensation but there is now no record of this? Would Richard's army have been much more careful where it marched on the way to the battle?

The other two songs that I composed on the keyboard were rejected by Lord Zarquon, and he refused to help me finish the recordings that I had started. One song was called 'The Sunne in Splendour', and I used the idea of Richard being lost in the forest from the opening chapter of Sharon Penman's novel. With the benefit of hindsight I think it was the right decision not to include it on the 'Loyaulté me Lie' album. The other rejected song idea was a very short introductory song called 'A Musical History of Richard III.' I was trying to recreate an Edwardian music hall feel with this song idea, but Mr—or should I say Lord!—Zarquon didn't like it. I still feel that this rejected idea might have worked.

I can remember that he and I had quite a debate about the song called 'The Lord Protector'. He didn't like it that the middle section starts with a G minor chord and then goes to G major towards the end of the instrumental part. We reached a compromise and just used the first half of the song for this track on 'Loyaulté me Lie'. On the album this song ends after the second chorus, just before the instrumental section. There was some very nice acoustic guitar and mandolin played by my neighbour Rob Blaikie on the recording. For the version on the album, Lord Zarquon decided to just use his piano and my vocal. I did record two other versions of the song, and one of those is on a Christmas CD that I gave to some of my friends.

'THE LORD PROTECTOR'

Edward the Fourth lay dying
By his death bed they gathered round
And he named the lord protector
Who he hoped would see his son crowned

He named the lord protector
In whom the queen she had no faith
She feared the Duke of Gloucester
Would not keep her two boys safe

And so history is written
And Prince Edward was never crowned
And Richard a man of honour
In a sea of treason was drowned

I got the idea for the song about Anne Neville while I was on holiday in Yorkshire with my wife, Elaine. Some of the words came to me while we were walking around Middleham Castle. Our friend Graham Moores was with us that day. He lives in Leeds so it was a good opportunity to meet up. At the time I was reading a very good novel by Alison Weir called *A Dangerous Inheritance*. I know that most people in the Richard III Society think that she hates Richard III and is in love with the Tudors, but her portrayal of Richard in this book is quite sympathetic. Her book is quite thought-provoking and intriguing, but it wasn't this novel that inspired the song about Anne Neville, it was the eclipse on the day that she died. This is mentioned in *The Red Queen* and *The Sunne in Splendour* novels. My step daughter's partner, Ashley Dyer played some brilliant trumpet parts for this song and Elaine is singing on the track. Around about this time I had started to do a few gigs where I would sing my songs about Richard III accompanying myself with my acoustic guitar. One evening I made the audience laugh when I said, "Just for a change I'm not going to sing a song about Richard III. Instead I'm going to sing one about his wife!"

'THE LADY ANNE NEVILLE'

We will never know how she felt
In the chapel where she knelt
Nor see the letters that she read
The Lady Anne Neville

The sun went out on the day she did die
Blocked by the moon in the sky
A bad omen on the day she did die
The sun extinguished in the sky

We can guess at the sorrow she felt
In the chapel where she knelt

A message that her son had died
The Lady Anne Neville

The sun went out on the day she did die
Blocked by the moon in the sky
A bad omen on the day she did die
The sun extinguished in the sky

We can't hear the passing bell
The end of joy that does foretell
The burden of a royal wife
The Lady Anne Neville

Just imagine all the letters that were written and read by Anne and Richard, if only these letters could have survived so that we could read them today.

I asked Elaine if she could write some words for a song about Richard's grave being discovered in a car park, and after she had written the words I composed a tune to go with them. I did change two of the lines to read "King Richard a tourist attraction" and "King Richard of England what crowds he could draw" because I felt that the main reason that York and Leicester argued over where his remains should be reburied, was on the basis of the income that could be generated from tourism. I can sympathise with both cities but I preferred the reburial in Leicester on purely selfish grounds as it is closer to where I live. So I am quite happy that I haven't got to travel a greater distance to visit his new tomb. I imagine that Richard would have preferred York and a friend of mine has warned that there will be howls of indignation from some people when they read this.

'THE KING IN THE CAR PARK'

In the choir of the priory hurriedly buried
No casket beneath the tiles of the floor
Silent beneath them unheeded underneath them
King Richard of England, he of the white boar

Car doors slamming, wet feet splashing
Running across to the office door
Silent beneath them, unheeded underneath them
King Richard of England, he of the white boar

The king in the car park, no peace for poor Richard
Will York and Leicester dispute ever more?
Where to rest poor King Richard, a tourist attraction?
King Richard of England, what crowds he could draw

I decided to try using the recording that I had made for the 'Dorchester Fair Song' on the Podtastic abum for the 'Loyaulté me Lie' project. I recorded some new singing and changed the song title and some of the words to 'York City Fair'. Lord Zarquon recorded new drums and added his Mellotron keyboard sounds. Although Guy Bolt had played the drums on the 'Dorchester Fair' recording and there was nothing wrong with his drum playing, we decided to replace his drums with new drum beats because the quality of the sound would be better. Our recording techniques had improved vastly since the recording of 'Dorchester Fair.' Another friend, called Mike Middleton added a new bass line to replace the bass guitar I played several years ago. My guitar, Rob Blaikie's mandolin playing and part of Elaine's backing vocal were retained from the original recording.

A new version of the instrumental 'Fanfare for the King' was also recorded. As I had mentioned in the first chapter it had been previously included on my second album on Golden Pathway. My stepson had composed and played the lead guitar part on the Golden Pathway version and I based my guitar solo on his solo on the new version of this instrumental piece. There was also an instrumental called 'Tudor Danse' that I had started to record a few years ago but never finished. I added a Chinese gong sound and Lord Zarquon worked his musical magic on the track to finish it.

'Sans Charger' was a new instrumental I composed for the album. The title of the track comes from the motto of Lord Thomas Stanley, who was the third husband of Margaret Beaufort, mother of Henry VII. I have seen his motto spelt differently as *San Changer*. I now understood why he had betrayed Richard at Bosworth.

All of the songs were mostly recorded in a similar method to the 'House of York'. I would start off by recording the acoustic guitar on my music computer in my basement, then record the singing, bass guitar, lead guitar and anything else such as mandolin etc. If anybody happened to be around who could sing or play a musical instrument then I would ask them to join in on the recordings. Lord Zarquon would then transfer the music file from my computer to his and add drums and keyboards. We both use Apple Mac computers and Logic music software.

While we had been recording the album, Lord Zarquon had contacted his friend Georgie Harman, who is a professional artist and does the artwork for a magazine called *Wargames, Soldiers and Strategy*. Lord Zarquon approached her to see if she would be interested in creating an album cover for our Richard III music project. She told him she would help us, and I asked her if she could paint the album cover in a style similar to the illustrations of Alphonse Mucha. I particularly like the style of artwork that you see on adverts for the late Victorian, and the Edwardian periods.

Georgie Harman produced a lovely cover for the album and the style of the 'Loyaulté me Lie' lettering was just what I had wanted. To me it looks like a cross between a Mucha painting and a cover from a 1920's edition of *'Argosy All Story'* magazine. Georgie based the portrait of Richard's head on the bust created by Caroline Wilkinson that was shown on the channel four documentary. In the background you can see the inside of Leicester guildhall. You can also see a modern radiator if you look closely!

This is the press release wording for the 'Loyaulté me Lie' album

Pastime Records breaks new ground with the release by The Legendary Ten Seconds of a Richard III Concept Album 'Loyaulté Me Lie'

Pastime Records have just announced their 30th CD release which charts new territory for the Exeter-based independent record label, as The Legendary Ten Seconds release their medieval folk-rock-inspired Richard III concept album 'Loyaulté Me Lie'.

The innovative CD release, the brainchild of the guitarist of The Morrisons and Session 75, Ian Churchward.

In this brilliant collection of songs, the Legendary Ten Seconds reveal the unquenched fighting spirit of the House of York and the steadfast loyalty of Good King Richard. They also bring to life the haunting sadness of death itself. This album is indeed worthy of King Richard III's motto.

Whilst this may seem like a change of musical direction for Ian Churchward, the music of The Legendary Ten Seconds has always been heavily influenced by folk rock and it is an influence on the Byrds' inspired jangly indie pop of Torquay act The Morrisons, for whom Ian has plied his trade as lead guitarist for many years.

The Morrisons, who have strong musical credentials and whose credits include airplay by the late great John Peel and a five star review for their Rainy Day EP from national magazine Artrocker, *now perform under the changed name of Session 75 following a recent change in line up.*

Exeter indie label Pastime Records, set up to promote and support indie acts recording and performing in the South West, has been attracting growing national and international recognition for its quality indie

releases, with radio airplay around the world and glowing reviews from music critics, with Artrocker magazine a particularly vocal supporter. Among the label's acts are nationally reviewed artists Falling Trees, The Morrisons, National Pastime and Andy B, plus new act The Thought Clouds, and recent releases include 'Brush Strokes on Canvas – the South West Music Awards 2012 Official Showcase Compilation CD'. Loyaulté Me Lie by The Legendary Ten Seconds, the 30th release by Pastime Records, is already available for download from such outlets as CD Baby and iTunes and is released on CD shortly.

Musicians performing on the CD are as follows:-
Ian Churchward lead vocals, 6 & 12 string guitars, bass guitar and mandolin
Lord Zarquon Mellotron, Hammond-Nord Electro 3, Roland XP50, MTron Pro and Mini Moog keyboards
Percival Thirlwall drums
Guy Bolt drums on 'Fanfare for the king'
Elaine Churchward backing vocals
Phil Helmore backing vocals on 'The Battle of Barnet Song'
Tom Churchward backing vocals on 'The Battle of Barnet Song'
Ashley Dyer trumpet on 'Fanfare for the King' & 'The Lady Anne Neville'
Rob Blaikie mandolin
Mike Middleton bass guitar on 'York City Fayre' & 'Wheat in the Field'
Songs in historical order
'York City Fayre' written by Ian Churchward & Elaine Churchward
'The Battle of Barnet Song' (April 1471) written by Ian Churchward & Lord Zarquon
'Loyalty Binds Me' (1472) written by Ian Churchward
'Lord Anthony Woodville '(April 1483 there is a theory that he poisoned King Edward IV in early 1483) written by Ian Churchward & Lord Zarquon

'The Lord Protector' (the death of Edward IV early April 1483) written by Ian Churchward

'Fanfare for the King' (coronation of Richard III July 1483) written by Ian Churchward

'The Lady Anne Neville' (death of the wife of Richard III 1485) written by Ian Churchward

'The Wheat in the Field'(August 1485) written by Ian Churchward

'Sans Charger' (new instrumental, it was the motto of Lord Stanley who betrayed Richard III at the battle of Bosworth in August 1485) written by Ian Churchward

'The Mystery of the Princes' written by Ian Churchward & Elaine Churchward

'Tudor Danse' written by Ian Churchward

'House of York' (Richard of York) written by Ian Churchward & Lord Zarquon

'The Fellowship of the Whyte Boare' (a song about the Richard III society) written by Ian Churchward

'The King in the Car Park' (2012 discovery of the grave of Richard III) written by Ian Churchward & Elaine Churchward

PROCEEDS FROM THE SALE OF THE MUSIC WILL BE DONATED TO A SCOLIOSIS CHARITY

Recorded at Rock Lee Studios, Torquay, Devon, by Ian Churchward, and produced and mixed by Lord Zarquon at Rainbow Starshine Studios, Torquay, 2013.

Inspired by the discovery of the grave of Richard III in a car park in Leicester.

Artwork by Redfox illustrations.

Copies of the new CD will be available for £10 and for download from CD Baby, Amazon and iTunes

For further information, photographs and review copies of 'Loyaulté Me Lie' by The Legendary Ten Seconds, contact: Pastime Records, C/O Andy Botterill

Additional Press Release Notes written by Ian Churchward:-
RICHARD III

Richard was born on 2nd October 1452 at Fotheringhay castle. He was the 11th child and youngest to survive into adulthood of Richard Plantagenet, the 3rd Duke of York and his wife Cecily Neville. His oldest brother reigned as Edward IV. Richard fought bravely with Edward at the battles of Barnet and Tewkesbury in 1471 after they both returned from a brief period in exile in Burgundy. At the time Richard was only 18 years old. Edward IV had fallen out very badly with Warwick the Kingmaker who had changed his allegiance over to the house of Lancaster during the period known to us as the Wars of the Roses. This falling out with Warwick had largely stemmed from Edward's secret marriage to Elizabeth Woodville.

Throughout the reign of his brother, Richard was a loyal and faithful supporter and held the title of the Duke of Gloucester. Edward IV died rather unexpectedly after a short illness and Richard was named as Lord Protector upon the Kings death, as Edward's oldest son and heir to the throne was only 12 at the time.

It appears that Richard's interests, property and also his life would have been put at severe risk if his nephew Edward V had been on the throne as the boy King would have been heavily influenced by his mother and her Woodville family. The Woodville's in turn probably felt threatened by Richard as Lord Protector. Richard may have had fears that England would have been plunged into another civil war. These reasons may largely be why he took the step to make himself King when he discovered that his older brother had already been secretly married to Lady Eleanor Butler when he married Elizabeth Woodville, thus making Edward's marriage to Elizabeth bigamous and his heir Edward V illegitimate.

After a brief reign of just over 2 years Richard III was killed at the battle of Bosworth in August 1485 and his victorious opponent took his place as the new King Henry VII. Most simple history books quote the traditional view that Richard was a very cruel and evil monarch and amongst his many supposed crimes was that he killed his 2 young nephews so that he could take the throne. Careful examination of the confusing information from the records of the late fifteenth and early sixteenth centuries casts severe doubt over these traditional views. In fact it actually appears that Richard was a much more just ruler than the usurper Henry VII and that Richard's name was blackened by the victorious Tudor King who had an extremely poor claim to the throne. These are the words for my song called 'The Sunne in Splendour' which was not included on the album.

'THE SUNNE IN SPLENDOUR'

I used to think my brother was as tall as the trees
The trees in the forest that so scared me
For Edward was fair and Edward was strong
I used to think my brother could do no wrong

For my brother was like the sunne in splendour
A hero he seemed to me
My brother was like the sunne in splendour
But he declined in luxury

I used to see my brother as a knight so bold
A king so dashing he would not grow old
For I was young and so naive
He could do nothing wrong I did believe

For my brother was like the sunne in splendour
A hero he seemed to me

My brother was like the sunne in splendour
But he declined in luxury

Initially the album was released in digital format and soon we received some very nice reviews on Amazon. About a month later the CDs of the album were duplicated and the covers printed. Here is one of the first reviews on Amazon

5 out of 5 stars Terrific 20th Dec 2013 by Jazzycat "Gloucester Girl"
If you like good folksy music with a modern slant, excellent production, originality and King Richard III, here's where to find all four. As a Ricardian, I wondered what this could possibly be like, but the word is SUPERB. I have played the whole thing a number of times already, even though I only bought it this morning and it's not yet even 1pm. I must congratulate whoever created the excellent cover art.

We even saw our album in the top 100 Amazon folk music chart although it didn't stay there for very long. It was only there for about one day! In the morning it was in the top 50 section, which also included a Steeleye Span album. It gradually fell down the pecking order in the afternoon and into the evening. By the next day it was no longer there. You've heard of one-hit wonders, well we were a one-day wonder, but at least it lasted longer than ten seconds!

The 'Loyaulté me Lie' album cover which was created by Georgie Harman of Red Fox illustrations.

Chapter Three
Tant le Desiree (I have longed for it so much)

Even before the recording of 'Loyaulté me Lie' had been finished, I had written nearly enough Ricardian songs for a second album about Richard III. Lord Zarquon and I decided to put another one together and call it 'Tant Le Desiree'. At some point during the recording sessions for this album we brought in Rob Bright to play lead guitar, who had previously played in Strange Red Earth with Lord Zarquon. Rob then introduced me to the great Thursday evening acoustic music nights at the Red Rock Brewery near Bishopsteignton, where I decided to perform my songs about Richard III on a fairly regular basis. These Thursday evening music nights would also see me singing cover versions of 'Midnight Hour' (Wilson Pickett) and 'Heart Full of Soul' (The Yardbirds). I seem to have been playing those two songs on and off for years. I first started performing 'Midnight Hour' in the late 1980's with The Morrisons, and I can remember Graham Moores showing me how to play the opening riff to 'Heart Full of Soul' in about 1988.

It was my idea to ask Camilla Joyce to join The Legendary Ten Seconds. We became friends when we first met in the building where I worked in Exeter. She was a secretary for a firm of quantity surveyors who were on the floor below my office. By a strange coincidence it is the same firm for whom my stepson works, although he is based in the Plymouth office. Camilla is a professionally trained actress but I found out that she could sing as well and I showed her some of my songs. She seemed to like them, and sings on some of the recordings produced after the initial 'Loyaulté me Lie' album.

That first album was reviewed by a Ricardian novelist, Sandra Heath Wilson, for the Richard III Society quarterly magazine and the *Murrey and Blue* blog. I later found out that she had also written the first review that was published on Amazon and that I mentioned in the previous chapter. Sandra made contact with me via Facebook and I asked her if she would be interested in writing an audio Ricardian novel which would also include my music. My initial idea was that this would be a novel in audio format, written by Sandra, with my music at the beginning of each Chapter. I then came up with another idea and suggested to Sandra that perhaps she could write some short fictional narratives from the perspective of Richard's mother, Cecily Neville, which might introduce each song for the new album that I was recording.

I sent Sandra an email with a link to a Dropbox file on the internet where I had placed my recordings and Word documents of the lyrics of the song ideas for the next album. Sandra was able to download it all and within a short space of time she sent me the resultant narratives that she had written. I met up with her at a holiday cottage in Tewkesbury in July 2014, where Elaine and I were staying for a week to attend the Tewkesbury Medieval Festival. When she visited I used my portable recorder to record her reading the narratives. Sandra is a staunch Ricardian and I thought it was rather amusing when she told me that her daughter is married to a Stanley!

By about September 2014 we had finished recording the second album about the life and times of Richard III. Unfortunately the Tewkesbury recordings turned out to be poor. Sandra's reading performance was excellent, but you could hear the sounds of the modern world everywhere, such as aeroplanes flying overhead and cars driving past outside. I tried to cover up those present-day sounds by adding some mandola in the background, but you could still hear those intrusive modern sounds. Fortunately Sandra agreed to visit me in Torquay, so we could try again, which we did in my studio basement. I kept the mandola that I had recorded to go underneath the narratives and Lord Zarquon also added some atmospheric keyboard sounds.

Here are the words for the songs and narratives on our second Ricardian album. The words are old French for 'I have longed for it so much', which was another one of the mottoes of the Duke of Gloucester, later Richard III. It was written in his own hand, together with his name, on a page of a book he owned of the story of Ipomedon, the best knight in the world.

'SHAKESPEARE'S RICHARD 1592'

Master William you have shown
A tyrant on the english throne
A hunchback with a withered arm
His reputation has been harmed

Shakespeare's Richard to see and hear
A villain to loath King Henry to cheer
Plantagenet tragedy
History, rhyme and mystery

Master Shakespeare for your queen
With sonnet and drama you did dream
Morton's tale you had read
By Thomas Moore you were misled

Shakespeare's Richard to see and hear
A villain to loath King Henry to cheer
Tudor rewritten history
Richard's charge the death of chivalry

This is a song about Shakespeare's version of Richard III. The lyrics were written by Elaine and myself, and the music was composed while on holiday in Tewkesbury in July 2014. Rob Bright plays the guitar solo on this recording.

"My name is Cecylle, and I was wife unto the right noble Prince Richard, late Duke of York. Many children had we together, daughters as well, but only four sons who lived to manhood. Two of them ascended the throne as Kings of England and France, and Lords of Ireland. Now I have no sons, but of them all, it is the youngest, my beloved Richard, who will always be closest to my heart. He was the third king of that name, and was called after his father, my dear lost duke."

'THE RAGGED STAFF 1470' – Instrumental

The 'bear and ragged staff' was the emblem of Warwick the Kingmaker. I was inspired to compose this mainly because of the encouragement I received via email from Judy Thomson in Chicago. The tune was written and recorded for her. Rob Bright is playing the electric guitar, with some very nice keyboard sounds produced by Lord Zarquon, while I play acoustic guitar and mandola. I may as well say it here (and try not to repeat it over and over) that Lord Zarquon plays particularly fantastic keyboard sounds on all the songs.

"It was at Tewkesbury, on a spring day in the Year of Grace, 1471, that Richard truly proved himself in battle against the Lancastrian enemy. He was young, only eighteen, but he bore his arms like the soldier and commander he had already become. He fought valiantly for York, for his brother King Edward IV, and alongside his other remaining brother, George, Duke of Clarence. Oh, my three sons of York. There was Yorkist glory that day, in the meadows where the rivers Severn and Avon come together. My prince and duke would have been so proud of his sons, but

it was Richard of whom I was the proudest. He was so very deep in my heart."

'TEWKESBURY TALE 1471'

An old man told me of deeds he had done
Of Tewkesbury field fourteen seventy one
King Edward the Fourth and his brothers too
One Richard of Gloucester his lord that he knew

To you this tale I will confide
When he spoke of Duke Richard
He fought by his side
To you this tale I will confide
When he spoke of Duke Richard
A man now despised

'Twas after Barnet's morning mist
King Edward's army he did dismiss
Then came the news of a queen from France
For the fate of her son she would take a chance

To you this tale I will confide
When he spoke of Duke Richard
A man now despised
To you this tale I will confide
When he spoke of Duke Richard
He spoke with pride

Margaret of Anjou she had returned
Of this grave news King Edward had learned

A call to arms in the cousins war
And a frantic march to battle once more

To you this tale I will confide
When he spoke of Duke Richard
He spoke with pride
To you this tale I will confide
When he spoke of Duke Richard
He fought by his side

The Duke of Somerset close by her side
Queen Margaret of Anjou she did decide
To march from the West into Wales
With Jasper Tudor she might prevail

To you this tale I will confide
When he spoke of Duke Richard
He fought by his side
To you this tale I will confide
When he spoke of Duke Richard
He fought by his side

At Tewkesbury field the armies engaged
And Edward the Fourth unleashed all his rage
Somerset smashed in Lord Wenlock's head
And Margaret's son was killed when he fled
And so ends this tale of Tewkesbury
Where Richard of Gloucester fought so bravely

I especially like the sound of the melodeon on this recording which my son Tom is playing. It is a melodeon that used to belong to

Elaine's father. Camilla Joyce is singing with me on this song. There is a key change for the last verse. Matthew North recorded a guitar solo for this song, although it wasn't included on the final version of the song because Lord Zarquon preferred an alternative guitar solo that I had recorded. I'd met Matthew at the Picture House venue in Exeter where I had seen him play guitar and the Morrisons had also performed there. Apologies to Matthew for not using his solo.

"No king could have had a more faithful and reliable brother than Richard, but Edward was not always worthy in return. He threatened war with France, and even assembled an army to go there to join with his allies Burgundy and Brittany, who proved shabby friends. Then the French king offered a treaty with Edward, who permitted himself to be bribed with French gold. I was ashamed of him, and of my other son, George. Richard was too honest and incorruptible to attend. He alone showed English honour when that humiliating treaty was sealed."

'THE GOLD IT FEELS SO COLD 1475'

Clarence took a thousand archers
I took a thousand more
We sailed across the sea to Calais
Not such a distant shore

No honour in the treaty
No honour in the gold
I didn't join them on the bridge
The gold it feels so cold

King Edward took his men at arms
And I took mine as well
I was thinking of Agincourt
When for France we set sail

No honour in the treaty
No honour in the gold
I didn't join them on the bridge
The gold it feels so cold

My brothers took their share of wealth
and I took mine for sure
A heavy heart I still have
When that day I recall

No honour in the treaty
No honour in the gold
I didn't join them on the bridge
The gold it feels so cold

On 'The Gold It Feels so Cold' I am playing a mandola for the first time. I purchased the instrument via the internet and recorded myself playing it in the evening of the day that it was delivered to me. Camilla Joyce is singing with me on this song. Along with 'White Surrey', this was one of the first songs to be completed for the album. I am singing it from the first-person perspective of Richard, taking the view that he went to France with his brothers hoping for glory, but returning very disappointed. Edward IV seems to have been rather relieved that a profitable treaty had been signed after Brittany and Burgundy failed to support the English army in the short-lived campaign of 1475 against the French. The chronicler Philippe de Commines wrote that Richard refused to participate in the negotiations. That is why I state in my song that he didn't join them on the bridge (at Picquigny). I first learned of the Treaty of Picquigny several years ago, when my son Tom was still a young boy, and Elaine and I took him to visit Windsor Castle. I recall that somewhere in the castle there is a carving with a depiction of this treaty. We stayed with our friends Wendy and Ian Watts at their house in Bracknell, and also visited Legoland. Windsor Castle was very interesting and Legoland was good fun and it reminds me that I used to enjoy making castles out of Lego bricks when I was a boy. Another childhood pastime was making sand castles during summer holidays. I was always disappointed if we got to the beach to find that the tide was just going out as I wanted an incoming tide so that I could try to build the strongest sand castle and then do battle against the waves of the sea.

"In 1476 King Edward fixed upon bringing home unto Fotheringhay the bodies of his father, my revered prince, the Duke of York, and my second son, Edmund, Earl of Rutland, who had both died at the Battle of Wakefield in 1460, the Year that was ill Grace to me. Richard was charged to escort the cortège unto the family castle. Fotheringhay was where Richard had been born. So frail a baby he had been. I feared I would lose him. But he fought, oh, how he fought. He was indomitable then, and remained so throughout his life."

'TO FOTHERINGHAY 1476'

My dear trusted Richard I charge you this day
Bring our father and brother to Fotheringhay
To the church, near our castle of Fotheringhay
The church near our castle at Fotheringhay

And I will make certain the chapel of rest
For the reinterment invite royal guests
Matins at midnight and mass at each dawning
Four hundred poor men with torches in mourning

My dear trusted Richard I charge you this day

Bring our father and brother to Fotheringhay
To the church, near our castle of Fotheringhay
The church near our castle at Fotheringhay

The Duke of York's effigy in purple ermine
The royal progress each sign will determine
Mark out the way the procession will follow
My subjects shall share in the depth of our sorrow

My dear trusted Richard I charge you this day
Bring our father and brother to Fotheringhay
To the church, near our castle of Fotheringhay
The church near our castle at Fotheringhay

And I will assemble the great of the land
Ambassadors, envoys and all I command
Nine Bishops to pray for our father and Edmund
Lay them to rest and our prayers we do send them

My dear trusted Richard I charge you this day
Bring our father and brother to Fotheringhay

This song, for which Elaine wrote most of the lyrics, is in the form of an instruction from Edward IV to his brother Richard. The inspiration came from reading a book about Richard III by David Baldwin. I felt really sad when I heard of the death of this author in April 2016. One of so many Ricardians who have sadly died during the few years I have been writing and recording my Ricardian songs. My wife and I really enjoyed reading his book, and also attended one of his lectures in Leicester in March 2015. Camilla Joyce is singing a backing vocal on this track. I recorded a guitar solo, which Lord

Zarquon deleted and replaced with the sound of his Minimoog. I have to admit that the Minimoog solo sounds much better than my deleted guitar solo. I remember not realising that there is a letter 'h' after the 'g' in Fotheringhay and I only discovered my mistake just in time to have the track list spelling amended just before the album covers were due to be printed.

"But Richard was lord of the north, where he was loved and respected. York he may have been, but to all, Yorkist and Lancastrian alike, he was a good, fair and generous lord. The north was his comfort and joy. It pleased him to be away from court, from the plotting, subterfuge and sordid cunning he hated so much. He did not want to be embroiled in such dishonourable matters. But embroiled he soon would be, by events that were not under his control, and would change his life forever."

'CONFORT ET LIESSE 1480'

The title of this instrumental, (Comfort and Joy), is the personal motto of Edward IV. I have based the music around a guitar riff that I made up years and years ago, and was finally able to utilise. The idea for the riff came from watching a band called Innocence Lost in Torquay, sometime in the mid-1980's, and a part played by the lead guitarist. Rob Bright plays the banjo on this track. I remember sitting down in my basement one morning—probably a Sunday—absent-mindedly picking up the guitar with no intention of writing a tune, actually composing it quite quickly, and then spending most of the rest of the day recording the instrumental.

"On his deathbed, Edward named Richard as Lord Protector, to watch over the new boy-king, Edward V. The so-called queen was frightened of Richard's strength and integrity, and wanted her own Woodville family to control the realm. She ordered that her son, the new king, be brought from Ludlow before Richard knew anything. But Richard learned of it,

took charge of his nephew and brought him to London to be crowned.
The Woodville woman fled to sanctuary at Westminster Abbey, taking
her remaining children with her. She blamed others for her downfall . .
. but was herself to blame."

'BY HEARSAY 1483'

By hearsay she heard of his riding to town
For she feared Lord Gloucester would steal her son's crown
This thing to prevent Earl Rivers tried
To ambush and kill him before he arrived

Of treacherous men she would quickly name
She felt Lord Hastings was largely to blame
For giving him warning of her true intent
To comply with her wishes they were not content

King Edward her husband was buried and gone
In mourning and sorrow she did not linger long
In his codicil the protector he named
Of her anger at this she was not ashamed

By hearsay I'm told the ambush did fail
Earl Rivers arrested so that is the tale
To sanctuary she did run and hide
Her next plan of action she would later decide

This song recounts some of the events in the spring of 1483, after
the death of Edward IV. Written several years ago, it was originally
a song about the 17th-century English Civil War. There were some
verses of an English Civil War poem in a book I read about Prince

Rupert, by Charles Spencer, and I made up a tune to go with the words. Eventually I made up my own words to go with the tune so that it is now a song about Elizabeth Woodville in the spring of 1483. In a novel by Reay Tannahill the Woodvilles try to ambush Richard on his journey south after receiving the news of the death of his brother, but in my song it is probably just hearsay.

I am playing the guitar solo on my son's Gretsch guitar, bought for him as his 21st birthday present. We bought the guitar in a shop called Mansons in Exeter, and then walked across the road with it to a cafe where we had a Session 75 gig later that day. At the gig, my stepdaughter took some photos of Tom playing his new guitar. There are fantastic harmony vocals on the 'By Hearsay' track by a sister duo called Gentian. I met them at a local radio station in Paignton one evening. Camilla and I were singing some of our songs on an episode of the Jackson Cooper radio show on Riviera FM.

"After his coronation, how glorious was the royal progress Richard made through his realm. How dazzling his banners and standards, how gracious his smiles as the people lined the way to cheer him. They knew he saved them from more years of war and strife during a minority rule, and they did not believe he had harmed his nephews or done away with them. It was the disaffected nobles who sought to believe such lies, and he already had an enemy within. I speak of his foul toad of a cousin, Buckingham. But Richard prevailed, and Buckingham's rebellion was crushed. And so was the first ignominious and presumptuous venture of one Henry Tudor, of whom I will soon say more."

'ROYAL PROGRESS 1483'

Upon his royal progress he travelled through the land
From London to Reading and on to Nottingham
Long live our good King Richard they shouted to the sky

With cries of acclaimation as the new king rode by

Upon his royal progress he travelled through the land
From Gloucester to Tewkesbury and on to Nottingham
His royal coronation was just two weeks ago
But of a foul conspiracy he was yet to know

To see his royal progress for miles they did walk
To greet their new King Richard when he arrived in York
Of Buckingham's betrayal he would soon be told
The schemes of Bishop Morton would very soon unfold

The idea for the words for this song came from the description of the royal progress in the book about Richard III by David Baldwin. Lord Zarquon composed most of the music, with a bit of help from me. The tune came first and then I wrote the words. I changed the tune slightly to go with the lyrics. The lead guitar is played by Rob Bright and my son plays melodeon.

When I started writing songs about Richard III I didn't know that he had visited Exeter in November 1483. I later discovered the Exeter cathedral rondels, which include details of the reign of Richard III. I hadn't realised there was a local connection to this King, but it was there in the city where I worked all around me! There is an image of Henry VII by a footpath next to the Cathedral which I must have walked over many times before I finally saw it. There used to be a statue of Henry VII on a building called Eastgate House, but it was taken down when the building was demolished and as far as I know it has been stored away somewhere. My good friend Sandra Heath Wilson in true devoted Ricardian fashion has told me that she hopes this statue of Henry VII has been stored somewhere deep, dark, dank and smelly! I can remember seeing the statue on the wall of the building when I used to visit Exeter with my parents and sister. There still exists the Bishop's Palace gatehouse, through which Richard probably rode as he arrived in the city after a brief stop at nearby Bridport.

When I was a child my father often took me around so many of the historic places of interest in Exeter yet only this year I have just discovered by accident a stained glass window of Richard III in the Mercure Exeter Rougemont Hotel. It is only a few minutes' walk away from my office in Exeter. How could I have not known about it for so long? I happened to find out about this window by accident when I stumbled across a reference to it on an obscure web page which had been posted by the USA branch of the Richard III society. The window depicts Richard visiting Rougemont castle in Exeter. The hotel was originally called the Rougemont Hotel and the window was designed by Frederick Drake. There is an inscription under the window which recalls a scene from Shakespeare's play about Richard III in Act 4, Scene 2. I mentioned this window to Shirley Stapley, one of the founding members of the Devon & Cornwall branch of the Richard III society and she was most surprised that she had also not known of it's existence.

During the Second World War the window was removed and placed in a cellar for safety. This was a wise precaution because the centre of Exeter suffered considerable damage due to German air raids in the 1940's. It can be found on the first floor level at the top of a central staircase. The hotel is in Queen Street just off the main shopping high street and opposite Exeter Central railway station.

My parents were both children growing up in Exeter when it was bombed by the German air raids in the Second World War. The glass in the windows of the house where my mother lived in Hoopern street lost much of it's glass windows which were shattered by the bombs exploding nearby. When the German bombers had departed after one of the night air raids my mother's family were using a torch so that they could sweep up some of the broken glass. They were told off by an air raid warden for breaking the black out "Put that light out Jerry might see it!". The Germans had used incendiary bombs and the night sky was full of flames from the city centre which was ablaze. It makes me think of the Hodges character in the episodes of Dad's army.

I decided to put some of my songs on YouTube and wanted some images to go with the music, and not just the album artwork, so I was able to take photos of items of medieval interest in the Cathedral Green area of Exeter. How lucky I am to be surrounded by history. Even in my home town in Torquay there are the remains of a medieval monastery. Just think, if Richard III had won the battle of Bosworth, there might have been much more of the original monastery structure remaining, for there would not have been Henry VIII to bring about its demise. That theme is mentioned in one of my other songs.

"There was such celebration and joy at Richard's court. He loved music and dancing, loved to entertain and be a gracious and engaging host. With his wife Anne at his side, and their little son, also named Edward, he might have been born to wear the crown. The Woodville woman and her daughters came out of sanctuary into his protection. They now trusted him, and that trust was well founded. These were his last months of true happiness. He would have been a great king, but there were those who hated him, and who now looked across the sea to Brittany, to the Lancastrian coward named Henry Tudor, who falsely called himself the Earl of Richmond. They wished this . . . this quaking fraud to invade with French money and men, and dispose of my last and most beloved son! The anointed and rightful King of England. Tudor was not fit to speak Richard's name then. Nor is he now."

'THE COURT OF KING RICHARD III 1484'

Blind John plays the sackbut

No sight since his birth
He sees the music in his head
The notes are filled with mirth

In the court of King Richard the Third
The loveliest music I've ever heard

A choir like a host of angels
Sing in harmony for the guest
A knight from far Silesia
Another song he does request

In the court of King Richard the Third
The loveliest music I've ever heard

In the shadows there is treason
Lord Stanley takes his leave
A message for the lady Margaret
From her son she will receive

This song is about the visit of the Silesian knight, Nikolas von Poppelau, to the Court of King Richard III. The second verse is based on fact but the other verses are historical fiction. Camilla Joyce sings the chorus on yet another song inspired largely by David Baldwin's book. There is a nice bass keyboard intro by Lord Zarquon, and I am playing the guitar solo on my Fender Telecaster. On a fifth Ricardian album we recorded a new version of this song with David Clifford playing the bass guitar and the bass intro. The fictional character that I created, who plays the sackbut, is included in the second novel by Joanne Larner. Her book is called *Richard Liveth Yet (Book II) A Foreign Country*.

"The wheel of fortune turned upon Richard. Death took his wife and son, and left him surrounded by baseness and treason, alone, beset by immeasurable personal grief. Oh, how I feared for him, how I wept . . . and prayed for his safety. May God forgive those who set themselves against him, for I, his mother, will never forgive. Or forget. As the Almighty is my witness, I will protect his name. With this, my testimony, I point my accusing finger at all who were soon to set themselves against him on the battlefield. All of them, because they all bore the name of Judas. Those who lived, still bear that shame now."

'FORTUNE'S WHEEL 1485'

The goddess Fortuna spins the wheel
And our good Fortune she may steal
The goddess Fortuna spins the wheel
And our bad luck she may seal

Fortune's wheel has spun Richard low
And fate has dealt him a mighty blow
Not only has Richard lost his son
It"s a hollow crown that he has won

The goddess Fortuna spins the wheel
And sees your fate chasing at your heel
The goddess Fortuna spins the wheel
See the cards that she will deal

Fortune's wheel has spun Richard low
And fate has dealt a mighty blow
Not only has death claimed his wife
Soon treachery will claim his life

The line about Richard winning a Hollow Crown came from thinking about a book I had read called *"The Hollow Crowns"* by Geoffrey Richardson. I borrowed the book from my friend Graham Moores. This was also inspired from reading the White Queen series of books by Philippa Gregory. There is a scene in one of the books where Elizabeth Woodville's mother Jacquetta talks about the wheel of fortune. This is where I learnt about the goddess Fortuna.

"Richard faced his foreign foes at a place called Bosworth. He was two and thirty, my peerless son, and how proudly he defended his crown, his realm and his life against this shabby French invasion. Mounted on his fine white courser, leading as a true king should lead, he was betrayed by the Stanleys and others. God condemn them all to burn in Hades! Richard ordered a charge that had been carefully planned, to force his way through and cut the craven Tudor down. Tudor, who lifted not a finger throughout the battle. But then Richard's supposed ally, that snake Sir William Stanley, who had been party to the planned charge, deserted my son in the final moments and went over to Tudor. Richard, was hacked down and murdered so bloodily that, that . . . I cannot speak of it. The grief is too much. My eyes fill with tears and my heart sorrows again."

'WHITE SURREY 1485'

His standard proudly on display
The burnished armour shines
Richard upon White Surrey
His knights fall in behind

My horse, my horse my White Surrey
For York and England my White Surrey
My horse, my horse my White Surrey

For York and England my White Surrey

The medieval cannons blast
At Henry Tudor's men
Richard upon White Surrey
Facing death again

My horse, my horse my White Surrey
For York and England my White Surrey
My horse, my horse my White Surrey
For York and England my White Surrey

The horses reaching gallop
The lances coming down
Richard upon White Surrey
Thunder on the ground

My horse, my horse my White Surrey
For York and England my White Surrey
My horse, my horse my White Surrey
For York and England my White Surrey

Sometimes I make fun of my own songs, and change the titles so
that White Surrey becomes White Slurry. This often happened when
I was going through the list of songs during a rehearsal with Rob
Bright and Lord Z. I used to rename quite a few of the tunes in the
Phoenix band set list in the same way.

I am playing the guitar solo on this recording. At rehearsals and
gigs Rob used to play the solo. His solo was different to the one
I played on the album, Rob is a much better, talented and fluent
musician. Camilla Joyce is singing the backing vocal. The chorus was

inspired from the famous line in the Shakespeare play *"My horse, my horse, my kingdom for a horse."* I have never seen a performance of the Shakespeare play about Richard III, because the Bard's version of him does not appeal to me. But I *have* read sections of the play.

"The horses reaching gallop, the lances coming down" was in an article that I read somewhere on the internet. Cavalry charges in the Wars of the Roses were a rarity, because the English men at arms and knights usually fought on foot. My belief is that Richard either longed to lead a cavalry charge in battle, or planned to use his mounted household knights to pursue Henry Tudor, to avoid him escaping after defeating him. The song idea came to me after reading a book about the search for Richard III's grave by Philippa Langley and Michael Jones. It is a most interesting book with alternating chapters by Philippa and Michael.

When I played this song at the Red Rock near Bishopsteignton I started by saying, "This is a song about Richard III on his horse, White Surrey, at the battle of Bosworth." I heard a lady in the audience cry out and thought she was going to faint. Later I learned that she was a Ricardian and had never heard anyone sing a song about Richard III.

On the anniversary of the battle of Bosworth in August 2017 I released a new version of the song featuring a new bass part played by David Clifford, new keyboard parts played by Lord Zarquon and a new lead vocal sung by myself. We combined this with some of the original parts of the recording such as my lead guitar and the backing vocal of Camilla Joyce. We also used the recording I had made with my 12 string electric guitar which hadn't been included on the Tant le desiree album but had been recorded during the original recording sessions for the song.

In 2017 I wrote a comedy song about one of my colleagues who I work with. I took the tune of my White Surrey song and made it into a song called 'He's off to Yoga.' To fully appreciate the humour I need to tell you that my colleague Chris Greenway sometimes used to take about an extra hour for his lunch break so that he could go to a yoga class. He also catches the train every day from where he lives in Exmouth because the traffic is so awful from his home to our office in Exeter. If he's ever late then we say that it must be due to leaves on the line. He has got a precious blue stapler and a large calculator that are relics from the 1970's. The bit about the two screens in the song is his refusal to have two screens which would make his work so much easier rather than having just the one linked up to his computer. Also at work my nick name is Chuffer which comes from another colleague called Malcolm Bowen giving everyone Bertie Wooster sounding nick names. Andy Fenn was Fudger Fenn, Chris is Greeners Greenaway or sometimes he is Christal Palace Greenaway because he loathes Crystal Palace. Chris is a Charlton Athletic supporter and I don't know how on earth he coped when they ground shared for a period of time with Crystal Palace. Young Craig Skinner who also worked at my office for a while was called Stilton Skinner because we felt he was very mature for his age. Bounder Bowen is the nickname I gave to Malcolm.

'HE'S OFF TO YOGA'

His two screens proudly on display
The polish on his shoes shines
Greenway working at his desk
Listen to him whinge and whine

His desk, his stapler, his calculator
He's off to yoga he'll see you later
His desk, his stapler, his calculator
He's off to yoga he'll see you later

Late for work it's the same excuse
There were leaves on the line
Or the train from Exmouth was cancelled
Good lord is that the time

His desk, his stapler, his calculator
He's off to yoga he'll see you later
His desk, his stapler, his calculator
He's off to yoga he'll see you later

The completions are piling up again
Another loan reversal yippee
Here's hoping that chuffer Churchward
Will make him a cup of coffee

His desk, his stapler, his calculator
He's off to yoga he'll see you later
His desk, his stapler, his calculator
He's off to yoga he'll see you later

"I have longed so much and so often for the survival of my last son. Would that his life had been happy and that his dear soul were still here on earth. I yearn for his arms to embrace me again, and his lips to press lovingly to my forehead. He always asked how I was, in French, because it pleased me. "Comment vas-tu, ma chère mère?" "How are you, my dear mother?" He was all to me, my Richard, Duke of Gloucester, so fine and delicate, so loving, and such a brave and dauntless warrior."

'THE BOAR LAY SLAIN 1485'

The boar lay slain on Bosworth Field

Too brave to flee, to proud to kneel
And then a dragon claimed the land
With poisoned tongue and crooked hand

And those who welcomed him would rue
When the red drake took his due
And then they laboured neath his claw
As greed and lies replaced the law

The boar lay slain on Bosworth Field
Too brave to flee, to proud to kneel
And then a dragon claimed the land
With poisoned tongue and crooked hand

Five centuries would pass before
The resurrection of the boar
As scholarship and loyalty
Free him from earth and calumny

The boar lay slain on Bosworth Field
Too brave to flee, to proud to kneel
And then a dragon claimed the land
With poisoned tongue and crooked hand

A song about Richard's death at the battle of Bosworth. The words
were written as a poem by the talented artist Frances Quinn, who
lives in Ireland. I saw the words on Facebook via the internet, and
made up some music to go with the poem. I am trying to make
psychedelic noises (inspired by the 'Piper At The Gates Of Dawn'
album by Pink Floyd) using a metal slide against the guitar strings on
my Fender Telecaster electric guitar, with lots of echo in the middle

of this song. Frances told me she liked my musical interpretation of her poem, and she created a painting to go with the song.

'The woman I most despise of all is the Tudor's evil dam, Margaret Beaufort, who feigns piety but is godless. She and Morton, that scheming, conscienceless bishop—now Archbishop of Canterbury and Lord Chancellor, no less—did all they could to bring Richard down. They, more than anyone, were responsible for the treachery that killed him. God will punish them for the evildoers they are. More than that, my baseborn granddaughter, Bess, is pronounced trueborn again, in order to be married to the Tudor, who makes a display of uniting York and Lancaster after so many years of war. The usurper—misbegotten himself, from all accounts—cannot marry a Yorkist bastard, even the daughter of King Edward IV. Oh, that such villainy should prevail. I am glad my dear duke is not here to see. So glad. But I will defend Richard's name. Loudly. Always."

'THE ROSE OF TUDOR 1509'

She knew her father had died in shame
A lasting slur on the Beaufort name
And her grandfather he was bastard born
The truth concealed distorted not worn

Secret ambition and deep desire
So strong her feelings, a holy fire
The rose of Tudor risen from the earth
For the hope of her son at his birth

Margaret Beaufort she did foresee
For her son Henry on bended knee
For her red rose she did claim
To bring glory to Tudor's name

Secret ambition and deep desire
So strong her feelings, a holy fire
The rose of Tudor risen from the earth
For the hope of her son at his birth

She lived to see her grandson crowned
At dissolving the monasteries he was renowned
An evil man on a tyrant's quest
For his six wives he is known best

Driving ambition and deep desire
So strong her feelings, a holy fire
The rose of Tudor risen from the earth
False hope for a grandson at his birth

The idea for the lyric for this song about Margaret Beaufort, mother of Henry VII, came after reading a book called *The Women of the Cousins' War*. I remember working out the sequence of the chords for this song in the board room of my office in Exeter one evening, while waiting for Camilla where we used to sometimes rehearse.

We have great hopes for our children and what joy it must have been for Margaret to live to see her son crowned as king of England. But she must have turned in her grave during the later years of her grandson's reign and especially with the dissolution of the monasteries.

One thing that I really recall about the song is that I was suffering with a very bad cough when I was recording my singing. It was a real struggle to sing it properly without coughing all the time.

"How my sleep is haunted by what might have been. I dream that Richard had not died at Bosworth, but left the field in triumph. There was never a cunning, spineless Tudor, only the glory of my youngest

son's long reign. How England would have prospered, and such a happy land it would have been. What a king was lost to us that black August day. What a king. My son. May his dear soul rest in peace, and may I meet him again in Heaven. He will take me in his arms and kiss my forehead, and I will hear again his loving greeting. 'Comment vas-tu, ma chère mère?' *My tears flow again. I am not strong enough to go on. Not now, when all that I hold most dear has been taken from me. Rest in peace, my husband and my sons. Rest a while, the House of York, one day to rise again. But most of all, rest in peace King Richard III, my most beloved son. My comfort and my joy."*

'YORKIST ARCHER 1513'

My grandfather he was an archer
For Edward the Fourth he did fight
In the snow in a battle called Towton
He spoke of many arrows in flight

My father he too was an archer
In the army of Richard the Third
Both died at the battle of Bosworth
Fighting bravely so I have heard

And me I too am an archer
With my bow I was at Flodden field
And though in my heart I'm a Yorkist
For the Tudors I have surely killed

My Yorkist Archer song, the last to be recorded for the album, is about an archer reflecting upon his grandfather, father and the battle of Flodden. There is a key change on the final verse. Lord Zarquon has used the same Mellotron sound on parts of our recording, as the sound that you can hear on the Pink Floyd song called 'Julia Dream', which is on their 'Relics' album. I believe the same sound was used on 'Ha Ha Said the Clown' by Manfred Mann. The keyboard sound is a mark two Mellotron flute sound, which was recorded onto tape in the early 1960's. The Mellotron uses tapes, a bit like cassette tape with recordings of each note of various instruments to produce the sound when it is played. Mike Pinder used a Mellotron keyboard on the late 1960's and early 1970's albums of The Moody Blues. A Mellotron keyboard from the 1960's, in good condition, would be worth tens of thousands of pounds. Unfortunately Lord Zarquon does not own a Mellotron but his keyboards have the sounds of the tapes that were used in the Mark Two and Three Mellotrons.

The Yorkist archer song was composed in Tewkesbury in July 2014 and was inspired by all the archers at the Tewkesbury medieval festival that we had attended. I remember working out some of the lyrics while driving during the week of that holiday. It was a very inspirational time, meeting Sandra Heath Wilson and seeing all the banners and coats of arms of many of the participants of the battle of Tewkesbury on display in the town. I sang some of my Richard III songs to Sandra when she visited the house where we were staying in Tewkesbury. I also met up with another friend called Judy Jacobs, who has done quite a lot to help promote my music, for which I am very grateful. It was a lovely spot by the river. While staying in Tewkesbury we also went to a very interesting and enjoyable lecture about George, Duke of Clarence, given by Dr John Ashdown-Hill. It was a fabulous holiday.

"Tudor—that vile faintheart!—has perpetrated many cruel lies against Richard, upon whose innocent shoulders are heaped charges so vile it grieves me to speak of them. At least Bess, the new Queen of England will not speak out against her lost uncle, much as Tudor wishes it. Richard did not harm his nephews when they were sent into the palace

in the Tower. Nor did he poison his wife in the hope of marrying Bess, towards whom he was never other than a fond uncle. They even claim Richard's back was hunched, his arm withered, his whole self a monstrosity. Monstrosity? My Richard? He had true beauty, both within and without, and possessed all the fine qualities Tudor will never possess, because Tudor is a craven wretch, a creature of bile and corruption. Both within and without."

'THE ROAD TO MIDDLEHAM'

This is another instrumental, and the idea for this tune began while I was playing the mandola. My lead guitar on this one was played on my Fender Esquire (not to be confused with the budget Fender Squire), which is easier to play than my Telecaster, but I must admit I prefer the sound of the Telecaster.

The 'Tant le Desiree' album cover portrays Richard in a full suit of armour upon a white horse, riding past his army, which stands in the background. It is a fantastic piece, although on reflection I wonder if his sword in its scabbard, might be too long and a possible health and safety tripping hazard!

Graham Moores painting the album cover for 'Tant le desiree' at his house in Leeds in 2014. I first met Graham when I was working in Sherborne in the early 1980's. Graham played in a band that was part of a really good live music scene in that part of north Dorset. I also got to know Andy Perry in Sherborne. Andy used to write articles for a local music fanzine called *Feeding the Fish* and he is now a well established music journalist. I occasionally see Andy at Plainmoor (the theatre of pain!) when Torquay United Football club are playing at home.

Chapter Four
Richard III

After finishing the recording of 'Tant le Desiree', we still had unused Ricardian songs and we carried on recording additional songs for a third album. Matthew Lewis let me use some historical narratives he had recorded, some specifically for my songs and others from his Ricardian history podcasts.

This narrative was written for my song called 'Sheriff Hutton' but was not used and I think it was not recorded by Matthew. It is a shame it isn't on the album as it is an excellent piece.

"In 1472 Edward IV, the first Yorkist king, established the Council of the North to administer areas around Yorkshire, Lancashire, Cumberland, Northumberland and Westmorland. The royal writ barely reached such far flung areas and the north had been the stronghold of the Neville affinity that had prised Edward from his throne for six months. Warwick's death at Barnet left a vacuum in a dangerously unruly region. Edward needed to fill that vacuum and there was only one person that he could entrust the job to. Richard, Duke of Gloucester was appointed as the first Lord President of the Council of the North. He was also granted the huge Warwick lands in the north so that he could represent the king's will. During more than a decade in the region Richard worked hard to improve the financial situation of the region, obtaining tax breaks from his brother. He sat in the courts to see impartial, equitable justice done under his keen eye. This service is the root of the love the north held for Richard III as duke and king, an affection that lingers still. The Council was initially based at Sheriff Hutton Castle and Richard stayed there frequently. The castle had been a Neville fortress in North Yorkshire, close enough to the city of York to be a convenient base of operations. Walking the walls of the ruin that remains to us today it is easy to imagine the hustle and bustle

of a working castle at the heart of government, with Richard standing, overseeing it all, as his own brand of justice was granted to a grateful region."

These are the songs that were recorded for the third album which we called 'Richard III':-

Song One:

Rob Bright plays the lead guitar solo. Lord Zarquon & David Clifford were quite impressed with my bass playing on this song. 'Sheriff Hutton' was partly inspired when I heard from a lady called Susan Buonaparte that this was her favourite castle. Susan has her own business called Loyalty Binds Us, which specialises in merchandise related to the Wars of the Roses. I met Susan at the Tewkesbury Medieval Festival in 2013. She had a stall there and sold some of my Loyaulté me Lie CDs at the festival. I also met Pam Benstead of the Worcester branch of the Richard III Society, who also agreed to display and sell my CDs on the stall she was helping to manage.

'SHERIFF HUTTON'

Of Sheriff Hutton I have been told
A sense of wonder did unfold
Of Richard's council of the north
Its lonely ruins I see henceforth

On the castle walls he must have walked
To his affinity he must have talked
Where distant echoes still resound
That which is lost may still be found

To Middleham Castle I have gone
It's broken walls once so strong
The strange white statue standing there
A twist of fate hanging in the air

On the castle walls he must have walked
To his affinity he must have talked
Where distant echoes still resound
That which is lost may still be found

To the Tower of London one fateful day
The crown of England one step away
At Bosworth Field, once Redemore Plain
Where Richard fought and lost in vain

On the castle walls he must have walked
To his affinity he must have talked
Where distant echoes still resound
That which is lost may still be found

Song Two:
The idea for this song came after reading the pages in a novel called
Stormbird by Conn Iggulden, which describes the birth of Richard.
In *Stormbird*, I feel that the Duke of York comes across as a rather
evil person, but in the next book of the series he seems to be quite a
noble character. Another source of inspiration for this song was yet
again David Baldwin's book about Richard, where I first learnt of the
Clare Roll, which states that "Richard Liveth Yet". My stepdaughter
sings with me on this song, my son Tom plays the melodeon, and
Rob is playing the banjo.

'RICHARD LIVETH YET'

The first cry of a new born child
And the delight at the birth of a son
The Duke of York full of pride
And a new life has now begun
And Richard liveth yet

The youngest son of the Duke of York
Born at the castle of Fotheringhay
October fourteen fifty two
Was the sun shining on that autumn day?

Song Three:
This is a song about the letter that Richard wrote at Castle Rising in
June 1469, to the Chancellor of the Duchy of Lancaster, Sir John Say.
It is another song inspired by David Baldwin's book about Richard
III, and some of Richard's original words from the letter are included
in the song.

There is a scene in another book, one of fiction, called *We Speak No
Treason* by Rosemary Hawley Jarman, in which the young Duke of
Gloucester dictates this letter which is written by his scribe. I read
her book about a year *after* I had written my song.

On July 4th 2015 Rob Bright, Lord Zarquon, Camilla Joyce and I,
as The Legendary Ten Seconds, played a selection of songs from the
three albums in Guildford for the West Surrey branch of the Richard
III Society. With a friend, Judy Jacobs, I wrote some narratives which
Camilla read as an introduction to each song when we performed in
Guildford.

This is the narrative that Camilla read as the introduction for
'Written at Rising', which was the first song on the set list

"My name is Margaret of York, Dowager Duchess of Burgundy. I am a daughter of the late Richard Plantagenet, Third Duke of York, and sister to, among others, Edward, Earl of March, George, Duke of Clarence, and Richard, Duke of Gloucester, known as the Three Sons of York. Edward and Richard both went on to ascend the Throne as Kings of England and Lords of Ireland. In the summer of 1469, my brothers, Edward (now King Edward IV) and Richard were staying at Castle Rising in Norfolk whilst travelling to Yorkshire to put down a rebellion in that county. From here, Richard wrote to Sir John Say, the King's Under-treasurer, requesting a loan of £100 to enable him to supply arms and men to assist his brother the King."

'WRITTEN AT RISING'

From Castle Rising fourteen sixty nine
To Sir John Say this letter I sign
Right trusty and well beloved we greet you well
And of my lack of funds I do sadly tell

The kings good grace has appointed me
To attend for his highness I did not foresee
My urgent request for one hundredth pound
Until next Easter when repayment is found

For at this time I am in great need
and I must show you good lordship indeed
The bearer hereof shall inform quite soon
Written at Rising the twenty fourth day of June

Song Four:

Rob Bright plays the guitar solo on 'Gold Angels', in which I have imagined the Duke of Gloucester visiting the court of King Edward IV at Christmas in the late 15th century. It was inspired by finding out there were coins called Gold Angels. I would like to think that I've written the first ever Christmas song about Richard III. My memory is uncertain about exactly when it was composed. It may have been in the spring or summer of 2014, it certainly wasn't written approaching or during the festive season. The song was initially released as a single download for December 2014. Graham Moores painted a fantastic picture of a Gold Angel coin for the song. When I showed the computer image of the painting to Elaine and Lord Zarquon, they thought it was a photo, and didn't believe me when I told them that it had been painted.

It may seem a bit odd to write a Christmas song when it isn't anywhere near the season of goodwill. One Christmas Elaine gave me a mandolin. I spent most of that day in my basement, writing and recording a comedy song called 'Santa Was Grumpy' complete with mandolin solo. Fortunately it was a quiet Christmas, with just Elaine, my son Tom and I in the house. Tom and Elaine were quite happy for me to be unsociable in my basement while they watched Christmas programmes and DVDs on the TV.

'SANTA WAS GRUMPY'

Santa was grumpy on Christmas Eve
His elves had too many tricks up their sleeves
Somehow they ended up ina fight
Delivering Christmas presents all through the night

Ho ho
Ho ho ho
Bah humbug I hate all the snow

Santa's feeling grumpy on Christmas Day
He's got a bad back after riding on his sleigh
You know he had a late night
Got stuck in a chimney on the Isle of Wight

Ho ho
Ho ho ho
Bah humbug I hate all the snow

Santa's feeling grumpy on Boxing Day
All of his reindeer have run away
He ran out of hay so they told him where to go
They're somewhere in Lapland enjoying all the snow

Ho ho
Ho ho ho
Bah humbug I hate all the snow

Santa got drunk at the party last night
It was New Year's Eve, he was high as a kite
Now he's hungover please get him a bucket
Roll on next Christmas he's going to throw up in it

Sandra Heath Wilson had written a narrative for the 'Gold Angels' song, and I recorded her reading it in Tewkesbury. I think that I may have intended to include the song on the 'Tant Le Desiree' album, but it wasn't finished in time for that album. I did use a segment of her narrative in an alternative version of the song, which I included on the Legendary Ten Songs Christmas album. This was something that wasn't professionally duplicated. I made the copies of the album at home and gave the CDs to some of my friends with a Christmas card.

This is the narrative that Matthew Lewis wrote and recorded for 'Gold Angels.'

"The medieval Christmas could be a raucous affair, often attracting the dismayed disapproval of the religious community who saw the true meaning of Christmas lost in debauchery. How little some things change across the centuries. One tradition lost to us is that of the appointment of a Lord of Misrule. The position could be found at the royal court, in the households of nobles and lords, at the Inns of Court and even in universities. The Lord was appointed to oversee the festivities, ruling for weeks and even months. He was responsible for organising all of the feasts and dances during the Christmas season. The Lord of Misrule was usually a peasant, overturning the social structure for a brief time as he received mock homage from his traditional betters. Recently a coin was sold in London for £36,000. It was a gold angel, minted around 1484 and bearing the boar badge of King Richard III along with an image of St George spearing a dragon. Valuable in its own time, it was a precious find that trebled its estimate."

'GOLD ANGELS'

The lord of misrule was dancing
The duke he did conceal
In his purse he had gold angels
For gifts he would later reveal

It was Christmas Day in London town
Snow covered the filth in the streets
There was ice on the banks of the river Thames
And his barge the duke he did seek

Here's a gold angel for Christmas Day
Richard handed his bargeman the gift
Now steer me to Westminster thank you, sir
For your service now let's be swift

The duke's barge on the river Thames
Steered to the royal court
Departing from Baynards Castle
Richard Gloucester deep in thought

The lord of misrule was dancing
The Duke of Gloucester did kneel
To the Queen Elizabeth Woodville
True feelings they were concealed

And the lord of misrule kept dancing
The duke he did conceal
In his purse he had gold angels
For gifts he would later reveal

Song Five:
The words for this song are taken from Act 3, Scene 4 of Shakespeare's play about Richard III. It describes the meeting just before the arrival of the Lord Protector, and the dramatic accusation of the treason of Lord Hastings followed by his execution. I did try to write my own lyrics, based on Shakespeare's words, but I couldn't get that idea to work and in the end just put my own music to Shakespeare's prose to create the song. At school I found the Bard incomprehensible in English literature lessons, but now I appreciate the eloquence and meaning of his words, even though most of the play about Richard III is bad history. Matthew Lewis could very well

be correct in his theory that the portrayal of Richard III is based on a hunchbacked politician from the reign of Elizabeth I, rather than Richard himself. All this is told in one of the narratives read by Matthew Lewis, which is on the album. I am playing my mandola on the intro to this song. The lead guitar parts are played by Rob. My stepdaughter sings the words of the chorus.

'ACT III, SCENE IV'

Now noble peers
The cause why we are met
Is to determine
Of the coronation
In God's name speak
When is the royal day
Are all things ready
For that royal time

Song Six:
After reading a book called *Richard III and the Murder in the Tower* by Peter Hancock, I came up with the idea for a song which I called 'The Year of Three Kings'. The guitar solo is mine, and my friend Phil Helmore is singing on the chorus. I gave Phil a pint of beer to put him in the right frame of mind for singing along on the chorus, which I imagined would sound good as a drunken sing-along in a pub, with tankards of ale swinging in time to the music. In fact the chorus has become quite popular for singing along to at the regular acoustic music Thursday evening session at the Red Rock.

Matthew Lewis wrote this narrative for 'The Year of Three Kings', but as far as I think he never recorded it.

"The few months of the spring of 1483 are a mystery, wrapped in an enigma and cloaked in mystery and paradox. Those who will tell you

that they know exactly what happened and why do not. Whether they paint Richard as an ambitious demon or a wronged saint their certainty is an illusion. On the 9th April 1483 King Edward IV died. His 12 year old son Edward was proclaimed King Edward V and Richard was appointed to be his nephew's Lord Protector. Richard took possession of his nephew and arrested members of his Woodville family. Preparations were made for a coronation and oaths of loyalty were sworn. In June, Edward and his siblings were declared illegitimate and Richard was proclaimed to be the only heir of the House of York who could take the throne. The motives of all parties and the contents of men's hearts cannot be known. Was Edward IV a victim of his wife and her family? Had he been pre-contracted to another? If so, his son was illegitimate and not capable of inheriting. Had Richard wanted the crown for years, harbouring a dark ambition that saw an opportunity to grow in the light of the upheavals of 1483? Were other hands at work to dismantle the House of York? Bishop Morton, Margaret Beaufort, Lord Stanley? We cannot know, but we can take a journey toward an opinion that takes consideration of the fact that these were real people, complex men and women with hopes, fears, triumphs, disasters and dreams that shaped them and their world."

'THE YEAR OF THREE KINGS'

Edward the Fourth his lust for life flown
With the hated Woodvilles the seeds of strife sown
The cronicles tell us of conspiracy
In a struggle for power in the year of three kings

The year of three kings, the year of three kings
The chronicles tell us of the year of three kings

Edward the Fifth a boy never crowned
With his disappearance the rumours abound
The chronicles tell us of conspiracy
Amidst all the rumours in the year of three kings

The year of three kings, the year of three kings
The chronicles tell us of the year of three kings

Richard of Gloucester an heir to the throne
But of the pre-contract he had not known
The chronicles tell us of conspiracy
In a text of confusion in the year of three kings

Song Seven:
Part of the idea for this song probably comes from thinking about
what I had read in one of Geoffrey Richardson's books. The words
are partly written by Susan Lamb. My initial recording of the song
was altered considerably. In the verse sections of the final recording
there is only one chord when originally there were several. My
stepdaughter is singing a backing vocal on this track. The mp3
version, which was released before the CDs of the album were
duplicated, differs to the one on the CD. On the physical version
of the album there is a backwards guitar feedback piece underneath
the keyboard solo in the middle instrumental section of the tune and
this is absent from the digital version of the song.

'HOLLOW CROWN'

You see this crown how it does shine
A golden crown and it is mine
I wear it for England which I hold dear

A cry of usurper I did hear

This hollow crown upon my head
They say my brother's sons are dead
Whispers at court behind my throne
In my reign seeds of doubt are sown

You see this body is it truly mine
My back is bent like a twisted vine
You speak of evil to tarnish my name
For the death of Hastings I am to blame

This hollow crown upon my head
And now my youngest son is dead
My grief at court upon my throne
The queen and I feel so alone

You see this sword in my hand
Against Tudor I defend this land
Of news from France I wait to hear
Within my armour I hide my fear

This hollow crown upon my head
They say Queen Anne will soon be dead
The sky is dark though it is day
With my book of hours I do pray

Song Eight:
Here is a narrative written, read and recorded by Matthew Lewis for
my song called 'Hollow Crown'. However, on the 'Richard III' album
the narrative was used to introduce 'Remember My Name'. I changed

the words for this song, from what I had originally written so that it was no longer my thoughts about the First World War, but instead about an archer departing to join an army to help defend the crown of a king. My step daughter is once again singing with me on this song. I did record a guitar solo for the instrumental section but this was replaced with a keyboard solo.

"As King Richard III took the field at the Battle of Bosworth in his gleaming, polished armour a golden crown sat atop his helm, glinting in the bright sunshine. It was a bold and defiant gesture of right and authority. 70 years earlier at the Battle of Agincourt King Henry V had done the same thing as his small band of bedraggled refugees faced the flower and might of French chivalry. The accomplished leadership of Henry V against the ill ordered and pompous French was already the stuff of legend. Not only had Henry gained a famous victory that defined his reign and opened the doorway to an empire but he had answered once and for all the critics of the Lancastrian dynasty who had plagued his father for over a decade as a usurper. Henry proved that God had accepted Lancastrian kingship. Who was left to argue now? As Henry Tudor invaded Richard's kingdom this Yorkist king had a similar point to prove. Facing an army largely comprised of French soldiers and charged as an undeserving usurper, Richard lowered that symbol of kingship atop his helm to mark himself out to all on the battlefield. A rallying point to allies and a challenge to foes. He offered himself for judgement as Henry V had done but was destined not to leave that patch of English earth alive."

'REMEMBER MY NAME'

The king has commanded and to battle you must go
From our home to a fate I'd rather not know

So if I never see you again

I won't forget you
I'll remember your name

With my longbow I hope my aim will be true
For war clouds have gathered and I must leave you

So if I never see you again
Please don't forget me
And remember my name

The king has commanded and to battle you must go
From our home to a fate I'd rather not know

Our lives once so happy
Could be shattered and torn
Some will rejoice but others will mourn

Song Nine:
Judy Thomson of Chicago wrote these words. She asked me if I could turn her words into a song. I had to change a few to fit the tune that I concocted. Her words were written to go with a novel she was writing. There is a chapter set sometime after the battle of Bosworth when Lord Lovell is singing a lullaby to help a young child to sleep.

'LORD LOVELL'S LAMENT'

Pray sleep thou tender child
I hold you to my breast
Defended from the wild
And slumbered in thy nest

Oh let sleep be so mild
Without dreams of strife
Sleep hold thee undefiled
Sweet innocent young life

Remember those now reviled
Whose faith had wavered not
Their honour has been defiled
They lie in earthen plot

Oh let sleep be so mild
Without dreams of strife
Sleep hold thee undefiled
Sweet innocent young life

Song Ten:
The idea for 'Requiem' came to me when I was driving home from a ballroom dancing lesson in Torquay. If you think that is a rather strange moment to get an idea for a Ricardian song then wonder no more since I spent quite a bit of my time thinking about ideas for songs about Richard III. Pity my poor family, especially Tom and Elaine when they were trying to have a conversation with me about something that had nothing to do with the late fifteenth century. Quite often I was not paying attention, quite lost in the mysteries of the Wars of the Roses.

Matthew Lewis wrote this narrative, but for some reason, probably a lack of time, it was not recorded for the album.

"Margaret of York was the fifth child of Richard, Duke of York and Cecily Neville to live to adulthood. She was the sister to two kings of England, aunt to another king and to Henry Tudor's queen consort. Her marriage to Charles the Bold, Duke of Burgundy, who died in 1477, left her wealthy and powerful as Dowager Duchess. Her youngest

brother's death at the hands of the first Tudor king and the loss of her family's throne left her embittered and determined. At the close of the Wars of the Roses, at least one thorn remained to torment Tudor. After Bosworth Margaret worked tirelessly to undermine the new Tudor regime. She supported Lambert Simnel's invasion with men and money and her hand was at work in the Perkin Warbeck affair that seriously threatened Henry VII. The Dowager Duchess's court at Mechelen became a haven for those who retained their Yorkist loyalties or who became disaffected with Henry VII's rule. Margaret lived until 1503 and although Henry Tudor worked to reduce her influence she remained utterly unreconciled to the regime that she believed had stolen her family's throne. She caused trouble wherever and whenever she was able in the belief that she could, or at least had a responsibility to try to, regain her family's birthright."

'REQUIEM'

Her heart was full of sorrow
The news somewhat delayed
Her younger brother Richard
In battle he was betrayed

A requiem mass for Richard
She had to prepare
Her heart was full of sorrow
Anger and deep despair

A usurper Henry Tudor
How she would hate that name
Did steal the crown of England
Her brother cruelly slain

A requiem mass for Richard
She had to prepare
Her heart was full of anger
Margaret's deep despair

A Greyfriars church in Mechelen
In the choir her body to rest
For in her will was written
This burial request

Song Eleven:
Here is another song that resulted from reading Annette Carson's *The Maligned King*, although the idea came to me a couple of years after reading the book. Rob Bright plays lead guitar on this song, and as well as playing acoustic guitar, I also play mandola. Sometime after recording this song I managed to borrow a copy of *The History of King Richard III*, edited by Arthur Kincaid. The original manuscript written by George Buck, had never been published as the author had intended, and had been damaged in a fire. Somehow Arthur Kincaid was able to assemble how the manuscript should probably have been published. The amount of time and skill required to have done this is truly staggering. It is an intriguing piece of work. The story about the manuscript is very interesting as it was published in a corrupted form by a great nephew of the author who was also called George Buck and he passed the work off as his own. Because of all the errors that were added by the nephew, the work of Sir George Buck was never taken seriously when in fact the original manuscript was the work of much painstaking and careful research.

'ROYAL TITLE'

I am descended from Sir John Buck

Executed after Bosworth Field
For loyalty I will write a book
And the truth will be revealed

For I have found the Croyland Chronicle
Written out by scribes
Within the missing royal title the truth it has survived

I have climbed the social ladder
And I went to the Inns of Court
Served the Tudor Queen Elizabeth
But the truth I have now sought

For I have found the Croyland Chronicle
Written out by scribes
Within the missing royal title the truth it has survived

The lords spiritual and temporal
Did petition a mighty prince
To be the ruler of this land
Shown dishonour ever since

My name is Sir George Buck
And now a Stuart king I serve
For King Richard I will write a book
Truth and honour he does deserve

For I have found the Croyland Chronicle
Written out by scribes
Within the missing royal title the truth it has survived

Song Twelve:

My Ricardian friend Susan Lamb told me this story of her visit to Ambion Hill in 2014.

"This happened back in late March, on a whim a friend and I decided to go to Bosworth Battlefield (it was actually the first day of the judicial review over his burial) it was a lovely spring day, we walked to Richard's Well, we noticed how very quiet it was there, but then it's always quiet there! We then walked up to Ambion Hill, the roses were just coming into bloom, and we walked around the sundial and read the account of the battle. Then we started walking back down, I turned to look towards Ambion Wood which is below Ambion Hill because something had caught my eye it seemed to be a glimmer of bright sunlight and we both turned to look, well my first thought was that, oh, bikers in the area as the light seemed to be reflected off their helmets, however...as we looked properly we realised that they were not bikers, they were knights, and as we stopped to look, they stopped and came to the edge of the woods...we noticed that one wore a wine coloured cloak over his armour which moved in the breeze, we watched them for several moments (there were four) when the one wearing a cloak gestured towards where we were standing, it was an open handed gesture, he seemed to hold his hand in the middle of his chest, then sort of reach towards us, he quite possibly was indicating towards Ambion Hill, or was he literally reaching out to me as that is how it felt!!"

Her story was the inspiration for this song called 'Ambion Hill', which was written in 2014. Lord Zarquon and I won silver boar badges after I submitted it to a ghost story and poem contest which had been organised on Facebook by Judy Thomson in Chicago. I think our song was voted as the best entry in the competition.

Matthew Lewis wrote this narrative for it.

"Many have stood on Ambion Hill, perhaps sat at the sundial that can be found there today, beneath the fluttering banner of King Richard III. There is a sense of ancient anticipation at that spot, long believed to

have been the site of the Battle of Bosworth. Recent archaeological study suggests that the main melee in fact took place about a mile to the south west of Ambion Hill where Europe's largest clutch of medieval cannon balls was found mingled with fragments of armour and a prize find; a silver boar badge that must have been worn by a prominent member of Richard III's household. Medieval battles were sprawling and sporadic affairs, punctuated by breaks to allow increasingly tired men at arms to draw breath and a mouthful of liquid. They could roam the countryside as the upper hand was passed back and forth and end far from where they were begun. It is still likely that King Richard's army mustered along the ridge of Ambion Hill to look down upon the landscape that would claim the lives of a king and his friends. The battlefield walk will lead you to the final destination of England's last Plantagenet king, England's last king to die in battle, England's last true warrior king. Ambion Hill remains drenched in memory, soaked in the expectation of those who formed their ranks there. As you stand with your eyes closed you might feel the earth's remembered dread, but Ambion Hill recalls no fighting."

'AMBION HILL'

I saw a knight up on Ambion Hill
His armour did shine in the sun
He wore a surcoat of murrey and blue
It felt like a dream had begun

He beckoned me to follow him
I blinked and he was gone
A ghost I think I had seen
But you say I must be wrong

I heard a voice up on Ambion Hill

He said the battle wasn't here
I looked around I was quite alone
But the voice it was quite near

He told me to turn around
I turned to walk that way
A ghostly voice I think i heard
Are you sure I hear you say

Song Thirteen:
Over what seemed like a long period of time (at least a year), there
was much discussion in the *Ricardian Bulletin*, about how the
reburial of Richard III should be conducted. There was much
argument as well, and I felt it was an obvious subject for a song.
I visited Leicester for the second time on the weekend before the
reburial ceremonies started. Why on earth I didn't stay for the actual
reburial week I do not know. Perhaps it was simply difficult to book
accommodation because of the huge number of people visiting
Leicester for that week.

'HOW DO YOU REBURY A KING?'

How do you rebury a king
When winter turns into spring
Soil from a field where he died
Can the old history be denied

Some came to gaze
Some came to praise
Some criticised
And some were wise

How do you rebury a king
When winter turns into spring
Soil from a place called Fotheringhay
In his tomb forever to stay

Some came to gaze
Some came to praise
Some criticised
And some were wise

How do you rebury a king
When winter turns into spring
Soil from Middleham in his grave
English heritage to try and save

Some came to gaze
Some came to praise
Some criticised
And some were wise

I have now described all the songs on the album. A very kind lady in the USA wrote a review on a website called *Murrey and Blue*.
"Richard III' by the Legendary Ten Seconds by Elke Paxson Feb 2016
"A few months ago I discovered the music of The Legendary Ten Seconds and I'm thrilled that their third and newest album of the Richard III trilogy (the first one being 'Loyaulté me Lie' and the second 'Tant le Desiree') is also out on CD. The songs are again pithy and meaningful. It also comes with historical and highly interesting narrations between all of the songs and it makes the CD all the more special.

"The first two songs 'Sheriff Hutton' and 'Richard Liveth Yet' are dynamic songs with a beautiful swinging rhythm. 'Written at Rising' has some cool sound effects and the instrumentation gives it a beautiful medieval feeling with a modern touch. 'Gold Angels', the next song is an interesting story about an old medieval Christmas tradition. 'Act III, Scene 4 William Shakespeare' is striking with its beautiful harmonies. 'The Year of 3 Kings" and 'Hollow Crown' are extraordinary. They are accompanied by diverse instruments, but the acoustic guitar and a lively flute stand out nicely as does an electronic keyboard. The sound is superb and they just have a great, lively swing to them. Then there is 'Remember my Name'. It is also filled with beautiful harmonies and lyrics that strike a chord inside. 'Lord Lovell's Lament' is a slow song that stands out in its touching presentation. 'Requiem Mass for Richard' tells the story of his sister Margaret after getting the news of her last brother's death. It's a heartfelt song with some definite rock elements. 'Royal Title' is about Sir George Buck finding Titulus Regius and the truth that deserves to be known! Sound effects and the sound of a beautiful acoustic guitar accompany the haunting song called 'Ambion Hill'. The last song of the CD is called 'How do You Rebury a King' and it is a catchy rendition of the events of Richard's reinterment. It rounds out the album quite well and it's a final song that leaves you wanting more. This album brings together English folk with a modern flair and some rock elements. Hard to imagine such a combination? Maybe so, but it's a combination you likely won't be disappointed in. Ian Churchward and his musicians of the Legendary Ten Seconds have created an astonishing set of thrilling, thoughtful, sometimes soothing and always professional songs that I wouldn't want to miss anymore."

Next, you will find one of the narratives written and read by Matthew Lewis for my 'Richard III' album. In fact it is the final narrative on that album, and was actually composed for my song called 'A Ricardian Dream', which did not make it onto the album.

The narrative is quite thought-provoking, and sets the scene perfectly for the last song on that album.

"Part of the lament of many Ricardians is that Bosworth Field denied King Richard of time during which he might have proven himself a great king and may even have solved the mystery of the fate of his nephews one way or another.

"Why King Richard led that fateful, thundering cavalry charge is another enigma. The main battle was going against him and he perhaps spied an opportunity to end his troubles once and for all. Henry Tudor was the last threat to the Yorkist throne and Richard had a chance to place his right to his crown into God's hands for judgement. He did not receive his vindication.

"As a man who had lost his only child and his wife in quick succession and was facing threats to his crown, perhaps Richard simply had nothing left to live for. We cannot know his deepest thoughts and fears at this distance. The charge failed and Richard lost his life in the mud of Bosworth Field.

"Had the battle ended differently we might never have had a Tudor dynasty. Henry VIII would never have been king, there would have been no Great Matter to drive seismic change in England. Monasteries might still stand proud and whole across the green fields and ancient towns of England. Would this be for good, or for ill? We can never know."

The artwork for the third Ricardian album painted by Georgie Harman showing the ruins of Middleham castle in the background.

Chapter Five

Sunnes and Roses

Song One:
The following song about the Battle of Towton, was written sometime in 2015 after reading a book called *Fatal Colours* by George Goodwin. It was released as a single via CD Baby so that it could be purchased in digital format via Amazon and iTunes on 29th March 2016, the anniversary of the battle. I hadn't planned to do this, but Graham Moores had shown me a painting he had done many years ago of a scene of the battle, and Lord Zarquon had recently finished recording the song. It coincided with the month of the historical event and Graham agreed to create an amended version of his artwork by adding the name of the song and the band name.

'TOWTON'
York's white rose and Lancaster's red
The white snow at Towton, thousands left dead
York's flowering rose and Lancaster's dead
The white snow at Towton turned to blood red

Oh Towton field
Such grim loss of life
A new king's revenge
Such meaningless strife

The river Cock in full flow
Men in armour dragged down below

The fast running water turning blood red
York's flowering rose and Lancaster's dead

Oh Towton field
Such grim loss of life
A new king's revenge
Such meaningless strife

This song is also the first one on the album Sunnes and Roses with
a theme of the Wars of the Roses. I understand that the title of this
conflict is a Victorian invention and the red rose wasn't used as a
Lancastrian emblem until the reign of Henry VII. Like many others I
am guilty of continuing this Victorian myth. The title of the album is
a play on words, similar to the rock band Guns N' Roses, combining
Edward IV's Sunne in Splendour with the Roses from the Wars of
the Roses. I asked Georgie Harman to create another album cover
in the style of a pulp magazine from the 1920's or 1930's. I have
had a passion for pulp science fiction magazine covers from this era
ever since I read a book called *Before the Golden Age*. To this day the
opening story by Edmond Hamilton in that volume, called *The Man
Who Evolved*, has remained the most exciting piece of science fiction
writing that I have ever read. I know the story is flawed, but this was
not apparent to me when I read it as a boy in the early 1970's. This
anthology of science fiction was compiled by Isaac Asimov and it
is by far and away the book I have most enjoyed reading. I can still
recall when by a happy chance I came upon on it on a bookshelf in
the Torquay Boys Grammar school library. I can clearly remember
flicking through the pages and reading a snippet about the Zoromes
visiting the solar system. While I write this I am in the middle of
reading the first half of a two-volume autobiography of Isaac Asimov,
who kept a diary that obviously helped him recount the dates of

when he wrote his science fiction stories. Incidentally he mentions Richard III in his book which is called *In Memory Yet Green*.

Song Two:
My song called 'List of the Dead' is about the first half of the Wars of the Roses, and was written in May 2016. I had a spell of about two months (March and April 2016) when I didn't write any songs because my music computer had stopped working and couldn't be repaired. Without it I couldn't record any songs, so I couldn't summon up any enthusiasm to compose. In May I got a replacement second-hand music computer and so I felt the urge to write this new song which I really enjoyed being able to record. I have actually recorded two versions of this song. When Lord Zarquon listened to my first attempt at recording the song he suggested a slight chord change in the verses, a slower tempo and a different ending. I therefore recorded a second version incorporating these changes that he had suggested.

'LIST OF THE DEAD'

Several battles in this song
The list of the dead goes on and on
First St Albans fourteen fifty five
The Duke of York he did strive

At Northampton the king was betrayed
With Lord Grey of Ruthin a deal was made
By the Earl of March and Warwick too
It allowed their troops to break through

Several battles in this song

The list of the dead goes on and on
Blore heath in fourteen fifty nine
The Earl of Salisbury's battle line

At Wakefield a Duke lost his head
And so more noble blood was shed
At Micklegate Bar his head on a spike
With many others such a dreadful sight

Second St Albans 1461 Lord Bonville executed
Ferrybridge March 1461 Lord Fitzwalter
mortally wounded
Towton March 1461 Sir Andrew Trollope killed
Hedgeley Moor April 1464 Sir Ralph Percy killed
Hexham May 1464 the Duke of Somerset executed

Several battles in this song
The list of the dead goes on and on
Ludford Bridge fourteen fifty nine
To fight the king they did decline

At Mortimers Cross three suns were seen
For the uneducated what did this mean
The Earl of March declared "a good sign"
For the three sons of York at that time

Song Three:
The idea for this song came after I read an article about the
Middleham Jewel written by Susan Troxell in the *Ricardian
Chronicle,* newsletter of the USA branch of the Richard III Society.
The article was later included in the March 2016 edition of the

Ricardian Bulletin magazine. Ashley Dyer plays some lovely trumpet on this song after I showed him the notes that I played on my guitar

'JEWEL OF MIDDLEHAM'

From Jervaulx Abbey to Middleham
On an ancient path she did ride
And there lost her precious jewel
For her lost jewel her tears she could not hide
For her lost jewel her tears she could not hide

Where did you lose that wondrous jewel
And will it ever be found
Were you a duchess what was your name
No one saw it lying there on the ground
No one saw it lying there on the ground

From Barnard Castle to Middleham
To a path Ted Seaton did go
And there found a precious jewel
When washed and cleaned the gold it did glow
When washed and cleaned the gold it did glow

Where did you find that wondrous jewel
By luck it has now been found
Who lost it we will never know
They had not seen it lying there on the ground
They had not seen it lying there on the ground

A double sided pendant of gold
So intricately engraved

In a museum for us to see
It is now safely displayed

From Jervaulx abbey to Middleham
On an ancient path she did ride
And there lost her precious jewel
for her lost jewel her tears she could not hide
For her lost jewel her tears she could not hide

Song Four:
Matthew Lewis also wrote and recorded the next narrative, for my
song 'Good King Richard', which I thought might be included on
the 'Richard III' album. The narrative was included on that album
but not the song, and the final paragraph echoes the sentiments in
the final section of the book about Richard III by David Baldwin.
*"King Richard III divides opinion every bit as much today as he did
during his reign. In life he inspired the kind of devoted loyalty amongst
his close friends that saw them follow him even to their deaths at the
Battle of Bosworth. For many others, though, he remained a usurper,
suspected of murdering his nephews and a target to be struck at.*
*"During the sixteenth century his reputation was deeply tarnished by
Sir Thomas More, the work completed by William Shakespeare. Early
in the next century a revision began, led by Sir George Buck, and ever
since this controversial king's reputation has swung back and forth,
dividing opinion wider and wider.*

*"The 20th century saw Richard's reputation revitalised in historical
fiction. Josephine Tey's 'Daughter of Time' and Sharon Penman's
'Sunne in Splendour' sought to paint Richard in a more positive light.
The discovery of his remains and subsequent reburial have been an
opportunity for the fresh light of popular attention to drive the shadows
from Richard's enduring reputation.*

"Shakespeare did his work well, but it is questionable whether the bard even meant to depict the king in his masterpiece in the study of evil. Shakespeare's King Richard bears more than a passing resemblance to Robert Cecil, son and successor to Elizabeth I's premier minister William Cecil, who was arranging the Stuart succession against the will of Shakespeare's Catholic patrons. Cecil, interestingly, suffered from kyphosis. In Shakespeare's own parlance he was a hunchback and his machinations were aimed at destroying the political certainties of the world to the condemnation of all. Society was watching it happen, helpless, just as the audience watches King Richard, who has told everyone of his dastardly plot.

"An impartial evaluation of King Richard is hard to reach. He was most likely no saint, but no monster either; a man of his times operating in the gulf between angel and devil that most of us inhabit."

'GOOD KING RICHARD'

Evil King Richard you did steal the throne
To prevent civil war and protect all I owned
Good King Richard you loved your wife
But some say I poisoned her to end her life

Evil King Richard from a widow you stole
An annuity I gave her from the lands I controlled
Good King Richard you gave justice to all
But so many in my realm wanted me to fall

Evil King Richard an uncle so cruel
I saw Edward the Fifth as a Woodville tool
Good King Richard so long despised
The daughter of time will win over lies

The last line of the song tells you that it was at least partly inspired by the intriguing book about Richard III written by Josephine Tey (the pen name of Elizabeth MacKintosh).

Song Five:
The chords for this instrumental are as follows

'SUNNES AND ROSES'

Part A

Dm, Bb, F, C
Dm, Bb, F, C, Dm
Dm, Bb, F, C
Dm, Bb, F, C, Dm

Part B

F, C, Dm, A
F, C, Dm, A, Dm
F, C, Dm, A
F, C, Dm, A, Dm

Part C

Gm, F, C, Dm
Gm, C, F, Dm
Gm, F, C, Dm
Gm, C, F, A, Dm

Mandola notes over Part A

D, E, F, A, G
D, E, F, A, G, F, E, D

Mandola notes over Part B

A, G, F, E
A, G, F, E, D, C, D

Song Six:
This is the second song that I have written about the battle of Barnet, which I called 'Battle in the Mist'. It is serious compared with my first song about that battle, and I had hoped that it would be included on the 'Richard III' album, but instead it was included on the Sunnes and Roses album. I feel that my comedy song about the battle is a much better tune but having said that, this serious one is still a worthwhile song. Matthew Lewis wrote this narrative for it.

"After a spell in exile King Edward IV returned to reclaim the throne that had been snatched from him in the name of the Lancastrian King Henry VI. The mastermind of the Lancastrian revival was Edward's cousin, friend and mentor Richard Neville, 16th Earl of Warwick, remembered as the Kingmaker. The two armies finally met outside Barnet, north of London.

"As darkness fell on 13th April 1471 the armies of Edward and Warwick pitched their camps. It was late and in the dusk the two camps were closer to each other than they thought. Warwick's cannons barked out angrily into the night, thundering over Edward's army at such short range. The cunning Edward kept his guns silent so that his position was not given away.

"As dawn broke on Sunday 14th April, Easter Sunday, the thin spring light strained to push through thick fog. It seemed that God had no

desire to see what was to pass on that spot. Unable to see the enemy, the opposing armies lined up off centre, each sides' right flank reaching beyond their counterpart's left.

"Edward's left flank was commanded by his Chamberlain and best friend, Lord Hastings, who was opposed by John de Vere, Earl of Oxford. Oxford's men swiftly flanked Hastings, who was routed, but Oxford's men gave chase rather than staying at the battle. On Edward's right his youngest brother Richard was leading that flank in his first taste of battle aged 18. He was able to flank and crush Henry Holland, Duke of Exeter at Warwick's left.

"In the centre the fighting was fierce. The tide turned when some of Oxford's men returned to the battle. Neville's men mistook Oxford's stars and streamers banner for Edward's sunne in splendour, and fired upon the approaching group, who cried treason. In the chaos Warwick's army was routed. The earl made it as far as the woods outside Barnet before he was caught and slain by his cousin's men. It was an ignoble end for a proud and mighty lord."

'BATTLE IN THE MIST'

Lord Hastings against the Earl of Oxford
Hastings left wing was outflanked
And a brave advance in the mist
Quickly turned into a rout

And the Earl of Warwick prayed for victory
Against foes who were once his protégés

The Earl of Oxford's men gave chase
They thought the battle had been won
Unaware of other Yorkist foes
Concealed in the morning mist

And the Earl of Warwick prayed for victory
Against foes who were once his protégés

In the centre of battle were King Edward's men
Pressing loyal John Neville hard
Further along the Duke of Gloucester
A brave young son of York

And the Earl of Warwick prayed for victory
Against foes who were once his protégés

The Earl of Oxford regrouped his men
And by mistake attacked John Neville's flank
By chance King Edward was victorious
In the battle in the morning mist

And the Earl of Warwick turned to flee
But was killed in the Yorkist victory

Song Seven:
While on a week long holiday in Scotland in May 2015, I wrote this next song on the mandola. The weather wasn't very good. It rained every day. Elaine and I travelled in one car from Torquay with our friends Phil and Debby Helmore, and their son George. There wasn't enough room in the car to take my guitar but I could take my mandola, which is a much smaller, so that I had a musical instrument to play while in Scotland.

'RICHARD OF YORK'

A prince of the realm
But how could we tell
Were you Richard of York

Were you telling the truth
And where is the proof
Were you Richard of York

And did you deceive
And did they believe
Were you Richard of York

A prince of the realm
With a rather tall tale
Perkin Warbeck of course

A pretenders claim
That you could not maintain
Perkin Warbeck of course

And did you deceive
And did they believe
Perkin Warbeck of course

Song Eight:
Judy Thomson asked me to write a soft instrumental for her, she wanted it to have a light female feel to it. These are the chords and notes for this instrumental.

'THE KING'S DAUGHTER'

Part A chords

C, F x 3 then C, F, C

Part A notes

E, F, G, F, E, F, A, G, F, G

Part B chords

Em, Am, F, C x 4

Part B notes

C, B, A, F, E, C, B, A, F, E, D, C

Middle section chords

G, F, Am, Dm, G, F, G

Notes at the end of the middle section

G, A, B, C, D, E, F, E, D, C, B, A, G

Song Nine:
The verses for this song, called 'Middleham Castle on Christmas Eve', were written by Frances Quinn. In December 2014 I composed the words for the chorus and the music. The verses are in the present but the chorus is in the past.

'MIDDLEHAM CASTLE ON CHRISTMAS EVE'

Frost diamonds glitter in the snow
Underneath the full moon's glow
Cold upon half fallen walls
Stark the silver moonlight falls

Middleham Castle on a winters night
The duke at prayer by candle light
Middleham Castle on Christmas Eve
For in gods power he did believe

Still and silent is the night
Save for the wind from the hills height
Sighing soft and moaning low
Stirring stardust in the snow

Middleham Castle on a winters night
The duke at prayer by candle light
Middleham Castle on Christmas Eve
For in gods power he did believe

But listen now and you may hear
So very faint the sounds of cheer
Echo round the crumbling walls
And sounds of hoofbeats rise and fall

Middleham castle on a winters night
The duke at prayer by candle light
Middleham Castle on Christmas Eve
For in gods power he did believe

Half seen shapes faint and frail
Insubstantial as a veil
Of finest silk pass to and fro
Echoes of the long ago

Song Ten:
In the following song, 'A Warwick', I was making a real effort to write songs relating to the Wars of the Roses, while trying to avoid the direct subject of Richard III. This was because I was beginning to feel it was time to slightly broaden the subject matter of my lyrics.

'A WARWICK'

As a captain of Calais a hero so bold
But sometimes a pirate so I've been told
To guard England's foothold in France he did strive
And thus his sense of pride stayed alive

A Warwick, a Warwick they cried
A Warwick, a Warwick they died

As Warwick the Kingmaker he is well known
For the influence he had on our country's throne
The men of Kent so tired of misrule
To his standard they flocked like thieves to a jewel

A Warwick, a Warwick they cried
A Warwick, a Warwick they died

The ragged staff and bear

This history book I will share
Near Barnet his cannons roared
Throughout the night for that mighty lord

At the second St Albans he suffered defeat
His archers killed in house and in street
King Henry the Sixth sat under a tree
Lord Bonville to guard him for his safety

A Warwick, a Warwick they cried
A Warwick, a Warwick they died

Song Eleven:
I have taken the motto of the Duke of Buckingham as the title of this instrumental. Here are the chords for it.

'SOUVENTE ME SOUVENE'

Part A

Am, C, G, Am
Am, F, Dm, Em
Am, C, G, Am x2

Part B

Dm. Am. Em, Am
Dm, Am Em

Part C

Am, G, Am
C, Em, Am
Am. G, Am
C, Em, Am

Song Twelve:
This song is about the betrayal of Richard III by the Duke of Buckingham, known in the history books as the Buckingham Rebellion in the Autumn of 1483.

'AUTUMN RAIN'

I thought the deluge would never cease
When the heavens opened it did release
Such endless rain I had never seen
That autumn rain and a traitor's scheme

Buckingham's betrayal in October
A rebellion so quickly over
The most untrue creature living
Richard's anger so unforgiving

I thought the deluge would never cease
When the heavens opened it did release
Such endless rain I had never seen
That autumn rain and a traitor's scheme

To Henry's ship we did shout
We tried to tempt the Tudor out
His fleet scattered by the storm
His own vessel looked so forlorne

Autumn rain, autumn rain, autumn rain

I thought the deluge would never cease
When the heavens opened it did release
Such endless rain I had never seen
That autumn rain and a traitor's scheme

As I recall the sky was grey
For Buckingham on that day
Executed in Salisbury
He'd betrayed King Richard quite dreadfully

Song Thirteen:
The verses for 'Herald's Lament' were written as a poem by Sandra
Heath Wilson, and I wrote the words and music for the chorus in
2015.

'HERALD'S LAMENT'

King Richard is dead such dread news I bring
No joy to cling to no hosannas to sing
I tell a tale so heart breakingly brief
A tale that can only convey pain and grief

A herald's lament King Richard is dead
And of Henry Tudor his reign I do dread

Treacherous Stanley and others with Percy
Did destroy our true king and offered no mercy
All grace did they forfeit as well as all honour

By callously raising to crown and to power

A herald's lament King Richard is dead
And of Henry Tudor his reign I do dread

A cowardly knave by the name of Tudor
A claimless joyless Lancastrian usurper
Oh England our anointed King Richard is lost
Betrayed deserted at what ruthless cost

A herald's lament King Richard is dead
And of Henry Tudor his reign I do dread

Now we have Henry he is numbered seven
Who will close upon us the gates of God's heaven
King Richard is dead such dread news I bring
No joy to cling to no hosannas to sing

Song Fourteen:
Well I expect that you have correctly and quickly realised that this song was inspired by a visit to the medieval fair in Tewkesbury. I watched the Battle of Tewkesbury being re-enacted on a Saturday, and then again the next day on a Sunday in July 2014. It was a very, very hot weekend and I do not know how the re-enactors could have endured wearing their full armour in such conditions.

'TEWKESBURY MEDIEVAL FAIR'

The re-enactors in their fine clothes
Of the late fifteenth century I do suppose
Go back in time yes you could be there

All found at Tewkesbury medieval fair

A pot of herbs or armour for sale
In the market music, dancing as well
A fabulous gown that your lady could wear
All found at Tewkesbury medieval fair

Entertainment throughout the day
And a dragon keeper did I hear you say
Displays of combat I do declare
All found at Tewkesbury medieval fair

Many come from all over the world
Across the field the banners unfurled
Fair maidens and knights you will find there
All found at Tewkesbury medieval fair

The stall of the Worcestershire branch of the Richard III Society at the Tewkesbury medieval festival, July 2014. You can see John Ashdown-Hill in this photo and I enjoyed his lecture about George Duke of Clarence (brother of Edward IV and Richard III) which I attended while staying in Tewkesbury that month.

Chapter Six
Murrey and Blue

The idea for the title of this album came from a Ricardian blog of the same name and once again Georgie Harman created a fantastic album cover. Probably her best one.

Song One:
This song was written in December 2016. I wanted to write a song for Christmas and suddenly realised I was running out of time. I went back to a book that I had recently read by Toni Mount about life in medieval London because I recalled that it had a very good chapter about the period of Christmas. I read through that chapter again and started to get some ideas which eventually turned into a song. The most difficult part was writing the words which were a bit of a struggle at first but became much easier after I picked a line saying "Bring out the boars head". As soon as I had the words the tune came to me quite easily.

'THE BOARS HEAD'

Bring out the boars head
Pour me some wine
Eat drink be merry
At this Christmas time

A brew of ale and spices
To drink to your good health
As your good and noble lord
This day I'll share my wealth

Drinking, singing, dancing
In my castle hall
You are all welcome
I welcome you all

Bring out the boars head
And the Christmas pie
Eat, drink, be merry
And raise your tankards high

Drinking, singing, dancing
In my castle hall
You are all welcome
I welcome you all

Eating, drinking, dancing
In my castle hall
You are all welcome
I welcome you all

The feast of Saint Nicholas
To the twelfth night
Christmas in my great hall
To fill you with delight

Drinking, singing, dancing
In my castle hall
You are all welcome
I welcome you all

Eating, drinking, dancing
In my castle hall
You are all welcome
I welcome you all

Song Two:
This song was also inspired after reading Toni Mount's book about life in medieval London.

'JOHN JUDDE'

Look at John with his culverin
For his service please pay him
Sulphur and saltpetre mixed as one
Smoke and fire from his gun

Remember John and his serpentine
That mighty cannon looked so fine
Near St Albans I've heard it said
He was listed amongst the dead

Take his body, take him away
And bury his body quickly today

Look at John with his culverin
For his cannon they paid him
Sulphur and saltpetre mixed as one
Smoke and fire beneath the setting sun

Take his body, take him away
And for his soul we will pray

Soldier, citizen, merchant too
A London Lancastrian that we knew

Remember John with his serpentine
That mighty cannon looked so fine
Near St Albans I've heard it said
He was listed amongst the dead
Yes near St Albans in a book I read
That he was listed amongst the dead

Song Three:
This song was written in the autumn of 2015, after I had been to Buckland Abbey at the end of August with Elaine and Tom. I wrote a short article about the visit which was included in the December 2015 issue of the *Ricardian Bulletin*. This is what I wrote about the visit.

"On Bank Holiday Monday, 31ˢᵗ August 2015, I visited Buckland Abbey near Plymouth, where a Wars of the Roses re-enactment group, who call themselves The Medieval Free Company, had set up their encampment. Buckland Abbey is a National Trust property which was founded by Cistercian monks in the 13ᵗʰ century and was at one time the home of Sir Francis Drake. The former abbey was the perfect setting for the medieval encampment with the tents of the Medieval Free Company set up next to a fabulous Great Barn.
"The Medieval Free Company specialise in the reenactment of a group of mercenaries during the Wars of the Roses and include a basket maker, scribe, cooks, archers and men at arms. They are led by a landless "hedge" knight. Members of the public are allowed to have free access to walk around the medieval camp site and ask questions. I chatted to the

scribe who told me that one could correct an error whilst writing on a sheet of parchment by using a knife to scrape off the mistake.

"I watched 2 fabulous displays of archery and we were informed that the archers were using longbows with a draw weight of about 40 lbs whereas the English longbow used in battle in the 14th and 15th centuries would have had a much heavier draw weight. One could only imagine how strong the archers must have been to be able to use the longbows with a heavy draw weight. The archers were timed to see how many arrows they could fire in one minute and one of the archers managed 14. Just imagine how many sheaths of arrows would have been used in a medieval battle and the devastation that would have been caused by the medieval equivalent of a machine gun.

"Towards the end of the afternoon the re-enactors put on a medieval fashion show describing their clothes and the materials that had been used to make them. We were informed that the white under garments could be cleaned by soaking them in urine and then rinsing in water."

'THE MEDIEVAL FREE COMPANY'

For hire we are in this land
And our hedge knight he does command
Of archery a fine display
Yes we will show throughout the day

Our camp site you may look around
Such wondrous items to be found
Hand crafted with all skill and care
Our master scribe writes over there

Divers, archers, men at arms
For adventure left their farms
See that lord he looks so handsome
Will his family pay the ransom?

Mercenaries one and all
Wars of the Roses we recall
Our landless knight he leads us well
As daylight fades we bid farewell

Song Four:

Out of all the instrumentals that I have written this is one of my favourites. I got part of the lead guitar idea after watching Rob Bright playing lead guitar at Red Rock.

'PLANTAGENET PAVENNE'

PART 1

D, Bm, A, D x2

PART 2

E, G, A, D
Bm, E, A
E, G, A, D
Bm. E, A

PART 3

Bm, A, E, A

Song Five:

I wrote my 'Francis Cranley' song after reading *The Woodville Connection* and *The Beaulieu Vanishing* by Kathy Martin. These novels are set in England during the reign of Edward IV. My song is about the main character in the books, Francis Cranley, and is my attempt to condense *The Woodville Connection* novel into a song. If you read or have read the book, then you will hopefully be able to understand the lyrics of the song.

You are reading a revised edition of my book. In the first edition I wrote that this was the second time that I had tried to write a song based around a book. Since the publication of the first edition of my book I have now remembered that this was actually the third time. I had forgotten a song called 'Mad Men Laughed' that was written while I was in Chapter 29. I think that I wrote most of the music for that song and Phil Andrews wrote most of the words. We had both read a book called *Warlord of the Air* by Michael Moorcock which is a science fiction/science fantasy, alternative history novel.

When I first started to play the guitar I had been reading a science fiction book called *Way Station* by Clifford Simak, and made up a simple tune based on this novel which I called 'Shadow Love'. This was my first ever attempt at writing a song. The words for it no longer exist and I can barely remember the melody. I've got a vague idea that there was a D7 chord in the tune and the rest of the chords would have been the easy ones that you first learn when you start to try to play the guitar. I do remember playing it on the guitar to my cousin Robert Temple when we were together in Exeter visiting my grandmother. At that time Robert seemed quite impressed that I had composed a song.

'FRANCIS CRANLEY'

I shall speak of the old century
Of my liege lord I will speak kindly
Francis Cranley is my name
Of my youth you do remind me

To Middleham Castle a stranger came
And Fielding was his name
Of a murder he did stand accused
Of his innocence he did claim

I shall speak of the old century
Of the life that is behind me
Francis Cranley is my name
With my memories you do find me

For Plaincourt Manor I did ride
To help kind Gloucester's friend
To find the truth of Geoffrey's death
My assistance I might lend

I shall speak of the old century
Of the Woodvilles I don't speak kindly
Francis Cranley is my name
In my old age you do find me

Lord Rivers so noble but evil as well
With his lover Stephen Plaincourt
Mistress Blanche they did use
With a promise she was bought

I shall speak of the old century
Of Fielding I do speak kindly
Francis Cranley is my name
In sadness you do find me

To Middleham Castle I did return

In time for Christmas day
With young Matthew by my side
Then to York where I did pray

I shall speak of the old century
Of my liege lord I will speak kindly
Francis Cranley is my name
In my old age you do find me

After recording the song I asked Kathy Martin if she could tell me about how she came to write her first novel about Francis Cranley, especially where she got the names of the fictional characters such a Will Fielding. She very kindly sent me this information

"Writers are often told to write about what they know. It's sound advice, it is equally important to write about what fascinates. Thts's why, when I began work on my first historical novel, I chose the era of the Wars of the Roses. The Woodville Connection took a long time to complete; the book was finally published in 2013, some 19 years after I devised the plot and wrote my first stumbling sentences. During those years I had a child and embarked on a demanding new career as a magazine editor, leaving little time for novel writing. Yet even so, Will Fielding and Francis Cranley refused to go away. Every few years I would return to my work in progress to read it, re-write sections, pen another chapter or so and then put it away again.

This might have continued indefinitely had chance not taken a hand. Around 2008 I was signed to write a series of non-fiction books for a a small but respected publisher and a sort while later this same publisher decided to launch a historical fiction imprint. Since I already had a relationship with them, I realised this gave me a golden opportunity to pitch The Woodville Connection. The trouble with this scheme was that publishers generally only consider completed manuscripts and at this point, Woodville was less than two-thirds finished. Happily, they took the unconvential step of agreeing to publish on the basis of my synopsis and the first three chapters. With a contract under my belt, I felt sufficiently confident to cut back on my editing work and concentrate on completing The Woodville Connection.

I have sometimes been asked where I get the inspiration for my characters' names and also for my fictional locations. The answer is usually a combination of historical research - looking upnames that were in common use at the time – and personal motives. Francis Cranley is a case in point; although not as common as William, Edward or John, Francis was used in England in the 15th century. This information will come as no surprise to Ricardians who will be well aware of the fact that one of Richard III's closest friends was a young noble called Francis Lovell!

In The Woodville Connection, I wanted my central protagonist to have a close bond with Richard but at the same time, for the purposes of the plot he needed to be entirely fictitious rather than a fictional rendition of a real historical figure. By calling my character Francis I was making oblique reference to Lovell although Cranley is in no way 'based' on him. As for his surname, that stemmed from personal reasons: my husband grew up in Cranleigh in Surrey. As for Will Fielding, his name was borrowed from a Lancastrian knight who perished at the Battle of Tewkesbury - I hope he will forgive the liberty I took in having him switch loyalties and moving him several pegs down the social ladder! Apart from Middleham Castle, the main location in the novel is the fictitious Plaincourt Manor. The layout of Plaincourt is based on a number of 15th century manors but the location is roughly the same as Alford in Lincolnshire.

Song Six:

This song is meant to have an Edwardian music hall feel to it while the middle section was inspired thinking about the chord sequence from the 'Interstellar Overdrive' instrumental by Pink Floyd. I think that it is one of the best songs that I have written. With the lyrics I tried to imagine the thoughts of Anthony Woodville being anxious to bring young Edward V safely to London. He would have been full of hope for the future and not knowing about the grim future that would so soon be realised. I sent the song in mp3 format to Mark Heaney who is the Captain of the Woodville Household reenactment group. He sent me an email with these comments about the song:-

"I found it actually quite chilling and vaguely creepy, as I'm sure the sentiments you mention regarding the young King in his care were probably uppermost in Anthony's mind on the way to London. But not to get too anal about it I thought it was rather ripping."

'THE WOODVLLE HOUSEHOLD'

The Woodville household I'm sure you agree
Contains the finest nobility
The Woodville household of Sir Anthony
Residing at Ludlow so pleasantly

Our young prince in Anthony's care
Royalty, culture, you'll find it there

The Woodville household do you disagree?
From common stock with no pedigree
The Woodville household of Sir Anthony
Attending Prince Edward so courteously

Our young prince in Anthony's care
Royalty, culture, you'll find it there

Of King Edward's death
We have received news
All Haste to London

With no time to lose

Edward the Fifth in Anthony's care
Quickly to London to crown him there

The Woodville household yes we hold the key
For a new king's future we can foresee
The Woodville household of Sir Anthony
So soon to meet our destiny

Song Seven:
This song is in the form of a succession of short fictional letters being
written by someone living in London to another person living at a
manor somewhere else in England during the spring and summer of
1483.

'THE MONTH OF MAY'

Dearly beloved I greet you good day
So much has happened in the month of May
The stench from the street assaults my nose
How I do long for the scent of a rose

The news of the queen is very disturbing
Remaining in sanctuary this we are learning
The coronation date has been set
One Sunday in June it's not happened yet

Dearly beloved I greet you good day
So much has happened since the month of May
Of true honesty there's nought to be had
And the stench from the Thames is terribly bad

The news of Lord Hastings is very disturbing
Of his execution this we are learning
The coronation date is so near
Of it's cancellation I really do fear

How is the manor where I was raised
Oh how I long for those childhood days
Moving to London I do regret
Fresh air in the country I might forget

Dearly beloved I greet you good day
So much has happened since the month of May
The heat of the summer feels like a curse
The stench of this town gets worse and worse

The news in the street is very disturbing
Of two lost princes this we are learning
The coronation date it was changed
The lord protector the throne he has claimed

Song Eight:
These are the chords for this instrumental

'JOHN NESFIELD'S RETINUE'

Part One

Dm, C, E, Am
Dm, C, E
Dm, C, E, Am

C, G, C, G, C

Part Two

Am, G, C, G, C, G, C, G, C x2

Song Nine:
The idea for this song came to me after reading a book about Bosworth and the birth of the Tudor dynasty by Chris Skidmore.

'THE SEVENTH OF AUGUST'

Landfall at Mill bay on St Anne's Head
An August sunset filled with dread
Returning to claim the throne
Leaving the exile he had known

A fiery red dragon on green and white
And a banner of St George under which they'd fight
The seventh of August fourteen eighty five
French mercenaries by his side

From France thirty ships had set sail
Now out of sight from the village of Dale
Returning to claim the throne
Leaving the exile he had known

A fiery red dragon on green and white
And a banner of St George under which they'd fight
The seventh of August fourteen eighty five
French mercenaries by his side

Kneeling down to kiss the earth
A few miles west of his place of birth
Returning to claim the throne
Leaving the exile he had known

Song Ten:
The idea for this tune came from thinking about a song that I had
recently discovered by a band called Stiff Little fingers. It had a
traditional Irish folk music feel to it with a great guitar riff and I tried
to work out how to play the main guitar riff but failed. However I
stumbled upon my own idea for a guitar riff. Eventually I turned it
into a song about Lambert Simnel after reading an article abut the
battle of Stoke by John Ashdown-Hill. Writing this song once again
made me realise that I find it easier to make up my own songs rather
than trying to learn to play one written by someone else.

'THE DUBLIN KING'

Was he really Lambert Simnel
A mere pretender to the throne
A Yorkist prince it has been claimed
And the truth it is still not known

He was crowned in Dublin city
With Tudor tales confusion reigned
Edward, Lambert and young Richard
Are those he has been named

Who was the Dublin king
The Dublin king to proclaim

Who was the Dublin king
What was his real name

So Lincoln led his rebel army
Across to the English shore
Lord Lovell announcing that
The true king they would restore

At Stoke there was wholesale slaughter
The Dublin king perished there
To then live on as Lambert Simnel
A name that came from nowhere

Who was the Dublin king
The Dublin king to proclaim
Who was the Dublin king
What was his real name

Song Eleven:
Here are the chords for this instrumental, the title is taken from the name of the manuscript which was at one time the Book of Hours of Richard III.

'LAMBETH MS 474'

Part A

Am, G, E, Am
Am, G, C, Am, D
Am, G, E, Am
D, G, E, Am

D, G, E, Am

Part B

C, G, D, Am
C, G, Am
C, G, D, Am
C, G, Am

Part C

F, Dm, A, Bb, E, A

Notes of Part A riff

A, C, B, G, E, D
A, C, B, G, C, D
A, C, B, G, E, D
D, C, B, A, G, E, D

Song Twelve:
The idea for this song came from a lady in Finland called Riikka Katajisto. She asked me if I could write a song about all the women in modern times that have fallen in love with a romantic image of Richard III. Between Riikka Katajisto and myself we wrote the words for this song.

'SHINING KNIGHT'

Oh where did it all begin
She will welcome the king of sin

His honour gone he could not win
She will welcome the king of sin

He reaches out from the grave
She will tremble as he was so brave
From the deepest depths and a starless night
To her he is a shining knight

To feel his presence, well almost
She will welcome this knight a ghost
He is the one she loves the most
She will welcome this knight a ghost

He reaches out from the grave
She will tremble as he was so brave
From the deepest depths and a starless night
To her he is a shining knight

Oh to touch his raven hair
She'll lose herself in despair
So much stronger than she'll ever be
In every dream it's him she'll see

My photo of the Medieval Free Company at Buckfast Abbey. This was one of their displays of archery which

I enjoyed watching on the 31st August 2015.

Chapter Seven
Stony Stratford

On 19th February 2016 I travelled from Torquay for an event at the York House Centre in Stony Stratford. I had been invited to bring my Legendary Ten Seconds band to play our Ricardian songs for the Beds & Bucks branch of the Richard III Society. We stayed overnight in nearby Milton Keynes and shared a very enjoyable evening meal and a few drinks with Jeanette Melbourne who is the secretary of the Beds & Bucks branch.

We discovered that Jeanette has a musical rock background. When she lived in London during the 1970's, she was the girlfriend of one of the band members of Thin Lizzy. I was able to talk at length with Jeanette about my favourite subject which is, of course, Richard III. Unfortunately I haven't come across many Ricardians in Torquay so I don't usually have the opportunity to talk much to anyone with this same interest. Jeanette showed us her collection of old photos of herself with various members of Thin Lizzy. She even had an old photo of herself next to Bill Wyman, the bass player of the Rolling Stones!

In Stony Stratford Jeanette showed us a plaque on the wall of a house on the main street which states the following:-

"This house was anciently the Rose & Crown Inn and here in 1483 Richard Duke of Gloucester (Richard III) captured the uncrowned boy King Edward, who was later murdered in the Tower of London"

Jeanette told me that the Richard III Society had tried to have the wording on the plaque changed, but unfortunately the lady who owned the property refused because the plaque was put up by her late husband and she felt that her husband would not have wished the plaque to be altered.

We had parked our cars at the York House centre, and before returning to the venue to prepare for the event I took the opportunity to visit the Cock Hotel where my band were booked to play on a Sunday afternoon, 12th June as part of the 2016 Stony Live Music Festival. Also located in Stony Stratford is the Bull Inn and it is believed that the phrase "cock and bull story" originates from when the Cock and Bull were the two main coaching inns located in Stony Stratford.

After a short look around the Cock Hotel we walked back to the York House centre so that we could set up our musical equipment and have a sound check before the audience started to arrive. At first we couldn't seem to get any sound out of our microphones which was a bit of a worry but eventually we solved the problem and we were ready to start. By about 2.30pm just about everyone had arrived and after a short introduction by a member of the Beds & Bucks branch we started to play our songs. In the audience were three Ricardian authors, Sandra Heath Wilson, Kathy Martin and Joanne Larner. I gave Sandra a special mention between playing the songs because she had written and read the narratives which are included on the 'Tant le Desiree' album. Kathy and Joanne had brought along copies of their books to sell at the event. The first song that we performed was 'Ambion Hill' for my friend Susan Lamb, as she was also in the audience and she had given me the inspiration for the song.

This is the list of the songs that my band played at the event:-

'Ambion Hill'
'Loyalty Binds me'
'A Herald's Lament'
'Francis Cranley'
'Written at Rising'

'Lord Anthony Woodville'
'The Lady Anne Neville'
'House of York'
'Fellowship of the White Boar'
'King in the car Park'
'How do you Rebury a King'
'Ragged Staff' instrumental
'The Gold it Feels so Cold'
'The Year of Three Kings'
'The Court of King Richard III'
'Shakespeare's Richard'
'The Lord Protector'
'Act iii scene iv'
'White Surrey'

In between singing and playing the songs I explained to the audience where the inspiration came from for composing the tunes. After we had finished performing 'White Surrey,' which was the last song in the set, everyone enjoyed having cups of tea, coffee and a slice of some delicious, exquisitely decorated cake that boasted an icing sugar white rose of York. Kathy Martin and Joanne Larner sold and signed copies of their novels and I also managed to sell some copies of my Ricardian albums. The 'Tant Le Desiree' album seemed to be the most popular one, probably because of Sandra being at the event. I would like to thank Jeanette Melbourne for making it all possible, and I was very impressed with how well she had organised everything.

Joanne Larner wrote this short article about it:-

"Having enjoyed the three CD albums of songs about Richard III by The Legendary Ten Seconds, I was very keen to attend when I heard

there was to be a live concert by the group, who comprise Ian Churchward on lead vocals and acoustic guitar (and writer of most of the songs), Lord Zarquon on keyboards and Rob Bright on lead guitar. The lyrics of the songs all deal with various aspects of Richard's life and reputation and the music is a combination of folk-rock and medieval – a perfectly unique sound. The concert was organised by the Bucks and Beds branch of the Richard III Society, so all who attended were pro-Richard.

"There was a modest but very appreciative audience at York House (appropriate name) in Stony Stratford (appropriate location). The performance began with the lovely song, 'Ambion Hill' which was inspired by a ghostly encounter experienced by Susan Lamb, one of the audience. It described someone searching for the site of the Battle of Bosworth and being 'guided' by a ghostly knight. This was followed by 'Loyalty Binds Me' which refers to the motto of Richard III and how he was true to it during his life. It has a nice rhythm and inspiring lyrics.

"The third song, 'A Herald's Lament', is a newer song and its lyrics were written by Sandra Heath Wilson, a Ricardian author who was also present at the gig. The words of this one are poignant and very sad and the tune is dramatic and moving. This was followed by a song I hadn't heard before, 'Francis Cranley,' which was inspired by the main character of 'The Woodville Connection,' a medieval mystery novel written by another Ricardian author, Kathy Martin, also attending the event.

"'Written At Rising' was the next offering, based on a surviving letter from Richard to Sir John Say, requesting a loan of £100 – it is another of my favourites, maybe because it includes the line 'right trusty and well-beloved'. 'Tis a pity we don't begin our letters like that anymore!

"The next two songs were about two other important characters from Richard's life – 'Lord Anthony Woodville' and the 'Lady Anne Neville'. The former is interesting as it uses the theory that Anthony might have had a hand in poisoning King Edward IV and the tune is fast moving *and dramatic and the latter, in contrast, is very sad, dealing with the tragedies in the life of Richard's wife and referencing the eclipse which occurred when she died.*

"'House of York', following these, was originally titled 'Richard of York', and was the first Richard III song Ian Churchward wrote with the help of Lord Zarquon. I find the lyrics 'Long gone to his death, long gone his dying breath, long gone the House of York...' extremely moving and the melody is lovely. Another favourite.

"Then followed three songs with a more modern twist, dealing with events after Richard's death. 'Fellowship of the White Boar' was the original name of the Richard III Society and tells of the principles of the Society and the struggle to counter Tudor propaganda. 'King in the Car Park' is about the King's remains lying under the feet of the monks who buried him and then the modern workers who were all unaware that he was beneath them in the car park. The lyrics were written by Ian's wife and they are brilliant ('Car doors slamming, wet feet splashing, running across to the office door, Silent beneath them, unheeded underneath them, King Richard of England, he of the white boar.') They bring such a vivid picture into the mind's eye – everything normal and yet a King is right there just feet away as if waiting for the right time to return, and the music is perfect to complement the words. The third song in this modern trilogy is called 'How Do You Rebury a King?' and is about Richard's re-interment and the different emotions and attitudes of the people attending.

"Then there was an instrumental, 'The Ragged Staff' (it refers to the cognizance of Richard Neville, Earl of Warwick). It is an uplifting and upbeat melody and the three musicians' contributions complement each other well, Lord Zarquon like a wizard of the electronic keyboards, Rob contributing skilful guitar solos and Ian himself providing the rhythm guitar part that gives the song its framework and holds it all together.

"Next came a song which relates how Edward IV's French campaign ended without a fight, as he allowed himself to be bought off by French

gold. Richard was not happy about this and hence the song title 'The Gold It Feels So Cold.' The tune is quite fast and the lyrics move the story on at a cracking pace. I am sure Richard was, indeed, 'thinking of Agincourt' when they set off for France.

"'The Year of Three Kings' recalled 1483 and each of the kings has a verse, with the chorus being suitable for audience participation, and we obliged with gusto.

"The next idea was inspired by the report of a foreign courtier who visited Richard's Court and gave a favourable report on it: 'The Court of King Richard III' is another great tune and the CD version has great harmonies with a female singer, Camilla Joyce.

"'Shakespeare's Richard' questions the portrayal of Richard that we know from the Bard, a 'Plantagenet tragedy'.

"The next one has a solemn and portentous feel, taking place on the deathbed of Edward IV, where he names Richard as 'The Lord Protector' and refers to Elizabeth Woodville thinking she was unable to trust him.

"The lyrics of the penultimate song were not written by Ian, but Shakespeare! There are not many composers who can say they co-wrote a song with Shakespeare, so good for you, Ian! 'Act III, Scene IV' is the scene where there is a council meeting to arrange the King's coronation and it has a very catchy chorus.

"Last, but definitely not least, was the wonderful 'White Surrey' which is my absolute favourite track, and I was honoured that Ian dedicated it to me, as he knows I love it. It tells of Richard's final heroic charge at Bosworth and the tune gradually builds the tension through the verses, 'The medieval cannons blast at Henry Tudor's men, Richard upon White Surrey, facing death again', releasing it during the chorus 'My horse, my horse, my White Surrey, for York and England my White Surrey'. The best thing is that it ends before Richard is betrayed and murdered and we are left seeing him magnificent, courageous and heroic on his noble white steed.

"After the concert we had refreshments in the form of hot drinks and a wonderful cake made to the design of the white rose of York. There was time to catch up with old friends and meet new ones and lots of photographs were taken, one of which is reproduced here.

"All in all it was a fantastic day and if anyone has the chance to catch The Legendary Ten Seconds in concert, I urge you to do so – you won't be disappointed."

The Legendary Ten Seconds with Kathy Martin holding a copy of her first Francis Cranley novel at York House in Stony Stratford, February 2016. From left to right, Ian Churchward, Kathy Martin, Rob Bright and Lord Zarquon.

Chapter Eight
A Trip to Denver

On the 24th July 2015 I received an email from a lady called Mary Jo Kalbfleisch in the USA asking me if it would be possible for me to arrange for The Legendary Ten Seconds to visit the USA as she really liked the songs that I had written about Richard III. I replied saying that I would love to bring my band over to her country but I explained to her that I did not think it would be possible due to the costs that would be involved. In a later email Mary Jo asked me if I could let the USA branch of the Richard III Society have some of my Ricardian CD albums for them to sell to help raise some funds to enable Dominic Smee to visit the USA to give a talk.

I then received an email from Bob Pfile of the Tidewater chapter of the USA Richard III society who advised me that they were trying to arrange for Dominic to attend their general meeting of the main USA branch for 2016 which would be held in Denver. Bob then visited the UK and had a meeting with Dominic at Bosworth. Bob had asked me to also attend the meeting but this wasn't convenient for me so my friend Susan Lamb attended the meeting on my behalf. Susan lives in West Bromwich which is much closer to Bosworth compared to where I live. After this meeting I agreed to send 20 copies of my CD albums to Bob in the USA.

Later that year I received an email from Jackie Hudson of the Colorado Rocky Mountain chapter in the USA who was helping to organise the Denver Richard III event. She also told me how much she liked my songs and I was persuaded to agree to attend the AGM which was planned for September 2016. By this time Dominic and Christina Smee had also agreed to attend. I decided to visit the USA after Jackie told me that she would be very happy for Elaine and I to stay at her home in Boulder which is a short distance away from

Denver. I decided that it would be a rather nice holiday. When Rob, the lead guitar player in my band heard about this he also wanted to go with us and Jackie and her partner agreed that we would all be able to stay at their house. Jackie did a brilliant job of hiring the musical equipment that we would need to enable us to perform our songs in Denver. We had decided that it would be a logistical nightmare to try to bring along our own musical equipment. She also bought herself a new harp and started to learn how to play two of my songs, Ambion Hill and Yorkist Archer. We would then see if she would be able to play her harp and sing with my band at the USA Richard III Society GMM in Denver,

After much preparation Rob, Elaine and myself drove to Heathrow from where we live in Devon. We then boarded a British Airways Boeing 747. We flew out of Heathrow in the afternoon and had daylight all the way to Denver. I was very lucky to have a window seat and enjoyed being able to see the icy landscape of Greenland below us. I also enjoyed looking at lots of the lakes of Canada and then the flat plains and fields which seemed to go on forever into the northern states of the USA. I also saw the Missouri river and was so pleased that there weren't too many clouds to spoil the view. When we reached Denver I was very surprised to find that the mile high city is on the edge of a high rolling plain and so it didn't feel like it was at a very high altitude. I discovered that Denver is near the mountains, not in them. Jackie's partner Richard Napier met us at Denver international airport with a sign that said:-

WELCOME IAN, ELAINE & ROB! THE LEGENDARY TEN SECONDS AMERIAN TOUR.

Richard took us in his car to Boulder and when we arrived at his house it was quite exciting to meet Jackie after exchanging so many emails with her for the previous 12 months. By that time we were really feeling quite exhausted after travelling without sleep for such a long time. Because of this we went to bed very early although just before this it was very interesting talking to Jackie and to learn that her interest in Richard III had come via her previous interest in the Tudor period of English history.

We had arrived in the USA on a Tuesday afternoon (20th September) and the next day Jackie showed us around Boulder. Later that day we picked up the guitars and amplifier that Jackie had hired from a music shop in Boulder and we had a couple of rehearsal's at Jackie's house so that we could get used to the guitars and for Jackie to be able to practice singing and playing her harp with Elaine, Rob and myself.

On the Thursday Richard drove us to see Buffalo Bill's grave and museum on Lookout mountain and I was amazed to discover that his wild west circus visited my home town of Torquay in 1904. In the previous year of 1903 on an earlier tour of England he had visited Newton Abbot where Elaine was born, Plymouth where my stepson works and also Exeter where I was born.

Most of Friday was spent hiring the rest of the musical equipment (such as microphones and the public address speakers etc that we would need for our performance on the Saturday evening) and for Richard to make two trips in his car to Denver to transport us and all the things that had to be taken along for the GMM.

The Richard III event was held at the Spring Hill Suites hotel and I then discovered that the official title of the event was General membership meeting and that it is now held every two years and not on an annual basis. There were quite a few historical novels and books for sale at the meeting in the hotel. I quickly spotted a copy of one of Sandra Heath Wilson's early novels called *Wife to the Kingmaker*. I managed to limit myself to only buying two books which were second hand copies of Ricardian novels which I had not previously heard of. These books are *Cry God For Richard* by Jean

Allison-Williams and *The Rose at Harvest End* by Eleanor Fairburn. I didn't buy Sandra's novel as Sandra had given me a copy of that book the first time she visited my house in Torquay. I have a tendency to be a bit of an obsessive collector of things and I was at that time trying to collect and read as many Ricardian books as possible.

We had arrived at the hotel on the Friday evening and the next morning we listened to Sally Keil's very informative talk about heraldry and I also learnt about the term blazonry of which I had previously been ignorant. This was followed by a really interesting presentation by Susan Troxell about the Middleham Jewel. This was of special interest to me because of Susan's article in the *Ricardian Chronicle* which had given me the inspiration for my song which I had written about this medieval piece of jewelry. By coincidence Lord Zarquon had very recently finished mixing and mastering the recording of the song just before we had set off on our American adventure. It was a real thrill to meet Susan and also take some photos of her replica copy of the Middleham Jewel.

After lunch Dominic Smee gave a great presentation and talk about his participation in a Channel Four documentary which I had seen on TV. This showed us how scoliosis might have affected Richard III because Dominic suffers from this back condition. Dominic told us that his scoliosis effects one less veterbra in his back compared to Richard III with Dominic's spinal curvature starting at the fourth thoracic verterbra (near the base of the spine) and Richard's at the third. I was sitting on the same table as the author Anne Easter Smith and I could see her making lots of notes during Dominc's presentation. She later told me that this would help with her research for a new novel about Richard III.

In the evening there was a banquet and most of the people attending the event dressed up in medieval costumes. I was particularly impressed with Sally Keil's outfit, especially her headdress. After the evening meal my band played our songs about Richard III. We performed a very similar set of songs to those we had previously played at Torquay museum and Stony Stratford earlier in the year. I was quite pleased with my performance and I didn't forget any of the words for the songs, well I did nearly forget the words for the second verse of the song called 'The Lord Protector'. I had to keep on playing the verse on my guitar for much longer than I should have so that I could give myself some extra time to remember the lyrics. There was a bit of confusion with the introduction section of 'Yorkist Archer' which I started to play on my guitar in the wrong key. We had to stop and start again and then when we did I made some more mistakes at the beginning of the song. One day I will hopefully be able to play an entire gig without making any mistakes. I remember after one gig with my Ceildah band many years ago. After we had finished playing and the leader of the band, Nigel Howells, was handing out everyone's cash payment for playing, Nigel turned to me and said " Ian here is your fifty pounds less £5 for all your mistakes so now you owe me £10!" I have to remind myself that I am not a professional musician, only playing occasional gigs. My day job as a bank clerk means that my music is really just an obsessive hobby.

The next day on Sunday morning Christina Smee gave a fascinating talk about her book called *The Rose of Middleham*. Also about the living history group to which herself and Dominic are members. I have now read Christina's book and I can honestly say that it is a real page turner and quite brilliant.

After Christina's talk there was a Ricardian quiz and I was the winner of this. The chairman of the USA Richard III society was sat next to me and congratulated me on winning. I think I clinched it by providing the correct answer to a question about Catherine Woodville's second marriage which happened in 1485 and which was to Jasper Tudor.

After the GMM finished Pete and Dawn Shafer drove us to their house in Breckenridge where we stayed for a few days. With us were

Jackie Hudson, Dominic Smee and Christina Smee. Pete and Dawn were fabulous hosts and took us to see lots of interesting places. On Tuesday 27th September 2016 it was time to catch our flight back to the UK with lots of happy memories which included wining a couple of Ricardian things in the GMM raffle.

I must say a big thank you to Jackie Hudson and Richard Napier, especially Richard for collecting the music equipment in Boulder and taking it to Denver. After the GMM had finished he then took all the equipment back to Boulder. When it was time to leave the USA he drove us to the airport. All this so that we could play some songs about Richard III for the USA branch of the Richard III Society and he isn't even a Ricardian!

Not long after we arrived home at the end of September I sang and talked about Richard III on a local radio station, presented by Jeff Sleeman on the 2nd October which is a very significant date if you are a Ricardian. Co hosting the show was Camilla Joyce who sang along on my songs and I even had Jeff Sleeman singing along by the time we got to the third chorus of "The Year of Three Kings'.

The Legendary Ten Seconds and friends in Breckenridge, Colorado, September 2016, shortly after the USA Richard III society General Members Meeting. From left to right, Dawn Shafer, Christina Smee, Rob Bright, Elaine Churchward, Jackie Hudson, Ian Churchward and Dominic Smee.

Chapter Nine
The Mortimers

After finishing the Murrey and Blue album I was thinking about recording an album of songs covering a wider aspect of English history. With this in mind I composed and recorded a couple of songs in the autumn and winter of 2017 and then I received an email from the secretary of the Mortimer History Society who had been listening to some of my Richard III concept albums. He asked me if I would be interested in recording an album about the Mortimer family in the middle ages for his society to mark their tenth anniversary for June 2019. My initial reaction was that I didn't feel capable of doing this because I couldn't have the same emotional interest in the Mortimers that I'd had for Richard III. Without the sense of inspiration I didn't feel that I could undertake all the reading that would be required to learn enough about their history to be able to write enough songs for an album.

I didn't respond immediately but thought about the request for a while and then decided that it was a good opportunity and I responded by asking the chairman if he could help by sending me some information about the Mortimers. He agreed to send me a book that he had written which is called 'On the Trail of the Mortimers'. So I read his book and started to get an idea for a song. I was also sent several song ideas, poems and lyrics from various sources. Most of them were from Ashley Mantle, and throughout a period of just under a year I recorded the songs for the album.

Philip Hume wrote historical narratives to introduce the songs and we recorded the actor John Challis reading these. My wife had briefly met John at a flower festival at Powderham Castle where he had a stall signing copies of a new book he had written. That evening my wife told me about this and said that John's book was about the garden he had created at his house in the grounds of a former abbey. She couldn't remember the name of the abbey but said it began with the letter 'W'. She said that John Challis had mentioned that it had something to do with the Mortimers and she told John that I was in the process of recording an album about the Mortimers. He then said that there was a Mortimer castle near his house. As soon as she told me this I knew that it must be Wigmore. I then sent an email to Philip Hume about this and he replied telling me that John Challis was the patron of the Mortimer History Society! I asked if it would be possible to arrange for John to be recorded reading the narratives. To cut a long story short, by happy chance we were able to do this when John visited the Palace theatre in Paignton, Torbay where he gave an especially amusing talk about his very interesting career as an actor, most notably as Boycie in Only Fools Horses. Lord Zarquon recorded John reading the narratives at the theatre in the afternoon before his show on Saturday 25th October 2018.

Here are the details of the songs that were recorded for the Mortimer album.

'MORTIMER OVERTURE'

Instrumental composed by Ian Churchward, recorded from June to August 2018
Ian Churchward guitars
Lord Zarquon keyboards, and drums

'MORTEMER CASTLE'

In the year 1054 a battle it was set
A lord led his army out to meet the threat

Roger de Mortimer the first of that name
Of that noble family of ever lasting fame

Mortemer his castle on it's man made hill
Defending Normandy with his sword of steel

For the Duke of Normandy Roger braveley fought
Defeated the French army,
Prisoners to his castle brought
Roger de Mortimer the first of that name
Of that noble family of ever lasting fame

Mortemer his castle on it's man made hill
Defending Normandy with his sword of steel

His prisoner Ralph de Crepi Roger did set free
And this did greatly anger the Duke of Normandy
Roger de Mortimer the first of that name
Of that noble family of ever lasting fame

Mortemer his castle on it's man made hill
Defending Normandy with his sword of steel

In the year 1054 a battle it was set
A lord led his army out to meet the threat
Roger de Mortimer the first of that name
Of that noble family of ever lasting fame

Mortemer his castle on it's man made hill
Defending Normandy with his sword of steel

Lyrics written by Ashley Mantle and Ian Churchward January 2018, music composed by Ian Churchward January 2018.
Recorded from January until February 2018
Ian Churchward guitars, and verse vocals
Anna Bolt lead chorus vocals
Guy Bolt tambourine and chorus backing vocals
Lord Zarquon keyboards, bass guitar and drums

'THE MARCHER LORDS'

On the border with Wales we stand
Defence and conquest we have in hand
Our king and country we may serve
Though it's our power we preserve

The Marcher Lords are we
Masters of our destiny
Oh the Marcher Lords are we
If you cross our path tread carefully
Oh the Marcher Lords are we

It's a land of opportunity
Join our raids in the Welsh country
Land and riches we always seek
We exploit the poor and despise the meek

The Marcher Lords are we
Masters of our destiny
Oh the Marcher Lords are we
If you cross our path tread carefully
Oh the Marcher Lords are we

See our castles made of stone
The seeds of strife that we have sown
Of our power you must take heed
Or on your knees you will soon plead

The Marcher Lords are we
Masters of our destiny
Oh the Marcher Lords are we
If you cross our path tread carefully
Oh the Marcher Lords are we

Private wars are our liberty
Don't interfere just leave us be
But bring unto to us a royal writ
And you will soon be eating it

The Marcher Lords are we
Masters of our destiny
Oh the Marcher Lords are we
If you cross our path tread carefully
Oh the Marcher Lords are we

Lyrics written by Ashley Mantle and Ian Churchward June 2018,
music composed by Ian Churchward June 2018.
Recorded from June until August 2018.
Ian Churchward bass, 6 & 12 string guitars, and vocals,
Lord Zaquon keyboards and drums

'WHEN CHRIST AND HIS SAINTS SLEPT'

For Matilda or Stephen where do you stand
Anarchy and civil war has plagued our land
The earth is ravaged crops cannot grow
In warfare how you reap what you sow

With civil war nobody wins
God has abandoned us for our sins
Oh how the monks lamented and wept
In England when Christ and his saints slept

The rich man thinks himself a king
Like locusts illegal castles did spring
To private warfare the nobles soon fell
The poor they oppressed, they made their lives hell

With civil war nobody wins
God has abandoned us for our sins
Oh how the monks lamented and wept
In England when Christ and his saints slept

Hugh Mortimer For King Stephen stood true
At Wigmore the king's banners he flew
But loyalty is such a fickle thing
Hugh's allies deserted him and their king

With civil war nobody wins
God has abandoned us for our sins
Oh how the monks lamented and wept
In England when Christ and his saints slept

With the death of Stephen there is a new king

For peace in our land the church bells will ring
Now that the anarchy comes to an end
King Henry the Second I do now commend

Lyrics written by Ashley Mantle and Ian Churchward July 2018,
music composed by Ian Churchward July 2018.
Recorded from July until August 2018.
Ian Churchward bass & 6 string guitars, and vocals
Elaine Churchward backing vocals
Lord Zarquon keyboards and drums

'DE MONTFORT'

Early in the morning
It was an august day
De Montfort awoke to be told
Of the troops not far way

Three lions of the royal arms
Up there upon the hill
Prince Edward's royal standard
With revenge to fulfil

It was murder at Evesham
A true battle it was not
No sanctuary was given
Of slaughter there was a lot

Once held in confinement
Prince Edward escaped in May
Roger Mortimer had helped him

In royal favour he then did stay

Three lions of the royal arms
Up there upon the hill
Prince Edward's royal standard
With revenge to fulfil

It was murder at Evesham
A true battle it was not
No sanctuary was given
Of slaughter there was a lot

Great feuds personal and bitter
De Montfort killed that day
By the Lord of Wigmore
Such fury on display

Three lions of the royal arms
Up there upon the hill
Prince Edward's royal standard
With revenge to fulfil

It was murder at Evesham
A true battle it was not
No sanctuary was given
Of slaughter there was a lot

De Montfort's body butchered
His head removed that day
Delivered to Wigmore castle
To Maud de Braose without delay

Composed by Ian Churchward, January 2018.
Recorded from January until the end of August 2018.
Ian Churchward 6 & 12 string guitars, and vocals
Fleur Elliott backing vocals
Lord Zarquon keyboards, bass guitar and drums

'THE ROUND TABLE 1279'

To Kenilworth you are invited
For my sons have been knighted
To honour them we shall recall
King Arthur's pageantry once more

Oh the splendour we shall dance
In this grand circumstance

At my round table please join me
The noble king you will see
Arthur's court we shall recall
The pageantry and so much more

Oh the splendour we shall dance
See the knights break a lance

As Arthur's knights some will be dressed
Sir Lancelot will look the best
The heraldry on his shield
All of this will be revealed

My lords and ladies please attend

With the king my royal friend
King Arthur we shall recall
The pageantry see it all

Oh the splendour we shall dance
In this grand circumstance

Lyrics written by Ashley Mantle and Ian Churchward August 2018,
music composed by Ian Churchward August 2018.
Recorded from August until September 2018.
Ian Churchward 6 & 12 string guitars, mandola and vocals
Lord Zarquon keyboards, bass drum and tambourine

'TWO THOUSAND MARKS'

Aged fourteen he was given a bride
In the church in Pembridge, Joan by his side
His wife was an heiress to half of Ludlow
But to Piers Gaverston a fine he would owe

Two thousand marks and five hundred more
Was the fine he paid of that I am sure
Two thousand marks and five hundred more
Not one farthing less of that I am sure

He was just seventeen when his father died
Because of a wardship it was justified
To pay the favourite of the king's son
Piers Gaverston was that favoured one

Two thousand marks and five hundred more

Was the fine he paid of that I am sure
Two thousand marks and five hundred more
Not one farthing less of that I am sure

Despite this fine his wealth it did grow
A knighthood upon him the king did bestow
Then to parliament he was called
The death of the old king, a new one installed

Composed by Ian Churchward April 2018.
Recorded from April until the beginning of September 2018.
Ian Churchward bass, 6 & 12 string guitars, mandolin and vocals
Jules Jones backing vocals
Lord Zarquon keyboards and drums

'THE PRIVY SEAL AND THE ROYAL SHIELD'

Roger led men from his estate
Defeat at Bannockburn was their fate
Protecting the flight of their king
Of Roger's honour I will now sing

I wll now sing
I will now sing
Of Mortimer honour I will now sing

The privy seal and the royal shield
Lost to Sotland on the battlefield
Left behind by the English king
Of Roger's honour I will now sing

I wll now sing
I will now sing
Of Mortimer honour I will now sing

Rather than a ransom given a task
Was it demanded or did someone ask
To return the seal and the royal shield
And the bodies of two nobles who had been killed

Roger returning with the shield
Two dead nobles who had been killed
And the privy seal lost by the king
Of Roger's honour I will now sing

I wll now sing
I will now sing
Of Mortimer honour I will now sing
I wll now sing
I will now sing
Of Mortimer honour I will now sing

Composed by Ian Churchward April 2018.
Recorded from April until the beginning of September 2018.
Ian Churchward guitars, mandola and vocals
Jules Jones backing vocals
Lord Zarquon keyboards, bass guitar and drums

'THE KING OF FOLLY'

During thirteen twenty nine
At Wigmore the king of folly did dine

At Wigmore Castle his son did declare
The king of folly you will find there

A great tournament
And a round table
A double wedding
Perhaps a fable

During thirteen twenty nine
At Wigmore the king of folly did dine
At Wigmore Castle his son did declare
The king of folly you will find there

Two of his daughters
Married that day
Displaying grandeur
In every way

Elaborate and wearing rich clothes
How could this be the path that he chose
How did it spiral out of control
A price to pay for his leading role

During thirteen twenty nine
At Wigmore the king of folly did dine
At Wigmore Castle his son did declare
The king of folly you will find there
The king of folly you will find there

Composed by Ian Churchward March 2018.
Recorded from March until September 2018.

Ian Churchward guitars, mandola and vocals
Elaine Churchward vocals
Ashley Dyer trumpet
Lord Zarquon keyboards, bass guitar and drums

'THE TRAGEDY OF ROGER MORTIMER'

At Berkeley Castle the legends stated
A crime so evil was perpetrated
Edward the Second a king deposed
Was he murdered cruelly no one knows

A Mortimer for the king's death blamed
As a traitor he would be named
Yet I hear there are those who say
That Edward did not die that day

The tragedy of Roger Mortimer
Grave news to Isabella brought to her
At Tyburn he was hung up high
So many came to see him die

Of secret plots I have been apprised
The death of a king to be contrived
A funeral effigy then to be made
With a copper crown to be displayed

The tragedy of Roger Mortimer
Grave news to Isabella brought to her
At Tyburn he was hung up high
So many came to see him die

From Berkeley Castle he was conveyed
At Corfe under guard Edward then stayed
To free him his half brother did try
The tale of regicide perhaps a lie

With Edward's whereabouts now revealed
To Ireland he was then concealed
In France and Germany he would travel
Wearing a far less royal apparel

The tragedy of Roger Mortimer
Grave news to Isabella brought to her
At Tyburn he was hung up high
So many came to see him die

Later in Germany it was so strange
A new king met William le Galeys
His father this stranger pertained to be
Received by the king most graciously

Lyrics written by Ashley Mantle and Ian Churchward,
music composed by Ian Churchward July 2018,
Recorded from April until the beginning of September 2018.
Ian Churchward acoustic guitar and vocals
Elaine Churchward vocals
Rob Bright lead electric guitar

'LEINTWARDINE'

To the church of St Mary Magdalene

A gift that a king did bring
He came twice in thirteen fifty three
To Leintwardine there came a king

Laying a cloth of gold
See it there unfold
Masses for the high born sung
For their souls yes this was done

To the church of St Mary Magdalene
A gift that a king did bring
Can you just imagine the scene
A pilgrimage to Leintwardine

Laying a cloth of gold
See it there unfold
Masses for the high born sung
For their souls yes this was done

Composed by Ian Churchward in May 2018.
Recorded from May until September 2018.
Ian Churchward guitar and vocals
Violet Sheer vocals
Rowan Curle vocals
Lord Zarquon keyboards and drums

'MER DE MORT'

Taken across the Irish sea
Will we ever be set free
My father has been laid to rest

Of good fortune we are not blessed

In my mind's eye the mer de mort
Oh so dark is that thought

Roger and I just young boys
Forced to be Bollingbroke toys
Mortimer heirs we are distraught
To Windsor we are now brought

In my mind's eye the mer de mort
Oh so dark is that thought

In Wales Glyn Dwr is uprising
Of Bryn Glas I am surmising
Our uncle's army was defeated
Many dead bodies badly treated

In my mind's eye the mer de mort
Oh so dark is that thought

So many see me as a king
But I dare not entertain such a thing

Lady Despenser rescues me
With my brother briefly free
But at Cheltenham we are caught
To Pevensey we are brought

In my mind's eye the mer de mort
Oh so dark is that thought

Song composed by Ian Churchward in March 2018.
Based upon a poem by Margot Miller called 'Sea of Dead'.
Recorded from March until April 2018.
Ian Churchward bass & 6 string guitars, mandola, and vocals
Elaine Churchward backing vocals
Lord Zarquon keyboards and drums

'MER DE MORT PART TWO'

My brother has no tomb
Such sadness to reflect
Who he was, how did he die
Only I will not forget

Misery to me brought
Beside the mer de mort

I've heard my mother died
Such sadness to reflect
Who she was, how did she die
Only I will not forget

Mourning to me brought
Beyond the mer de mort

My minority behind me
The future I will grasp
I've gained my inheritance
I ride freely at last
Contentment to be brought

Far from the mer de mort

Lyrics written by Margot Miller and Ian Churchward in March
2018, music composed by Ian Churchward in March 2018.
Recorded from March until September 2018.
Ian Churchward bass & 6 string guitars, mandolin, mandola, and
vocals
Elaine Churchward backing vocals
Lord Zarquon keyboards

'HENRY VI'

A once disputed king of France
A lack of authority was his stance
Civil war throughout his land
He showed no interest to command

Henry the Sixth his reign so weak
Henry the Sixth his thoughts so meek
Henry the Fifth's only child
Henry the Sixth so meek and mild

As a child his uncles ruled
By Richard Beauchamp he was schooled
The Duke of Suffolk came on the scene
And used a talent to exploit and scheme

Henry the Sixth his reign so weak
Henry the Sixth his thoughts so meek
Henry the Fifth's only child
Henry the Sixth so meek and mild

For a while Henry lost his mind
In a catatonic state he did decline
And then the Duke of York did rule
Till Henry woke up still a fool

Composed by Ian Churchward in December 2016.
Recorded from December 2016 until March 2018.
Ian Churchward guitars, mandola and vocals
Lord Zarquon keyboards, bass guitar and drums

'THE SUNNES OF YORK'

In fourteen twenty five Edmund Mortimer died
The right of inheritance was ratified
Thus given to Anne Mortimer's son
Claiming full inheritance aged twenty one

The sunnes of York, of York threes sons
So infamous one would become
Edward the Fourth, George and Richard
Their brother killed by Lord Clifford

Henry the sixth was a hapless king
To the greedy nobles he would give anything
Though anarchy the king did deplore
The Duke of York he chose to ignore

The sunnes of York, of York threes sons
So infamous one would become
Edward the Fourth, George and Richard

Their brother killed by Lord Clifford

We clearly saw three suns in the sky
Edward the Fourth told us the reason why
Richard was so noble don't believe the Tudor lie

At Wakefield the Duke of York was slain
To his son Edward fell that royal claim
At Mortimer's cross three suns were seen
A good omen before his victory

The sunnes of York, of York threes sons
So infamous one would become
Edward the Fourth, George and Richard
Their brother killed by Lord Clifford

Lyrics written by Ashley Mantle and Ian Churchward January 2018,
music composed by Ian Churchward Janaury 2018.
Recorded from January until June 2018.
Ian Churchward guitars, mandola, mandolin and vocals
Pippa West vocals
Lord Zarquon keyboards, bass guitar and drums

'CHAPEL OF SIR JOHN'

In the window above Sir John
A king, a crown he's seeking
Centuries slowly slipping by
Those secrets they lie sleeping

In the church, St Matthews Church

Sir John he lies a sleeping
Centuries slowly slipping by
His secrets still he's keeping

See the scold with the horrid tongue
Hidden in the screen
Clearly not a lady fair
Surely not a Woodville queen

In the face that holds a crown
Looks like he's been scheming
Centuries slowly slipping by
A kingship oh so fleeting

See the scold with the horrid tongue
Hidden in the screen
Clearly not a lady fair
Surely not a Woodville queen

Ancient tiles upon the floor
To be seen through the church door
To the chapel of Sir John
Where have all the answers gone

In the window above Sir John
A king, a crown he's seeking
Centuries slowly slipping by
Those secrets they lie sleeping

See the scold with the horrid tongue
Hidden in the screen

Clearly not a lady fair
Surely not a Woodville queen

Lyrics written by Elaine Churchward and Ian Churchward February 2018 after visiting St Matthews church in Coldridge.
Music composed by Ian Churchward February 2018.
Recorded from February until April 2018.
Ian Churchward bass, 6 & 12 guitars, and vocals
Fleur Elliott backing vocals
Tom Churchward tambourine
Lord Zarquon keyboards and drums

A very interesting thing happened at the end of January 2018 when I became involved with a project about the missing Princes of Edward VI. This was because of a stained glass window of Edward V in the church at Coldridge in Devon. I visited another church in Devon at Doddiscombleigh which has a large amount of intact medieval stained glass in it's windows. The stained glass is of a similar design to the Edward V window in the church at Coldridge. I had read on the internet that the windows were made in 1480 and I asked the churchwarden if this was true and she told me that it was because a stained glass window expert had come to the church from York minster to clean the windows and had been able to confirm the date. My friend Pippa West came over to my house a few days later to sing on one of my new songs and I mentioned to her about the church and I said that the churchwarden had confirmed the age of the windows because an expert had visited the church from York. Before I had hardly finished my sentence Pippa said "I know who that person would be, it would be Peter Gibson. He was the leading expert in the country on stained glass windows. I used to live in York and my father knew him really well". I then checked in the church booklet that I had purchased and sure enough it was Peter Gibson who had taken his team to St Michaels church in Doddiscombleigh in 1976

One of the illustrations that was created by Graham Moores for the
Mer de Mort album.

Chapter Ten
History Book Part One

This album was released on 1st April 2019, on Richard the Third Records, as catalogue number R40

It was recorded from 2017 & 2018 except for a new version of the 'King in the Car Park' which was recorded from 2013 to 2018. All the songs were composed by me except 'The Green Knight' for which most of the lyrics were written by Sandra Heath Wilson. Ashley Mantle wrote most of the lyrics for 'The Conqueror's Prophecy'. Most of the lyrics for 'Who Layeth There' were written by John Dike. Of course my wife Elaine wrote the lyrics for 'King in the Car Park'. All of the songs were recorded by Lord Zarquon and myself at our homes in Marldon and Torbay.

Here is a list of who sings and plays on the recordings:-

Ian Churchward vocals, guitars, ukulele, mandolin and mandola
Lord Zarquon keyboards, mellotron ghosts, bass guitar and drums
Jules Jones vocals on 'The Green Knight' and 'When They Came to Edinburgh'
Jackie Hudson chorus vocal on 'Back in Time'
Elaine Churchward backing vocal on 'The Conqueror's Prophecy' and spoken words on 'Who Layeth There'
Rob Bright lead guitar solo on 'When They Came to Edinburgh'
Ashley Dyer trumpet on 'For the Harringtons'
Fleur Elliott backing vocals on 'The Treachery of Sir William'
Pippa West backing vocal and tambourine on 'The Beaufort Companye'
Lis Durham violin on 'The Beaufort Companye'

HISTORY BOOK LYRICS

'BACK IN TIME'

Take a journey back in time
I wonder what we might find
The last ice age has departed
The history lesson has now started

Back in time, back in time
Back in time, back in time

Take a journey back through time
I wonder what we might find
The secrets of Stonehenge concealed
The mists of time now revealed

Back in time, back in time
Back in time, back in time

Take a journey back through time
I wonder what we might find
The Roman legions here then gone
Dark ages lingering for so long

'THE GREEN KNIGHT'

Twas Christmas at Camelot the feasting was grand
With Arthur and Guinevere and all their knights to hand
There seemed not a care nothing would spoil the day

When in rode a giant knight and he was heard to say

I challenge a knight to fight me
But you won't land one blow
And the knight was green
From his head to his toes
Green was his hair his beard and his clothes

Gawain declared his courage that he would show
And to that giant knight his gauntlet he did throw
The green knight did laugh such a terrible sound
Shouting *you can have a year to find my battleground*

I accept your challenge
But you won't land one blow
And the knight was green
From his head to his toes
Green was his hair his beard and his clothes

Green was his armour his surcoat and his shield
How many men had that giant killed
Green was his helmet, his sword and his lance
And only Gawain dared to try to meet his glance

The time it did come for the greatest fight
Gawain looked so tiny up against that giant knight
The giant dropped his sword and gave a great big grin
I like you young sir and so I'll let you win
My challenge has been met and my wrath does disappear
You have surely proved your bravery for more than a year

'SENLAC RIDGE'

At Stamford Bridge King Harold
Took the Vikings by surprise
But shortly after victory
From the south bad news arrived
William had landed
To claim the English throne
He had the pope's blessing
Men at arms and knights so bold

Harold raced back to London
His housecarls close behind
Receiving news of rape and pillage
In the English countryside
Harold was determined
Not to waste precious time
Though his army was depleted
He had courage he had pride

From the woods the Saxons gathered
Out on Senlac Ridge
Though they were weary
They would not give an inch
Up the slope the Normans charged
The shield wall held firm
The Normans they fell back
William had them charge once more

The battle raged on all day
An arrow took out Harold's eye
The shield wall was broken

Beneath the autumn skies
Yes the battle raged on all day
An arrow took out Harold's eye
The shield wall was broken
Beneath the autumn skies

'THE CONQUEROR'S PROPHECY'

Oh pity the plight of the youngest son
Prince Henry was born to be no one
With three elder brothers who came before
A life in the church was all that lay in store

Prince Henry was not content with his lot
And the conqueror prophesied and said worry not
"Let thine elder brothers go before thee
For you will be greater just wait and see"

And so those words rang in his ears
The conqueror's prophecy followed him through the years

William on his death bed did declare
For Robert there's Normandy I think that's fair
William Rufus in England crowned
To Henry my youngest I give ten thousand pound

And so those words rang in his ears
The conqueror's prophecy followed him through the years

His brothers came together in pretence of peace
To their youngest brother their fury unleashed

At Mont-St-Michael Henry made a stand
And was cast away from that land

And still those words rang in his ears
The conqueror's prophecy followed him through the years

Let your elder brothers go before
For you will be so much more
Weep not my boy you will be a king
And the prophecy in his ears did ring

Then lo and behold William Rufus is dead
Killed by Walter Tirel so it is said
To Westminster then Henry did ride
To be crowned king with Matilda as his bride

And still those words rang in his ears
The conqueror's prophecy followed him through the years

His brother Robert claimed England as his right
He landed with an army ready to fight
The brother's gave the kiss of peace
But Robert"s ill ways still did not cease

And still those words rang in his ears
The conqueror's prophecy followed him through the years

As the ruler of Normandy Robert did fail
For anarchy and disorder did prevail
To Henry the first the church did appeal
To restore peace with his sword of steel

In battle Robert was defeated at last
And then into prison he ws cast
Prince Henry was now duke and king
And the prophecy in his ears did ring

'THE LOST RING'

The lost ring
The minstrels sing
The duke's hawk on the wing
Oh what tales they could tell
The merchant with his goods for sale

The jigsaw puzzle has pieces missing
Lost history that once was living
So many memories that have died
And yet some fragments have survived

The drunken monk
The peasant poor
The archer with fingers sore
Oh what tales they could tell
The merchant's ship has set sail

The jigsaw puzzle has pieces missing
Lost history that once was living
So many memories that have died
And yet some fragments have survived

The men at arms
Medieval farms

The tailor with his fabric yarns
Oh what tales they could tell
The merchant's ship lost in a gale

The jigsaw puzzle has pieces missing
Lost history that once was living
So many memories that have died
And yet some fragments have survived

'WHEN THEY CAME TO EDINBURGH'

With countless sheaves of arrows
And ordnance from the Tyne
An army of twenty thousand men
Their intent this did define

And when they came to Edinburgh
The castle they could not attack
To James the Third of Scotland
The town they did give back

But for this English army
This time there was no fight
They found that the men of Scotland
Had disappeared out of sight

'FOR THE HARRINGTONS'

Draw close the time has come
The knot now tied stands firm
Though the enemy comes in it's thousands

We have had to learn

That we are for our master
Having been drawn to this field
For no one else save the king we must ever yield
And for our master Harrington
Our loyalty is sealed

So stand firm in the knowledge
That this knot will never break
Though they come with horse and lance
We bravely meet our fate

For we are for our master
Having been drawn to this field
For no one else save the king we must ever yield
And for our master Harrington
Our loyalty is sealed

This is our England on this field below this sky
We shall face today and if needed bravely die
Kiss your sweetheart and bow to the cross and cry
For England for the Harringtons
For glory do or die

'THE TREACHERY OF SIR WILLIAM STANLEY'

When Lord Strange failed in his escape
Twas then that the king learnt nearly too late
Of the treachery of Sir William Stanley
Such doubtful loyalty for his majesty

A very clear message from the king was sent
But with nothing to lose Sir William could not relent
Sir William the traitor had nothing to lose
In declaring support for the Tudor I presume

For a while Henry Tudor's nerve nearly failed
His demeanour so nervous his face so pale
He journeyed to Tamworth and his men must have feared
Just like in Normandy he had disappeared

From Leicester the king led his army out
Intent upon victory there is no doubt
Near Merevale Abbey close to Watling street
That's where Tudor's army he would meet

Thomas Longe"s duty his king to defend
But Roger Wake felt he was no friend
Threatened by his letters full sore against his will
Untested in battle the summons to fulfill

Flickering campfires not so distant
Tomorrow to die perhaps in an instant
Would they survive and who might they kill
The king's army camped on Ambion Hill

'WHO LAYETH THERE'

Upon the hill see the church
The history there to research
Bleak and grey for Tudor folk

Open the door of ancient oak

A corner of this church in devon
John Evan's chantry his bid for heaven
A missing prince in stained glass
An unsolved mystery of the past

The princes last seen in the tower
King Richard blamed for misue of power
But is the truth behind a screen
Lament, lament the Woodville queen

From Bosworth perhaps sir john had come
To Coldridge rewarded for deeds done
Deer park and manor his to keep
To resolve a mystery we now seek

My sons, my sons, i kiss your cheek
I gave my all - to give you life
To let you fly that stony keep
Tossed in a sea of angry strife
So understand my sins-
For love of you. for love of you

Did he feel a stony stare
Hear witches's tongues so evil there
In the stained glass window did he see himself
Guilt, praise, despair or something else

See the carved stone of Sir John
Did a queen save her son

Perhaps King Edward' s son and heir
Inside the tomb who layeth there

'THE BEAUFORT COMPANYE'

The men of the Beaufort company
Of the fifteenth century
Gentle women of our company
The Dukes of Somerset for to please

We will take part in st george's day
In may there is a foot tourney
At Haddon Hall a living history event
See the colours of our banners and our tents

The men of the Beaufort company
Of the fifteenth century
Gentle women of our company
The Dukes of Somerset for to please

On the seventeenth of June East Stoke to see
In July at Tewkesbury
At Lincoln Castle a history event
See the colours of our banners and our tents

The men of the Beaufort company
Of the fifteenth century
Gentle women of our company
The Dukes of Somerset for to please

See our armour on display

Our men at arms in fine array
Tales of trouble and of strife
Of the past brought to life

The men of the Beaufort company
Of the fifteenth century
Gentle women of our company
The Dukes of Somerset for to please

In August we will be on our Welsh tour
To Bosworth we've been many times before
At Raglan Castle a history event
See the colours of our banners and our tents

Artwork drawn by Graham Moores for the border of the History Book albums.

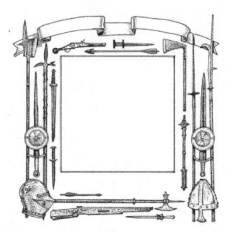

Chapter Eleven
Ian's Blog 2019

At the request of Lord Zarquon in April of 2019 I started to write a weekly blog which would be published on my website.

1st April 2019

Well I've written another song, I'm being lazy and only writing 2 verses with no middle eight, or is it a muddle eight or whatever, can't read music etc so don't really know?! I haven't decided which key to start recording for this one. Probably go for F# to make it awkward for Lord Z. Here are the lyrics:-

'THE DUKE OF YORK'S WIFE'

She saw her last son for the very last time
Though she didn't know it so soon he would die
Killed in battle fighting so bravely
And his body stripped naked for everyone to see
A twisted spine Henry Tudor then could see

When he came to see her he had plans for his life
From Portugal or Spain perhaps a new wife
From Portugal or Spain a new queen as his wife

She took communion for the very last time
She surely knew that very soon she would die
To join her husband who fought so bravely
He was killed at Wakefield so very brutally

IAN CHURCHWARD

His head put on a spike at York for everyone to see

When Ludlow was ravaged she prayed for her life
For she was the proud Duke of York's wife
For she was the proud Duke of York's wife

I submitted all the stuff to CD Baby last week for the History Book Part One album and it is now shown on their website. Also sent the artwork and master CD of the audio to Trade Duplication. The Richard III Society have agreed to take some CDs of this new album to sell to their members, which will be available on the shop page of their website. Pam of the Worcestershire branch will have some CDs on sale at the branch meetings and on her stall at the next Tewkesbury medieval festival.

8th April 2019

I spent Saturday afternoon promoting the History Book Part One album via my laptop while listening to Torquay United playing away against Woking on BBC Radio Devon. It was very stressful and I had difficulty concentrating on the promoting of the new album and the possible promotion of Torquay United football club. Despair when I heard that Torquay had hit the woodwork and then Woking scored, followed by elation when we equalised via Jamie Reid. Further despair when Woking went ahead with two more goals (I nearly switched off the radio, there's only so much that a Gulls football fan can take!), hope when Torquay got a second goal near the end of the game. (the vision of John Cleese in a ditch in the film clockwise comes back once again. "I can cope with failure it's the hope that I can't endure" or something along those lines. Any supporter of TUAFC should be able to relate to this sentiment). Then there was joy when Torquay get a very late equaliser, and total relief when I hear the game has finished. I could then get back to concentrating on The Legendary Ten Seconds. Well it was another crunch game! There's another one next weekend at home to Eastbourne.

Back to some music. The next day, Sunday afternoon, 7th April, I recorded myself playing acoustic rhythm guitar for my new song about Richard III's mother. I have recorded two versions, one in F# and one in E. I've done this because I'm not sure which is the best one for Jules Jones to sing. I went through this new song with Jules last week and I think we decided that E was better for her but I didn't make a note of it and it might be that it was F#. In the evening Fleur Elliott came over to my house and I recorded her singing some backing vocals on a song called 'The Act of Accord'. The song is about Richard III's father being killed at the battle of Wakefield, so yes another jolly tune with miserable lyrics. I recorded the song several years ago but have now decided that most of my guitar playing on it was total rubbish and have deleted the worst of it as well as my singing. I have retained Jules Jones as the lead vocalist. Also recorded Fleur singing on a track about the most famous of the Roger Mortimers (the one who deposed Edward II). The song is called 'A Rare Romance' and didn't make it onto the Mer de Mort album but perhaps it could be included on History Book Part Two? This morning Bridgit England visited me so that I could record her singing on some of my songs. She has let me record her singing lead and harmony vocals on 'I Greet You Well', lead and harmony on 'Fatal Match' and a harmony vocal on the chorus of 'The Act of Accord'. I have changed the lyrics and chords of 'Right Trusty Sister' and turned it into 'I Greet You Well'.

'I GREET YOU WELL'

Beloved brother I greet you well

Despite the fears in which we dwell
Our brother dead the news is grave
But in our hearts we must be brave

Right trusty brother across the sea
From my fair court of Burgundy
Prayers for Edward have been said
I can't believe that he is dead

Beloved brother if you please
Of your plans please tell me
For our house I do fear
Our House of York which we hold dear

Right trusty brother across the sea
From my fair court of Burgundy
Prayers for Edward have been said
I can't believe that he is dead

To you dear brother I do confide
For to London you must ride
To the Woodville affinity
Their plans for the boy king I can foresee

15th April 2019

The highlight of the week was Saturday afternoon at Plainmoor with
my friend Jerry Brimicombe witnessing Torquay United gaining
automatic promotion from the National League South. In the
evening I went over to Shaldon with Elaine to see the Estuary Buoys
playing some very good songs at the London Inn by the river Teign in

Shaldon. I particularly liked their version of 'I Fought the Law'. This was followed the next evening when Lord Z came over to give me the finished recordings of two songs for the Devon Roses album. These are 'I Greet You Well' and 'Less Fortunate Than Fair'. The lyrics for the latter song were mostly written by Sandra Heath Wilson and I originally envisaged this as a music hall type song. I hope Sandra likes the finished version of the song which is about Cecily of York, one of the daughters of Edward IV and uses the title of her book about this princess.

With regards to 'I Greet You Well', there are actually four different finished versions of this song with different bass guitar playing on each one so that Lord Z could see which bass guitar was the best for recording. It seems to be the least likely second hand Encore! Not so nice to play because of poor action but he says that it sounds much better than the much more expensive and playable Fender Jazz bass guitar. Anyway not only is Lord Z a legendary keyboard Mellotron maestro and Logic recording software expert, he is now an accomplished bass player! Lord Z is now in the process of trying to finish the recording of a song called 'Sanctuary' about the birth of Edward V. Work has also progressed on another song called 'Her Household Requires.' I think we now have nine completed songs for the 'Devon Roses' album. This includes 'Wife to the Kingmaker' which was inspired by the book of the same title by Sandra Heath Wilson. This very lovely lady has certainly given me lots of inspiration.

'WIFE TO THE KINGMAKER'

Hear the scratching of the quill
The smell of hot wax to make the seal
The betrothal of Salisbury's oldest son
To the daughter of an earl a bright future won

Now Anne was such a lovely child
Married at twelve she was not beguiled
By her husband too young for the marriage bed
To a younger boy she had been wed

Later in the shadow of her husband's fame
Richard Neville is his name
Gaining an earldom filled him with fire
The title of a Kingmaker he would acquire

Hear the scratching of the quill
The smell of hot wax to make the seal
The betrothal of Salisbury's oldest son
To the daughter of an earl a bright future won

22nd April 2019

On Monday 15th April I recorded a new guitar solo for an instrumental called 'Trinity'. I started recording this instrumental a few years ago but so far it's not been finished. Lord Z now wants to add a few more tunes to the proposed 'Instrumental Legends' album so perhaps we may be able to now finish the 'Trinity' instrumental. Anyway I felt inspired to go back to it and quickly worked out a guitar solo which I am quite pleased with. The next day Jules Jones came over in the morning and I recorded her singing three songs. Two of the songs, 'Over my Shoulder' and 'Bone Cupboard' (songs not written by me) are for a CD she is going to give to her mother as a present for Easter. The third song is the most recent one that I have composed called 'The Duke of York's Wife'. In the evening I recorded some lead acoustic guitar for the song and the following evening I recorded myself playing an electric guitar solo for it. Later in the week I managed to do some work on the revised edition of my book which I think I will publish after the Devon Roses album has been finished.

29th April 2019

Here are the lyrics for my latest song idea which is about Elizabeth Lambert who was a mistress of Edward IV. When Richard III became King she was found guilty of harlotry and for punishment she was made to walk from St Paul's Cross in London wearing only her petticoat. She was then imprisoned in Ludgate where Richard III's solicitor, Thomas Lynom, fell in love with her and was later allowed to marry her.

'WALK OF SHAME'

Once the wife of master Shore
Now that marriage is no more
The witty mistress of a king
To him her beauty she could bring

Public penance in the street
No shoes worn on her feet
For punishment the walk of shame
Jane Shore was not her name

Once the wife of master Shore
Now that marriage is no more
A concubine she became
Lambert was her maiden name

Her kirtle in an unkempt state
So this would be her fate
For punishment the walk of shame
Jane Shore was not her name

On Thursday evening I performed a version of a song called 'Pride of Man' (which is probably the best thing Quicksilver Messenger Service ever recorded) with Elaine singing along with me at Red Rock near Bishopsteignton. Someone asked me if it was a song I had written and I had to tell them I hadn't, it was composed by Hamilton Camp.

It was great to learn that Torquay United won their last game of the season on Saturday afternoon, beating St Alban's 0-4 away, Torquay also hit the woodwork several times, missed a penalty (again!), and broke a few of their records such as their fastest ever goal ten seconds (apart from an own goal in the 1970's!) after the start of the match. In fact they also nearly scored a second goal from the next kick off when Jamie Reed hit the cross bar.

Spent most of the afternoon at home making a video to go with the 2018 version of 'King in the Car Park' using the artwork that was drawn and painted by Graham Moores for the History Book Part One album. Did some more work on the 'Walk of Shame' song in the evening by recording some guide vocals but found it quite difficult to sing because the recording is a bit too fast for the lyrics. On Sunday afternoon I started recording version two with a slightly slower tempo and found it easier to record the guide vocal this time. On Sunday morning I met Graham Moores in Exeter and gave him a copy of the History Book Part One CD. He's done quite a bit of the artwork for Part Two. In the evening I recorded myself playing bass guitar for the first time for ages. Lord Zarquon has got so good at playing the bass that I've virtually given up trying to work out bass lines for my songs.

I've exchanged a few emails this week with John Challis and Philip Hume as we are trying to organise a recording session in the Ludlow for a comedy song about the Mortimers in medieval England. Philip mentioned this in one of his emails:-

"I met a medieval re-enactor recently who told me that Sunnes and Roses is the best CD that he has ever heard and that he plays it constantly in his car!"

5th May 2019

It's always quite exciting when Lord Z comes over on a Monday evening with one of my songs that he has finished recording and mastering. The most recent Monday evening was a particularly good one with three tracks finished for the next albums. One is an instrumental called 'Lady of the Rivers' for the Instrumental Legends album and the other two for Devon Roses. I was especially pleased with the finished version of 'Fatal Match' with some lovely singing by Bridgit England including lots of her nice harmonies and a backing vocal sung by Jules Jones. The other song is 'Sanctuary' which I started recording several years ago and at last it is finished! I am now hoping that Lord Z can finish my songs called 'Act of Accord' and 'Duke of York's Wife'. Jules is singing the lead on both of these songs with a backing vocal sung by Bridgit on 'Act of Accord'.

By coincidence I saw Sarah Gristwood on TV this week talking about Beatrice Potter with Alan Titchmarsh. Sarah is an author who wrote a book that I read earlier this year called *Blood Sisters* and it was this book that gave me the lyrics for the 'Fatal Match' song. I purchased the book with a Christmas WH Smith gift card given to me by Jerry Brimicombe.

'FATAL MATCH'

She arrived on the Cock John
Blown off course for so long
Battered and bruised by an angry sea
Carried ashore to her destiny

Oh peers of England this fatal match
Fatal this marriage and this dispatch
Grave news for our duke in France
Maine and Anjou lost perchance

Margaret of Anjou to Henry wed
By his queen he was led
Suffolk's advice the queen sought
She loved to have him in her court

I have finished reading a book about John Howard by John Ashdown-Hill. This book gave me the idea for my song about Elizabeth Lambert. I sent an mp3 of the song to Phil Swann (of the Estuary Buoys) to see if he might be interested in helping me with the recording of the song. He has recorded himself playing his 12 string acoustic guitar and mandolin for my song and has sent over wav files of the recordings. I have been able to import these files into the project of the song on my computer. I have been very impressed with his mandolin playing at the two gigs that I have seen of his band and he has told me that he also plays the bouzouki. I am always keen to record different instruments and it would be great if I could record him playing his bouzouki on one of my songs.

I am now in the process of recording a song about a science fiction story called *The Man Who Evolved* which was written by Edmond Hamilton and was published in 1931 in Wonder Stories. I remember reading this story in my early teens in my Dad's car in the car park of Torquay technical college. At the time the college was in Torre close to the site of Eden Philpotts house. His house was called Eltham which was knocked down, probably when the college was being built. A blue plaque is now located there. On the other side of the road was a hut where the boys grammar school teacher Mr Hopkins taught history and music. He was my teacher for these subjects in my first year at the grammar school.

'THE MAN WHO EVOLVED'

There were three of us in that place
Pollard talked of rays from outer space
Of the cause of evolutionary change
Doctor John Pollard then began to explain

From outer space, the cosmic rays
Hitting the Earth every night and day
Cast forth from an exploding star
The distance travelled so very far

What became of the man who evolved
The strangest tale that has ever been told
The evolution of the human race
To accelerate this with those rays from space

Fifteen minutes, fifty million years
He was in the cube with his hopes and fears
I closed the door and threw the switch
The cosmic rays made him writhe and twitch

What became of the man who evolved
The strangest tale that has ever been told
The evolution of the human race
To accelerate this with those rays from space

A god like creature we then saw
With such beauty we'd not seen before
But later on then just a brain
And what came next drove Dutton insane

What became of the man who evolved
The strangest tale that has ever been told
The evolution of the human race
To accelerate this with those rays from space

12th May 2019

Lord Zarquon has finished recording two more songs for the Devon
Roses album and there are now just two songs that need to be
finished. Phil Swann has recorded some electric guitar for my song
about the driverless car track at the site of the battle of Bosworth.
I hope that Lord Zarquon can complete the recording of this song
for the History Book Part Two album. Further recording sessions
are booked for Pippa, Fleur and Bridgit to sing on some more of my
songs and I have just purchased a new and better microphone.

'DRIVERLESS CARS'

For years we looked for that field
We thought the battle was on a hill
Then at long last it was found

With a boar badge buried in the ground

Now that we've found that historic place
A car track there would be a disgrace
With driverless cars driving round and round
How does that planning application sound

For years we looked for that field
We thought the battle was on a hill
Then at long last it was found
With a gold angel buried in the ground

Driverless cars is that a good idea
Such mayhem i can only fear
Imagine the people that could be killed
Far more than those at Bosworth Field

19th May 2019

On Monday morning Lord Z recorded Pippa singing for the song about the Household expenses of Elizabeth of York. Then in the afternoon I drove up to Ludlow with Lord Z and we stayed overnight at a Travelodge hotel. I spent most of the journey and evening listening to him going on and on about the Game of Thrones TV series. He's been telling me all about it ever since I composed the song about Elizabeth Lambert's walk of shame during the reign of Richard III. He says I should watch this programme but I think I'm too busy writing songs. The Game of Thrones also sounds even more gruesome than the battle of Towton and the Wars of the Roses!
On Tuesday morning we met up with Philip Hume, secretary of the Mortimer History Society and John Challis in Orleton. We were

there to record John's vocal talents for a comedy song about the Mortimers. We had booked the local village hall for this and John's wife Carol commented about the new kitchen there that John had opened. She said he had also opened the new toilet.

'HER HOUSEHOLD REQUIRES'

Two barrels of the Rheinish wine
Clothes for herself that look so fine
Pippins. puddings, pears and pork
Money for the keeper of her hawk

Conserves of cherries. wild boar and tripe
Candles needed to light the night
Wool, woodcocks, rabbits and quails
Pomegranates and a box of nails

These things her household requires
But not the love her heart desires

Almond butter for the time of lent
Baskets and bellows to her household sent
Bread, table and small beer
To be consumed throughout the year

These things her household requires
But not the love her heart desires

All funded from her moneybox
But when opened such a shock
Of the coins there were all too few

And so her debts would accrue

Two barrels of the Rheinish wine
Clothes for herself that look so fine
Pippins. puddings. pears and pork
Money for the keeper of her hawk

These things her household requires
But not the love her heart desires

26th May 2019

Lord Z came over last Monday evening and we listened to the finished and mastered recordings of 'Her Household Requires' and the Mortimer comedy song. Later in the week Phil Swann sent me the wav files of the very nice 12 string acoustic guitar and mandolin that he has recorded for a song about Gallants Bower. My wife wrote the lyrics for this song shortly after we climbed to the top of the hill above Dartmouth castle. Gallants Bower is a fort which was constructed during the English civil war. The song was actually written years ago, perhaps about 10 years ago? I did record a version back then with my wife, Elaine singing it, but we never did anything with the recording. I am now in the process of trying to finish a new version of the song.

'GALLANTS BOWER'

Looking down from the top of the hill
Out of breath waiting for you still
Who kept watch here so long ago
Dartmouth Castle so far below

A winding path to this Gallants Bower
So peaceful now in this sunny hour
The ruins and battles of the civil war
Look back through time what was it for

Dig up the past who won who lost
That civil war such a terrible cost
And no one remembers and no one ever will
Know the name of the watcher on the hill

2nd June 2019

I've written another science fiction song. This is based upon a story
written by Neil R Jones called *The Jameson Satellite*. It was first
published in Amazing Stories in 1931 and the author wrote a long
series of sequels about Professor Jameson and the Zoromes who
are friendly aliens. They have serial numbers and letters rather than
names. The story portrays our solar system in a far future in which
our planet is dead like our moon and the human race extinct.

'THE JAMESON SATELLITE'

Professor Jameson sought a plan
Some might think him not a wise man
After death his body to preserve
His solution we shall now observe

His coffin was the Jameson satellite
Propelled into space like a meteorite
For aeons revolving around the Earth

Where he had died and the place of his birth

Generation after generation passed away
The rule of mankind had it's final day
Other races would then arrive
But each in their turn would also die

Billions of years in a far off time
Our sun is no longer in it's prime
Stars are born and then they die
The Sun used up it's hydrogen supply

In the Solar System from far off Zor
A strange spaceship the Zoromes saw
It was the Jameson satellite
So small it was an intriguing sight

25X-987
Perhaps one with a number 11?
8B-52
These were just some of the Zorome crew

They removed the body, revived the brain
So the professor might live once again
They gave him a body like their own
Made of metal not flesh and bone

Unfortunately Fleur wasn't feeling very well on Sunday so I couldn't record her singing on this song. Hopefully she will be able to let me record her singing later in the month. However Bridgit England visited me on Tuesday and I recorded her singing on four songs.

This included the lead and harmony vocals for the 'Walk of Shame' song. Phil Swann has recorded himself playing his bouzouki and mandolin for my song about metal detecting. The inspiration for this song came from Ashley Mantle. One of Ashley's hobbies is metal detecting and my song describes some of the coins that he has found.

9th June 2019

Here is some information about the comedy song called 'the Mortimers' by Boycie and the Legendary Ten Seconds

Richard the Third Records June 2019, catalogue number R17. Recorded at Rock Lee 2018, Orleton Village Hall & Other World Studios May 2019

John Challis : Boycie vocals
Lord Zarquon : Mellotron flute keyboards
Ashley Dyer : Trumpet
Rob Bright : Lead guitar
Ian Churchward : Acoustic rhythm guitar, electric rhythm guitar, mandolin and bass guitar

Music composed by Ian Churchward. Lyrics written by Ian Churchward and John Challis

'THE MORTIMERS'

Far too many Rogers
Only two Hughs
With the Ralph's and Edmunds
I'm completely confused

Along came the first Roger
De Mortimer was his name
Next came a Ralph
A marcher lord he became
After Ralph a Hugh
A Mortimer lord through and through

Then another Roger
Then another Hugh
With those names
I bet you're confused

Along came a second Ralph
With that Mortimer name
Next another Roger
At Evesham he won fame
Edmund his second son
The Lord of Wigmore he did become

Then another Roger
An Edmund next
I must say
It's too complex

Usually I don't do this sort of thing of course
I'm more known for my second hand car expertise
I've got some lovely deals on my forecourt
at the moment that you should see
Most of them rejected by Del Boy which is probably not a good sign
I've got a lovely Skoda with a Laura Ashley interior and a clean ashtray
But no wheels, just a clean ashtray

Along came the fifth Roger
With that Mortimer name
Next a third Edmund
A royal wife he did claim
Then another Roger
Followed by an Edmund once again

Far too many Rogers
Only two Hughs
With the Ralph's and Edmunds
I'm completely confused
Come along Marlene get your coat we're leaving!

16th June 2019

I was given an Amazon gift voucher of £10 as a birthday present at the beginning of the month. I've spent a couple of weeks every night on the internet trawling through the vast amount of digital music on the Amazon website trying to decide which songs to purchase with the money. At one point I remembered two fantastic songs recorded by Denny Laine in the late 1960's that were on an album of obscure tracks on Decca records called Lost and Found. I spent quite a bit of time trying to find them and at one point my hopes were raised only to quickly realise it wasn't an original recording I had found from 1967 but a much newer version with boring modern keyboard sounds on it. Just to make sure I wasn't imagining it I found the 1960's versions on you tube, lovely acoustic guitar playing and orchestration. As far as I'm aware you can't buy the songs as mp3 downloads from you tube.

About 10 years ago I sold most of my records because they were taking up so much space and I didn't have a record player. I kept some of my most treasured ones like my Quicksilver Messenger Service LPs and from the money I got from the ones I sold I used the funds to buy CDs or purchase mp3 downloads. There were some songs that I particularly liked which were on obscure B sides that I owned ('Shame' by Dave Dee, Dozy, Beaky Mick and Tich is one of them) and so I borrowed a record player from my stepson and connected it to my computer.

I then digitised the songs into mp3 format. Remembering that I had done this and the fact that my stepdaughter bought me a record player a few years ago I thought that there was a chance that I might still have the precious Lost and Found Decca album which included those rare Denny Laine songs. So I went through all of the remaining albums that I still own that are located in various places in my house but unfortunately I can't find it. I can't believe that I could have been so stupid not to keep that album without at least checking to see if I could get those 2 songs on CD or on the internet. Surely not? What is so annoying is that the recordings of these songs do not deserve to be so obscure. The songs were on a single, 'Say you don't mind' was the brilliant A side and on the B side was the equally catchy and memorable 'Ask the people'. How on earth was this not a hit single? Probably due to the complete incompetence of the record label I would imagine. It's such a shame that you can't easily purchase these fantastic recordings on CD and the Denny Laine version is much better than the one recorded by Colin Blunstone.

Having got that whinge out of my system I am very pleased to announce that Georgie Harman has finished the album cover for the Devon Roses album and we've also finished recording the songs! So now we move onto the recording of History Book Part Two. Lord Z has got my latest offering called 'Gallants Bower' and he says he likes it. I've written lots of other songs that we haven't finished recording and I just hope he like these as well.

23rd June 2019

Since my last blog post I've been particularly busy with recording various bits for some of my songs. So here is a bit of an update.

New comedy song about myself called 'A Song About Me' which Elaine has told me I am not allowed to perform in public. It made Jules laugh when I played it to her and she agreed to sing a few silly bits on it. I have also recorded Ashley Dyer playing trumpet and Rowan Curle singing a very nice harmony vocal. I now want to put together an album of my comedy songs.

A song for the De Cobham 15th century reenactment group. Phil Swann has recorded some very good Irish Bouzouki for this song and I have recorded a short electric guitar solo for it.

The 'Knights of a King' is another Ricardian song which I wrote several years ago and started to record but then felt it was a bit lame after I started recording it so it never progressed. I nearly forgot about this song until I found it while I was in the process of trying to tidy up the files on one of my computers. Phil Swann has recorded some great slide guitar for the song and I have recorded Ashley Dyer playing trumpet and my step daughter is singing a nice backing vocal.

'Ricardian Dream' was written about 5 years ago and I have been recording the song on and off ever since then. I recently recorded Jules Jones singing a backing vocal part to it and I've just recorded a new version of my singing for it.

'Driftwood' is a song that was mainly written by Elaine when we used to play in a band called Just a Shadow (1988 – 1989). The song started off as a keyboard idea played by Jerry Brimicombe. He only really had just a very tiny intro for a song. I've got a recording of the song somewhere on a cassette which dates back to the 1990's and I thought it would be a nice idea to record a new version. I've recorded some acoustic guitar and Elaine's singing.

30th June 2019

I've started recording a new instrumental idea which I originally called 'History Book Part Two in Em' but now it's called 'The Old Bouzouki.' My stepson has been a great help this week as he brought his electronic drum kit to my house and we spent one afternoon recording him playing drums, bass and electric guitar for my 'Man who Evolved' science fiction song. Earlier in the week we recorded him playing drums for a few instrumental tunes composed by Graham Moores.

In my spare time at home I've spent a fair amount of time promoting the Mortimer comedy song via the internet. Last Saturday I attended a meeting of the Devon and Cornwall branch of the Richard III Society to hear a talk given by Philip Hume of the Mortimer History Society and this included him playing the comedy song which made everyone laugh when Boycie starts talking about used cars in between the confusion of the Rogers, Hughs, Ralphs and Edmunds.

Lord Z and myself have also been busy finalising the release of the Devon Roses album. I have had confirmation that my submission to CD Baby for the digital distribution has been accepted, I've made a master CD of the audio and the artwork has been submitted for approval before it gets printed.

I'm off to Kent for a week now and I needed to find a book to read while I am there on holiday. We were in Dartmouth yesterday and I found a second hand bookshop but nothing caught my eye. I've got a few Ricardian novels that I haven't got around to reading because I feel like I've read too many and most of them always inevitably end with Henry VII winning the battle of Bosworth. One of them is about Elizabeth Lambert and her sister so I started reading it last night and I'm now on page 46 and I'm rather enjoying it. I was afraid that it was going to have too much romance in it but that doesn't seem to be the case so far. In the book written by Vanora Bennett, I've just realised that Elizabeth Lambert is called Jane Shore which isn't correct and I wonder if the author mentions this in the historical notes at the end of the book? It feels quite interesting to be reading this novel having only recently finished recording a song about Elizabeth Lambert.

7th July 2019

Just got back from a very interesting holiday in Kent. I had no guitar, internet or TV so I read two books and went to lots of interesting places. I mentioned one of the books in my blog last week. Well I can't recommend it to fans of Richard III, he seemed to be a true hero until half way through the book you find out that he is really a villain. The section where Hastings gets executed was most upsetting.

14th July 2019

It was a good holiday in Kent with Elaine, Tom and his wife Sasha. We went to lots of interesting places that I hadn't visited before. Ightham Mote, Bodiam castle and Dover castle were the most interesting ones. We were staying in Sevenoaks and on the first night we went to a pub and there was a good band playing called Dead Man's Corner. The musicianship was excellent and so was the style of music. They started off with a psychedelic 60's style surf instrumental that they had composed which was probably the best live tune I've heard in ages and finished the first set with an amazing version of a Dick Dale instrumental called 'Nitro'. Two other songs really stood out, one was a version of 'Then I've got Everything' which was recorded by Johnny Kid and the Pirates and the other was 'Wondrous Place' by Billy Fury. I'd never heard of these songs before and when I got back to Torquay I checked them out. The Johnny Kid and the Pirates' one is excellent.

Last year I wanted to write a song about the battle of Blenheim and I went back to a book about this by Charles Spencer. It's a very good read and I decided to check it out again as I thought it would give me the inspiration for a song. I read it again and enjoyed it very much but unfortunately there was no song idea forthcoming. This week I started composing another song. I quickly realised that the new melody ought to be ideal for a song about the battle of Blenheim and then the words came to me

'THE BLENHEIM SONG'

We marched every day and camped every night
The size of our army was a splendid sight
From the Low Countries along the Rhine
A grim destination in this wartime

John Churchill our duke had a bold plan
To stop the French for his Queen Anne
With such skill over many a mile
His clever deception still makes me smile

The reason for fighting was not understood
As I held my musket of metal and wood
Of Spanish succession I heard it said
It makes no real sense when you count up the dead

And so to the battle the cannons roared
The steel of the bayonets the clash of the sword
At Blenheim the French made a fatal mistake
That village the English they must not take

The reason for fighting was not understood
As I held my musket of metal and wood
Of Spanish succession I heard it said
It makes no real sense when you count up the dead

The news of defeat hurt King Louis' pride
The Sun King's brightness had surely died
In England the victory greatly acclaimed
Whilst the French generals felt so ashamed

The reason for fighting was not understood
As I held my musket of metal and wood
Of Spanish succession I heard it said
It makes no real sense when you count up the dead

21st July 2019

It was the Tewkesbury medieval festival last week and I had an email from Pam Benstead of the Worcestershire branch of the Richard III Society to tell me that some of the Legendary Ten Seconds CDs were sold at her stall. This included the first CD sale of the Devon Roses album. I also received an email from the person who purchased it. He liked the songs so much he has also purchased it in digital format via itunes.

Here is some information about the album:-

To commemorate the 40th anniversary of the Devon & Cornwall branch of the Richard III Society. Songs recorded from 2015 to 2019 at Rock Lee & Other World Studios

The lady singers of the Legendary Ten Seconds:-

Elaine Churchward vocals
Jules Jones vocals
Pippa West vocals
Bridgit England vocals
Violet Sheer backing vocal on 'Wife to the Kingmaker'
Fleur Elliott backing vocal on 'Act of Accord'

The minstrels of the Legendary Ten Seconds:-

Ian Churchward guitars, mandolin, mandola & keyboards
Lord Zarquon keyboards, bass guitar, drums & percussion
Phil Swann mandolin & 12 string acoustic guitar on 'The Walk of Shame'
Ashley Dyer trumpet on 'Wife to the Kingmaker'
Rob Bright lead guitar on 'How do you Rebury a King'

All songs written by Ian Churchward except 'Eleanor Talbot' written by Elaine & Ian Churchward and 'Less Fortunate Than Fair' written by Sandra Heath Wilson & Ian Churchward

1)'Fatal Match' - a song about the marriage of Henry VI to Margaret of Anjou
2)'Charm and Grace' - the coronation of Elizabeth Woodville
3)'Kings of England' - a song about Henry VII's wife

4)'Less Fortunate Than Fair' - a song about Cecily of York, the daughter of Edward IV

5)'The Duke of York's Wife' - a song about Richard III's mother

6)'Sanctuary' - a song about the birth of Edward V

7)'The Walk of Shame' - a song about Elizabeth Lambert, mistress of Edward IV

8)'The Minstrels did Play' - Christmas 1484 in the court of King Richard III

9)'How do you Rebury a King' (2018 version) - about the reburial of Richard III

10)'Eleanor Talbot' - a very sad song about Eleanor Talbot

11)'The Month of May' - a song about the events in London in May 1483

12)'Act of Accord' - a song about the defeat of Richard Duke of York at the battle of Wakefield

13)'Her Household Requires' - a song about the household of Elizabeth of York

14)'I Greet you Well' - correspondence between the Duke of Gloucester and his sister Margaret

15)'Wife to the Kingmaker' - inspired by a novel written by Sandra Heath Wilson

'THE MINSTRELS DID PLAY'

Queen Anne wore a dress of velvet blue
Her niece wore the same colour too
There were rumours in the court that Christmas
I'm not sure if they were true

The minstrels did play
And the court was gay
There was sadness in the queen's heart

And the Lady Grey
Was heard to say
I told Dorset in France to depart

His lady kept the secret that she knew
Lord Stanley kept his secrets too
Lies were told of the court that Christmas
Of this I know to be true

28th July 2019

Last Saturday I visited Coldridge in Devon for the fifth time in the last two years. On the face of it this place is rather insignificant. I must admit I'd never heard of the village until I came across something on the internet written by John Ashdown-Hill. He mentioned a church in Devon which has a stained glass window of Edward V. This was news to me and I was curious because Mr Ashdown-Hill didn't say whereabouts in Devon that the church is located. Since reading about it I have now found out that there is an image of this uncrowned King in St Matthew's church in Coldridge. If you visit this church then you will find it in the chapel of Sir John Evans.

I've now become acquainted with John Dike who lives in Coldridge and he gave a presentation last week at St Matthew's church to the Devon & Cornwall branch of the Richard III Society which I attended with Elaine. I've recorded two songs about the mystery surrounding the tomb of Sir John Evans and the stained glass window of Edward V. One song written with Elaine and the other with John Dike. This mystery may be linked to the mystery surrounding the missing Princes of Edward IV and John Dike has become involved with Philippa Langley's missing Princes project. John is planning to undertake an investigation outside one of the windows in the church to see if he can find any fragments of broken stained glass which may provide some clues in respect of the original glass in the windows in the church. John went to Crediton library very recently and found an interesting description of the Coldridge church written in the early 1900's. This included a comment along the lines of

"Why would you find a portrait of Edward V in this remote place in Devon!"

So people have obviously been puzzled about this for quite some time. The reason must surely be linked to the fact that one of the sons from the first marriage of the Queen of Edward IV owned the deer park and manor in Coldridge.

4th August 2019

I have had a very busy weekend. On Friday evening we celebrated a birthday with a meal at the Premier Inn over looking Abbey Sands in Torquay. Saturday was spent attending the wedding of my niece starting off at the lovely church in Ipplepen and then onto Torre Abbey gardens and the Spanish Barn. Sunday morning I went to Holy Angels church in Chelston to witness a baptism. When we got home from the baptism I recorded my stepson singing some nice harmony vocals to go with the really nice guitar parts that Phil Swann has recorded for my song about the battle of Blenheim.

11th August 2019

I've been rehearsing some of my songs with Phil Swann once a week on a fairly regular basis so far this summer. To be honest if it wasn't for Phil's enthusiasm for my tunes I wouldn't be considering playing gigs again. Last year I was rehearsing about twice a week but after the disappointment of the arrangements at Bosworth last August (and only doing a couple of gigs that year) I decided to just concentrate on writing and recording songs. So since last August until this summer I haven't been rehearsing any of my songs. This may help to explain why 3 Legendary Ten Seconds' albums have been released during this period of time. There's another one we've actually finished as well which Lord Zarquon has called Instrumental Legends but I think he's forgotten that it needs an album cover. The intention was to create the artwork using a collage of photos so I must discuss this the next time I see him.

18th August 2019

Lord Zarquon came over on Monday evening and I forgot to discuss the Instrumental Legends album. Hopefully he will read this blog and remember that he needs to sort out the album cover! We somehow ended up talking about other things for ages, mainly about our old friend Roger Crompton who has an incredible musical talent yet seems content to keep it in a room in his house and strangle it with both of his hands. Also talked about care in the community or lack of it.

We have however started to make some real progress with the History Book Part Two album with the songs 'Driverless Cars' and 'Knights of a King' completed. I've written and partly recorded loads of songs for this album and as usual probably too many!!

'THE KNIGHTS OF A KING'

The knights of a king
Wore the badge of a boar
Rode to their death

At a place they called Redemoor

The knights of a king
The knights of a king
Of their bravery we will surely sing

The knights of a queen
Wore the badge of a swan
At Blore Heath
The Yorkists they did chance upon

The knights of a queen
The knights of a queen
Was their chivalry just a dream

The knights of a lord
Wore the badge of a hart
Of treachery Lord Stanley
Would play his part

The knights of a lord
The knights of a lord
A Tudor king was their reward

Had a very interesting evening on Tuesday which was quite enjoyable despite seeing Torquay United lose at Plainmoor to Maidenhead United. This was the second home fixture of the new season but I missed the first one because I was at a wedding. I thought Torquay looked very good and the scoreline flattered the away side so I am not disheartened, it was just one of those games. I normally go to Plainmoor with my disabled friend Jerry Brimicombe as his carer but is wheelchair is out of action at the moment so I went on my own. I bumped into Andy Perry who I haven't seen for ages and sat with him and he said we can sit with another friend who was there.... the one and only Steve Honeywill. Steve his quite a character. I will never forget the journey down to Plymouth to see the Cure gig and meeting him for the first time.

Andy Perry used to write articles about bands for a Sherborne based fanzine called Feeding the Fish and his Dad used to own the Livermead House Hotel in Torquay. He witnessed the 2-2 draw at Plainmoor in 1977 against Cambridge United when Torquay United entered the Guinness book of records for scoring the fastest own goal. We talked about this on Wednesday evening and about the book he wrote with John Lydon. I've seen it a few times in HMV and I really must get around to purchasing a copy of it.

25th August 2019

I didn't see Lord Zarquon this week, he was due to come over to see me on Monday but I wasn't feeling very well so we cancelled meeting up. A few years ago I recorded Camilla Joyce singing on my song about the Richard III Society. I thought I had lost that recording but found it last month and I gave it to Lord Zarquon earlier this month. He tells me he has mixed and mastered this recording and I will be interested to hear how it sounds.

I have recently written two new songs and one of the them is about the Stover canal between Bovey Tracey and Newton Abbot. Here are some of the lyrics

'JAMES TEMPLER'S LEGACY'

Transporting granite and ball clay

To Hackney Marsh throughout day
A once thriving industry
The old remains for us to see

Along the path the wild flowers
I could walk for hours and hours
And dream of days of a distant past
Of so many things that do not last

Beyond Teigngrace to Ventiford
The old canal may be restored
The sad remains of industry
James Templer's legacy

1st September 2019

Lord Zarquon came over on Monday and he gave me the finished
master of the new version of my song about the Richard III Society.
It differs from the original version which is on our first Ricardian
album because it features the recording that I made several years ago
of Camilla Joyce singing some of the lyrics. Lord Zarquon played me
a new keyboard part he has recorded for the 'Gallant's Bower' song
and we've decided that my singing on the song needs to be different
so I will have to have a think about that.
On Saturday morning I had a very nice walk with Elaine and our
friends Phil and Debby Helmore in Babbacombe. In the afternoon
I went to Plainmoor with Jerry Brimicombe and unfortunately we
witnessed Torquay United losing 1-2 against Hartlepool. Another
weekend ruined!!! Just as I was about to leave my house to go over
to Babbacombe to take Jerry to the football match, I found that the
September 2019 issue of the Ricardian Bulletin had arrived in the

post and I was very pleased to see that there is a positive review of the History Book Part One album on page 32. Included with the magazine is the Richard III Society mail order catalogue, issue number 17 which includes 7 Legendary Ten Seconds albums and takes up the whole of page 10.

8th September 2019

Lord Zarquon has now given me the finished digital version of the Instrumental Legends album cover for me to submit to CD Baby. I've used this to complete the album submission and I have requested a release date of 23rd September 2019. This gives me a bit of time to gear up for promoting it. I had a look at a Wars of the Roses website and saw that the 23rd September is the anniversary of the battle of Blore Heath which was a Yorkist victory so that date seems appropriate for the release date of the new album.

The album has got 13 instrumental tracks and it was really Lord Zarquon's idea. There are 3 instrumentals that haven't appeared on the previous albums listed on our website. Several of the other instrumentals have some new things on them such as a new bass guitar part played by Lord Zarquon. Apart from 'Mortimer Overture' all of the tunes have been remixed and remastered. The album has basically been recorded from 2013 to 2019.

Friday was quite an emotional day in my office in Exeter. My good friend Malcolm Bounder Bowen had retired on 30th August and we had a farewell party for him on Friday. I had recorded a comedy retirement song for him called 'Goodbye Mabo31' and made a video containing some silly photos which made us all laugh when we watched it. We all had a very nice meal at the Cosy Club and Malcolm gave a very funny speech containing some of the highlights of his career in Banking. He actually had me crying at the end of his speech which was partly crying with laughter. I should mention that his work email address was mabo31@handelsbanken.co.uk so that the title of the song will make a bit more sense.

Goodbye Mabo thirty one
Working with you was great fun
When you retire we'll miss you
In your retirement what will you do

I gave him 2 spicey pot noodles as part of his leaving presents. He is very partial to a spicey pot noodle but what he doesn't realise is that I carefully peeled off the lid of one of them, and filled it up with paper clips and the contents of the office hole punch. I then carefully glued the tin foil lid back onto it. If you shake the plastic container it sounds like the one that hasn't been tampered with and is about the same weight.

15th September 2019

Some information about the Mer de Mort album that we recorded with John Challis has recently been published on a website called the PRSD (The People's Republic of South Devon). This website was established in 2005 and is a not for profit media venture with news covering the county of Devon.

22nd September 2019

It was my son's wedding yesterday. This is the church version of the wedding having done the registry office version earlier this year. It hardly seems that long ago that he was born. Where do all the years go? It seems that as I get older the years fly by so much more quickly.

I must admit that yesterday was quite emotional at times and I am now feeling completely exhausted!

We arrived at Holy Angels church in Chelston early in the morning. A few minutes later, on the other side of the road Lord Zarquon arrived on his motor bike wearing his karate gear. Turns out he was giving a karate lesson in the church hall opposite to Holy Angels church that morning. I had a brief chat with him and he told me that he had finished the 'Man who Evolved' song so I am now looking forward to hearing the final version of this recording.

After the church marriage service finished we then moved on to the Berry Head hotel in Brixham. Photos were taken of the happy couple with various members of the family including the bride's father who had come all the way from Russia. He must have been feeling tired as it had taken him about two days to travel from Nizhny Novgorod to arrive in Torquay at about 4 pm yesterday. Before the afternoon meal we heard 3 very entertaining speeches which included John Bessant mentioning Quicksilver Messenger Service. Shortly after the meal I told John that I never expected that band to be mentioned in a wedding speech.

In the evening the Estuary Buoys played two excellent sets of songs and in between various friends and family performed some songs. Tom was the compere and he said the the performances after the Estuary Buoys had played their first set, and before their second, was called amateur hour! Having said that Emma Matthews in particular sounded amazing with her singing. This was definitely one of the highlights of the evening. The Estuary Buoys played lots of songs that I particularly liked and this was not surprising as I had given them a long list of songs that I wanted to hear them perform. Probably the best ones were their renditions of 'Apache' and 'Paint it Black'. The latter song was one that I would have liked to have requested but I felt that it wasn't appropriate for a wedding. So although I knew it was a song that they sometimes played and one

which I particularly like I hadn't included it in my list. I said this to
Phil Swann after they had finished their second set (which included
so many encores that I lost count). I also told him that it sounded
great.

29th September 2019

I have decided that it would be a good idea to make a list of the
songs that I am in the process of recording. The main reason for this
is to make sure there aren't any that get forgotten and then never
get finished. Of course I do realise that for some of these tunes the
recording process may not ever be finished due to a lack of time as
further new songs are composed. As I type out the list of songs I am
struggling to remember all of them so this list does seem like a quite
a good idea. Here is the list of songs in no particular order:-

'The Music Hall War'
'Wait Until the Harvests in'
'Goodbye Mabo31'
'Gallants Bower'
'The Jameson Satellite'
'Sunshine in the Rain'
'James Templer's Legacy'
'The Teign Valley
God aid the Marshall'
'Lease on Your Heart'
'The Blenheim Song'
'Sitting in a Trench'
'Capel Celyn'
'De Cobham'
'Darkest Hour'
'Charles Howard's English Fleet'

'Song of a Metal Detectorist'
'Jack the Ripper'
'St Albans Way'
'Cade's Rebellion'
'A Rare Romance'
'Ricardian Dream'

This list doesn't include some tunes that Lord Z has decided are a bit rubbish, however he has now finished my comedy song about myself and the CDs for the Instrumental Legends album have now arrived in the post.

6th October 2019

Several years ago my son Tom and his friends played a trick on me. It was one evening at my house in the kitchen. I was a little bit merry having drunk some beer and one of Tom's friends called Matteo, said that he was very good at magic card tricks. Matteo said that he had videos of his card tricks on youtube and that he was called the Great Edwardo. He then showed me one of his card tricks where I had to select a card at random from a full pack of playing cards without showing him the card. I then placed the card back in the pack and he got me to shuffle the cards. He then managed to produce the card I had chosen. I lost count of the number of times that he performed this magic card trick on me and each time producing the correct card I had chosen. What I didn't realise was that Tom and one of his other friend's, who stood behind me, could see the cards I was choosing and were secretly telling Mateo/the Great Edwardo which card I had chosen. I must admit that I am often pretty gullible and even more so that time because I was a bit drunk. Since then, whenever I see Matteo I say to him "How is the Great Edwardo?"

Matteo was the best man at Tom's wedding and this started me thinking about the Great Edwardo and it gave me the idea for a song about a magician.

'THE GREAT EDWARDO'

He's got tricks up his sleeve
Magic spells you just won't believe
Slight of hand and misdirection
On the stage with such perfection

Come and see the Great Edwardo
Come and see his magic show
Come and see the Great Edwardo
To his show you must go

His audience gather in a crowd
Hear them all gasp aloud
A puff of smoke and he appears
And just as quickly disappears

Come and see the Great Edwardo
Come and see his magic show
Come and see the Great Edwardo
To his show you must go

In top hat and black gown
The poster of him in the town
Advertising his greatest show
The one to which we all must go

13th October 2019

Guy visited for a few days last weekend and stayed at my place until half way through the week. He brought his drum kit with him and we recorded him playing drums for two of my new songs. Guy used his electronic drum kit which presented us with the opportunity to obtain a great drum sound with a huge amount of flexibility. In some ways I am not a big fan of electronic drums because they don't look as good as acoustic kits but the choice and quality of sound is now quite excellent. The first song that Guy played drums on was the 'Jameson Satellite' and the second song was the one about the magician called 'The Great Edwardo'. I then recorded him playing bass to these songs and I am very happy with how these recordings are progressing.

20th October 2019

Although the weather is wet and horrible most of the time so far this month, there is one good thing about it. Lord Zarquon isn't going out very much. When he's not at yoga, sorry I mean karate, he is in his music room working away on my songs. Last week he finished the 'Blenheim song', 'Goodbye Mabo31', and 'Ricardian Dream'. I was a bit startled by this, especially hearing the finished version of 'Ricardian Dream' which I thought he had placed in the rejected section. When I saw him on Sunday evening I played him the initial recording of my 'Great Edwardo' song, which he liked and he asked if he could have it to finish. I told him that I wasn't ready to give it to him as I was hoping to get a harmony vocal added to the recording and I also wanted to get something for it from Phil Swann. He said that he was working on the metal detecting song but after that he needed some more songs from me to work on. I assumed that all the other songs I had given him weren't good enough, however later in the week I received a text message from him saying that he was creating another masterpiece out of my 'Music Hall War' song and it was amongst some other recordings that I'd given him that he had forgotten about. I must admit that I've rather lost track of what songs I've given him and which ones I haven't. This is mainly because of the large number of unfinished recordings and I haven't kept a proper list (the one I posted on my blog fairly recently is now out of date and incomplete). I'm hoping that between the two of us we can make a list of what we've got and who's got it. If we're not careful we could end up nearly forgetting to release an album like what nearly happened with the Instrumental Legends album.

27th October 2019

Rowan Curle came to stay at my house on Friday evening and on Sunday morning I recorded him singing on my new comedy song called 'Sixtieth Birthday'. Then later on that day Guy Bolt visited and I recorded him playing drums on 'Lease on Your Heart'. In the evening Lord Zarquon brought over three more completed song files, The 'Music Hall War', 'Song of a Metal Detectorist' and 'Jack the Ripper'. On Monday morning Bridgit England visited my Rock Lee basement studio and I recorded her singing on 'Lease on Your Heart', 'The Jameson Satellite', 'Great Edwardo' and 'Sunshine in the Rain'. The next day I recorded myself playing bass guitar on 'Lease on Your Heart' and then an instrumental written by Graham Moores so it was a busy few days in the music world of Ian Churchward.

3rd November 2019

I saw Phil Swann on Monday evening and I showed him the chords on my guitar to a song called 'A Rare Romance'. It's a song about Roger Mortimer during the reign of Edward II that I composed last year but have not finished recording. Phil played along with me on his 12 string acoustic guitar and also his bouzouki. Playing the song on the bouzouki gives it a medieval feel so I hope that he will help with the recording of the tune with that instrument. I also really liked his finger picking style on his acoustic guitar.

I think we have decided to drop the idea of gigs for the Legendary Ten Seconds. Phil has got gigs with the Estuary Buoys and Lord Zarquon is busy rehearsing the Prophets of Zarquon. I'm going to continue to focus on writing new songs and recording them. My latest tune is called 'The Fastest Own Goal' about Torquay United entering the Guinness Book of Records.

'THE FASTEST OWN GOAL'

Remember when he made the news
That special own goal by Pat Kruse
We scored four goals in a two all draw
You'd surely not seen that before

It was in the Guinness book of records
An own goal scored in just six seconds

Cambridge came to Torquay
Another match for you to see
The third of January at Plainmoor
You still remember the final score

What a way to gain such fame
And how well you recall that game

The fastest own goal you'd ever seen

Pity our poor football team
Phil Sandercock then scored one more
But Willie Brown gained us a draw

10th November 2019

I have made some good progress with the recording of my 'Fastest Own Goal' song. I have recorded the rhythm guitar, lead vocal and Guy Bolt singing a harmony vocal on the chorus. Lord Z has created another masterpiece out of a song called 'Teign Valley'. The music for this instrumental was composed by Phil Swann. There is also another version with singing for which I have written the lyrics

Graham Moores has been exchanging emails with me on a fairly regular basis recently and he tells me that he has made good progress with the Thrilling Blunder Stories album artwork. I have been working on some guitar parts for one of his instrumentals and I spent most of Tuesday afternoon doing this.

On a less happy note I have been kicked out of Facebook. I think that my Facebook account was hacked but it doesn't look like a straight forward process to get myself reinstated. My main concern is the Facebook pages for the Legendary Ten Seconds and Richard the Third Records which I use to promote my music, so I am not sure what to do about this at the moment.

17th November 2019

I spent Tuesday evening looking through lots of old family photos that my cousin Joanne had given to me on a CD. There are lots of photos that I hadn't seen before, several going back to the 1920's of my grandmother, grandfather, Mum and Dad etc. The ones of my cousins, my sister and myself from the 1960's brought back memories of a very happy childhood but for some reason by the time I went to bed I was feeling quite melancholy. Maybe it's a feeling of longing for all those carefree days before the worries and stress of adult life arrived and missing members of the family that have passed away over the years.

I have recorded some bass guitar for another tune composed by Graham Moores and it's got a lovely melody and I have now written some lyrics to go with the tune after thinking about the old photos.

24th November 2019

On Thursday evening I gave an interview for a metal detecting podcast which was good fun. There was a long section of silence at the beginning of the interview for the listeners because the presenter forgot he had the mute button on his microphone. I talked about four of my songs which have a connection with metal detecting and archaeology. Richard III is discussed at great length and I also mentioned my new song about Torquay United.

1st December 2019

Inspired by a story in an article about metal detecting I have written another song. The article was written by Dave Sadler who interviewed me for his podcast. I have also learnt how to spell archaeology without using spell check or looking it up in a dictionary.

'C SCOPE 600'

My dad's C Scope 600, oh what a memory
Metal detecting, archaeology

When my dad passed away it was passed to me
My dad's C Scope 600, oh what a memory

My dad was my hero
He looked after me
Took me on detecting trips
Such fun he could guarantee

My dad's C Scope 600, oh what a memory
Metal detecting, archaeology
When my dad passed away it was passed to me
My dad's C Scope 600, oh what a memory

My dad and my uncle
Out there in a field
Dreaming of what we might find
What might be revealed

My dad's C Scope 600, oh what a memory
Metal detecting, archaeology
When my dad passed away it was passed to me
My dad's C Scope 600, oh what a memory

Beneath our feet we never knew
What might be concealed
When we dug into the mud
What might it yield

My dad's C Scope 600, oh what a memory
Metal detecting, archaeology
When my dad passed away it was passed to me

My dad's C Scope 600, oh what a memory
When my dad passed away it was passed to me

8th December 2019

Inspired by the disaster at Plainmoor last weekend when the mighty Gulls were put to the sword by Stockport County I have written another song. The title of the song came from an old school buddy called Chris Donovan.

'THE THEATRE OF PAIN'

Come along to the theatre of pain
Another season goes down the drain
We have such fun at the theatre of pain
Come and watch the gulls lose once again

No success in the FA cup
It seems we're always out of luck
It's enough to make a grown man cry
But you live in hope I don't know why

Come along to the theatre of pain
Another season goes down the drain
We have such fun at the theatre of pain
Come and watch the Gulls lose once again

Through think and thin you support your team
A mid table season just a distant dream
It's enough to make a grown man cry
But you live in hope I don't know why

Oh dear it's all gone pete tong
Why must it always go so wrong

Come along to the theatre of pain
Another season goes down the drain
We have such fun at the theatre of pain
Come and watch the Gulls lose once again

15th December 2019

I am now writing a Christmas song for Lord Zarquon.

All he wants for Christmas is a Mellotron
So i've written this song for Lord Zarquon
The Moody Blues had one and he wants one too
Though they're expensive you know that's true

He's got lots of keyboards but you'll hear him complain
That the price of a Mellotron is rather insane

Please can Lord Zarquon have a Mellotron
He'd play the damn thing all day long
The Moody Blues had one and he wants one too
Though they're expensive you know that's true

He's got lots of keyboards but you'll hear him complain
That the price of a Mellotron is rather insane

Dear Mrs Zarquon you could take out a loan
Or perhaps a large mortgage on your home

A Mellotron you could then afford to buy
And great tears of joy you would see him cry

All he wants for Christmas is a Mellotron
I'm singing all about it in this song
The Moody Blues had one and he wants one too
Though they're expensive you know that's true

Also there is a very nice feature that has just been published on the PRSD website about an instrumental version of 'God Rest ye Merry Gentlemen' which Lord Zarquon has just finished recording. This is my favourite Christmas carol and Guy plays a great guitar solo on it. I was singing and playing on it but my parts have all been deleted apart from a tiny bit of mandola.

22nd December 2019

I had better start off by wishing anyone who is reading this a very happy Christmas. I have now finished wrapping up lots of Christmas presents for Mrs Churchward and I am well and truly ready for the big day to once again arrive when I will probably eat too much.

This week I finally got around to changing all of the 12 strings on my Rickenbacker electric guitar. The last time I did this I changed 6 of the strings, and then couldn't face changing the other 6 and that must have been a few years ago! In fact the guitar was down to 11 strings for quite along time because one of the top E strings had broken. All of the other strings were very rusty. To prepare myself for the great string change I watched a tutorial on youtube on how to restring a 12 string Rickenbacker guitar.

At the beginning of the tutorial Terry of the Guitar Works Ltd, Illinois says "Today we're going to do the most daunting restring that there ever will be for any guitar player and that's a Rickenbacker 12 string". This confirmed what I had often suspected having owned my Rickenbacker for about 19 years. The tutorial is great and showed the easiest way to change the strings, most of which I had previously already worked out for myself through trial and error. Mind you changing all the strings this time still took me 4 hours and I wouldn't recommend it to the faint hearted.

29th December 2019

My good friend Andy England happened to spot that the name of one of my old bands, The Morrisons, is shown on the cover of a fanzine called Blast Off. He says that he spotted it on the website of the Go Betweens. I presume that this fanzine was printed in the late 1980's when The Morrisons were featured in several fanzines after 'Listen to Your Heart' was played on Radio One by John Peel.

The back cover of the Thrilling Blunder Stories album in a similar style to the 1930s pulp science fiction magazines Wonder Stories and Thrilling Wonder Stories.

1) The Man Who Evolved
2) Driverless Cars
3) The Fastest Own Goal
4) Sunshine in the Rain
5) Jack the Ripper
6) The Music Hall War

7) A Song About Me
8) The Great Edwardo
9) Goodbye Mabo31
10) Knights of a King
11) Teign Valley Jig
12) Farewell Nico02

Richard 3 Records R302   © 2019
www.thelegendary10seconds.co.uk

Chapter Twelve
Ian's Blog 2020

5th January 2020

Well it's happy new year 2020 and the sound of that feels like it is something to do with science fiction. I can remember reading 1984 in the 1970s and that future year seemed like the far future. I can still recall thinking about it walking up Shiphay Lane in Torquay and also thinking that in the year 2000 I would be nearly 40 and how old that seemed. Now that I am 58 years old 40 sounds quite young!

It's been an interesting start to the year. I went to a new years eve party and I think I am finding it a struggle to party until midnight. I would prefer to be at home reading a book if I stay up late. Yes I know I'm boring. The next day I saw Torquay United lose at the Theatre of Pain with my very good friend Jerry. Back to work in my office in Exeter the next day after being on holiday since 13th December 2019, but seemed to cope with it despite getting up early in the morning in the dark to drive to work. The next day on Friday I felt very very tired and it was time to say farewell to Nico02 also known as Nick Connors. He liked the A to Z of Ashburton that I had written out for him where he will be working. This included A for Ashburton and B for bus stop etc. Absolutely hilarious if you work in my office but undoubtedly not so if you don't!

Met up with Graham Moores after work in Exeter on Friday evening and finally got around to paying him for the Thrilling Blunder Stories artwork. We talked about our music which included when Graham recorded some of the songs of Iain Smith who I was at school with at Torquay Boys Grammar School. I can still remember parts of the first day at that school quite vividly. Queuing up in the car park outside the school first thing in the morning with Nadi Jahangiri a little further ahead of me in the queue. He had a brown satchel over his shoulder. Nadi would later be the guitar player in a local punk band called Das Schnitz. The drummer of Das Schnitz was Kevin Perry also at the same school and in fact I was also at Sherwell Valley junior school with him. I remember being sent to detention once at that junior school and Kevin was there in the same room, also on detention mucking about with some pencils that were on his desk.

One of the other things I remember about my first day at Torquay Boys Grammar School was sitting next to Iain Smith and when I got home after seeing Graham I found and listened to one of Iain's songs on youtube. About the same time as Das Schnitz were playing gigs in Torbay Iain formed his first band called the Gatecrashers with another school friend, Steve Rawson. This would have been in our last year at the Grammar school when I formed a strong friendship with Tony Graff who sometimes performed as Doctor Prufroct, singing with his acoustic guitar. On 20th December 1978 there was a benefit gig for a charity called Mencap at the Victoria Hotel and myself, and Sean Cannon helped Tony while he sang a song by bashing out a rhythm with rolled up newspapers. Das Schnitz, the Gatecrashers, the Hedgehogs and the System all played at this event. Martin Johnson was the singer of System with Steve Milton on drums who would later play drums for the Gatecrashers. I think that the singer of the Hedgehogs was John Shaw, all school mates at the Grammar School.

12th January 2020

I've recently been reading about the bread riots which took placed in Torquay in 1847 and 1867 and this gave me the idea for some lyrics to go with a new tune idea I had. There was an interesting article which mentioned the bread riots in a local magazine called the Beach Hut. The article was written by Jack Critchlow about Torquay Museum and having read this it sparked off the idea for a song. The idea for the tune came from watching a tutorial on youtube about playing a country and western style steel guitar riff. My tune idea sounds nothing like that style of music though.

'RIOTS IN TORQUAY'

The harvest was so poor
The price of bread it would soar
The potato crop had failed
Hope for the poor had not prevailed

There were riots in Torquay
In Union street like an angry sea
It was eighteen forty seven
Great discontent for the poor in Devon

The price of bread so high
Could this the baker justify
A mob in Union Street
The constables had to defeat

There were riots in Torquay
In Union Street like an angry sea
It was eighteen sixty seven
Great discontent for the poor in Devon

A sharp rise in the price of bread
Led to a riot the newspapers said
It was bonfire night when the shops were trashed
Broken into ransacked trashed and smashed

19th January 2020

It has been a very enjoyable weekend. Went for a nice walk with Phil and Debby Helmore in Babbacombe yesterday morning. In the afternoon had a very good recording session with Bridgit England. I have recorded her singing on three more of my songs. I think the best one is the 'Mayflower' song. At the end of the afternoon I found out that Torquay United had won away from home which put me in an even better mood. The day ended with a lovely evening celebrating Jerry Brimicombe's 60th birthday. Andy and Bridgit England played a great set of songs for Jerry. It was really good to see lots of old friends like Gary Long, Steve Honeywill and Steve Rawson. Lord Zarquon was also there.

26th January 2020

On Tuesday morning I went to a very interesting lecture at Torquay museum about the historical pageant which took place in Torquay in June 1924. This is something which I did not know about and it turns out that pageants were very popular just before the first world war and also in the 1920s. My wife has written some lyrics for a possible song about the Torquay pageant and I am also now seriously considering recording a concept album about the history of Torbay.

2nd February 2020

Here are the lyrics for two songs about the Torquay Pageant of 1924.
Elaine wrote the lyrics for the opening verses and I wrote the rest.

'THE TORQUAY PAGEANT PART ONE'

A passion for the past took the counties over
With historical pageants from sherborne to dover
In a seaside town in nineteen twenty four
There was a pageant Torquay had not had one before

Off to Rock End Gardens
In the June sunshine
To enjoy the pageant
To have a jolly time

Now Mr Arthur Aplin a hero from the war
He was the pageant master his novels I adore
A playwright and an actor he knew a thing or two
He said to the town now it's up to you

Off to Rock End Gardens
In the June sunshine
To enjoy the pageant
To have a jolly time

Vice Admiral Mccully happened to be in Torbay
He opened the pageant during his short stay

Off to Rock End Gardens

In the June sunshine
To enjoy the pageant
To have a jolly time

Now the pageant is forgotten and few will ever know
Of the many thousands who enjoyed the show
Yes the pageant is forgotten and few will ever know
Of the many thousands who enjoyed the show

'THE TORQUAY PAGEANT PART TWO'

Over looking Torbay on a perfect June day
Our pageant begins at a time
When mammoths still roam
And Torquay is home
To cavemen depicted in mime

Then next are displayed fair maidens afraid
For the druids to sacrifice
But what of the omens
Then enter the Romans
The maidens saved in a trice

In episode three an abbot we see
Torre Abbey is endowed
Children are playing
The monks they are praying
Of the abbey they are so proud

A noble man's wedding and then we are heading
To a challenge on fine steeds

Then Drake on the Hoe
With a fair wind to blow
We hear of his brave deeds

A princess arrives to our surprise
And also devon's high born
A triumphal parade
Of the actors is made
In all the costumes worn

9th February 2020

I recently decided to make my Podtastic album available in digital format and it can now be heard via all the usual places on the internet such as Spotify. I think that this was the last album I recorded as the Legendary Ten Seconds before I started to record songs about Richard III. I did record some further songs after this album was finished but I never got around to doing anything with them until I decided to put them on another album called Good Fortune which is also now available to be heard on the internet in digital format.
The sound quality of these albums isn't as good as my Ricardian albums, mainly because Lord Zarquon only started helping me with my songs just before we started doing the Ricardian stuff. Lord Zarquon is a wizard with recording songs and my albums have greatly improved since we formed our musical partnership.

16th February 2020

I was asked by a friend for some more information about who contributed to the Podtastic album. As far as I can remember it was mainly just myself and Guy playing on that album. One of my neighbours played some guitar on one track and I think he played the mandolin on 'Nothing is Going Your Way'. He also played keyboards on one track. Dave Clifford of the Morrisons played bass on one track, possibly 'Shoot the Moon' and Guy played bass on all of the other songs. The harmonica on 'Can't Live Without' you was played by someone called Simon Lane who was at school with Guy. There is even a very rare piece played and recorded by Roger Crompton of a tiny amount of electric guitar at the end of a song called 'Lose Control'. I think the best track on the album is 'The Travelling Medicine Show' which has Guy's sister singing on it. Elaine wrote the lyrics. I had found a really interesting article about someone who lived in the USA in the late 19th century who had joined a travelling medicine show and I asked Elaine if she could write some lyrics for a song based upon the article. The only problem with the song is that it really ought to be sung by someone with a strong American accent. The lyrics for the song are superb and Elaine was really impressed with the tune that I made up to go with the lyrics. I wish I could remember the name of the person in the article that inspired the song and unfortunately I appear to have lost the magazine which contained the article.

23rd February 2020

I've been thinking quite a bit about the way I go about recording my songs and the fact that I'm not in a band playing live music. In an ideal world I would be working with a dedicated drummer and bass player. As the Legendary Ten Seconds, I did try it for several years during which period there was an excellent performance at the Summer Moon festival in Kingsteignton. Unfortunately it was extremely difficult to find a drummer who was interested in my style of music and who wasn't already in another band. It was also very difficult to get gigs. When we did get the odd gig it was very time consuming and expensive . It was also very time consuming rehearsing and I ended up having two rehearsals a week because I couldn't get all of the same band members to attend the same rehearsal days. This meant that on one day I might rehearse with the bass player and then later on in the week I'd have a rehearsal with the lead guitar player. After being let down rather badly at the Bosworth festival in August 2018, I decided to stop doing gigs and cancel rehearsing. Sincd then I have mainly just concentrated on writing and recording new songs. Last year we recorded History Book Part One, Thrilling Blunder Stories, Devon Roses, released Instrumental Legends and recorded a comedy song with John Challis. Before that I was releasing a maximum of one album a year so on balance I think it was a good idea to scrap the gigs.

1st March 2020

There is a review of a Richard III novel called *Distant Echoe*s on a Ricardian blog called Murrey and Blue. I am mentioning this in my weekly blog because one of my songs appears to be the inspiration for the novel and for me this is quite exciting really.

8th March 2020

The recording for the History Book Part Two album has been completed and I've submitted everything that is required for the digital distribution to CD Baby. Graham Moores will shortly be completing the album artwork so that the CDs can be duplicated. I would like to thank the following for their valuable contributions to the songs on the album, especially myself!!!

Ian Churchward vocals, guitars, keyboards, mandola and mandolin

Lord Zarquon keyboards, bass guitar, drums and percussion
Phil Swann guitars, bouzouki and mandolin
Bridgit England vocals
Guy Bolt vocals
Jules Jones vocals
Elaine Churchward vocals and she also wrote the lyrics for Gallants
Bower
Tom Churchward harmonica
Fleur Elliott vocals
Ashley Mantle wrote most of the lyrics for Cade's Rebellion
The album was recorded from 2016 to February 2020 in
Kingsteignton, Marldon, and Torquay in South Devon. It was mixed
and produced by Lord Zarquon.

15th March 2020

I've made a promotional video for the new History Book Part Two
album which can be viewed on youtube. This then gave me the idea
to edit some photos using a combination of imovie and photoshop.
I discovered that if you
use the transition feature in imovie you can create a photo that looks
like a page which is in the process of being turned over. The CDs for
the album have now been duplicated and I am selling them for £10
each including p & p.

22nd March 2020

I have just finished reading a book called the *Billy Ruffian* by David
Cordingly about the Bellerophon that held Napoleon as a prisoner
in Torbay, just after the battle of Waterloo. Most of the sailors on
the Bellerophon couldn't pronounce the name of their ship so they

called her the Billy Ruffian. Here are the lyrics to my new song that I have just written after reading about Napoleon on that ship.

'THE BILLY RUFFIAN'

Aboard the Billy Ruffian
From France to Torbay
With the prisoner Napoleon
Such fame had come their way
Aboard the Billy Ruffian
From France to Torbay

Her hull was made of English oak
More than three thousand felled
Named the Bellerophon
And her keel was made of of elm

Aboard the Billy Ruffian
Arriving in Torbay
With Napoleon Bonaparte
And in England he hoped to stay
Aboard the Billy Ruffian
Arriving in Torbay

Of battles she had many
The bravest of the brave
Part of the Royal Navy
And England they would save

Sightseers came from Exeter
To gather in the bay

They'd come to see Napoleon
Get a glimpse of him that day

Aboard the Northumberland
Departing from Torbay
With the prisoner Napoleon
To exile on his way
Aboard the Northumberland
Departing from Torbay

Goodbye to the Bellerophon
And her claim to fame
The crew stripped her of everything
And a prison she became
Goodbye to the Bellerophon
And her claim to fame

29th March 2020

At the moment I am trying not to worry about the corona virus and trying to stay focused on music. With this in mind I have enjoyed watching Nick Mason's Saucerful of Secrets on youtube. I had listened to several recordings of some of the recent gigs over the last few weeks and it wasn't until yesterday that I suddenly realised that Gary Kemp was part of the band. I must admit I never thought that an ex member of Spandau Ballet would be performing some of Syd Barrett's songs in a band with Nick Mason.

This has reminded me of when I purchased the Relics album in the record department of what must have been John Menzies back in about 1980. I can't remember how I first heard about Syd Barrett, it may have been from a book, but I was intrigued by his story and I decided to listen to some of his recordings with Pink Floyd. I can still remember bumping into Stuart Gordon who I knew from school and when he saw what I had in my hand he called me a toad. I guess Pink Floyd wasn't considered to be very cool in the era of punk rock and new wave. I can clearly remember playing the record in my bedroom when I got home and the first song was 'Arnold Layne' which I immediately loved. There were loads of great tracks, especially 'See Emily Play', 'Interstellar Overdrive' and 'Bike'. Then I purchased Piper at the Gates of Dawn and I thought that album was even better. Syd Barrett had a very short and tremendously creative period and then almost straight away seemed to disappear into thin air. It's a shame that it didn't last longer and it makes those albums seem especially wonderful and precious.

5th April 2020

The Churchward household is now well and truly in lock down mode at the present time due to the horrible virus that is causing massive worldwide problems. This presents a good opportunity for me to write lots more songs which will hopefully keep Lord Zarquon busy. I've just finished writing another song which is about Isaac Merritt Singer who owned Oldway Mansions when it was built in the 1870s. It's not certain but quite likely that his last wife was the model for the Statue of Liberty. It was designed by the French sculptor Frédéric Auguste Bartholdi and I think his mother was the model for the initial sketch with the last wife and widow of Isaac Singer being the model for the final design. Isaac made a fortune from his patent of a sewing machine and I've called the song 'Patent 8294.'

'PATENT 8294'

He's got a complicated life
So he had to leave another wife
Took a ship to go to France
It's one hell of a merry old dance

His Patent 8294
A sewing machine we all adore
In Paignton he lives in style
And his massive fortune makes him smile

He was born in New York state
Ran away from a home he'd grown to hate
With a travelling carnival he had some fun
Got married and divorced when he was young

His Patent 8294
A sewing machine we all adore
In Paignton he lives in style
And his massive fortune makes him smile

He asked George Bridgeman for a plan
For a mansion a big wigwam
Oldway mansion his grand design
Using bricks from Dorset to look so fine

In Paris he married Isabella
She couldn't resist such a tall fella
Isaac Merritt Singer is his name
An inventor and an actor he will claim

Of children he's got at least twenty

And in his will they'll get plenty
Of the money from patent 8294
And they'll live in style of that I'm sure

I have also written another song after reading a book about the history of Torbay. I learnt from the book that there was a shipyard in Brixham that built a replica of the Mayflower which then successfully sailed across the Atlantic in the 1950's. The song is called 'The Brixham Mayflower.'

'THE BRIXHAM MAYFLOWER'

In Plymouth Massachusetts a special ship arrived
And a warm welcome would not be denied
Lining the docks was a cheering crowd
And I heard that their cheers were very loud

Such a triumph for Upham's shipyard
The ship sailing on when a storm hit her hard
With English oak and canvas sail
Mr Charlton's vision would prevail

In Plymouth Massachusetts a special ship arrived
And a warm welcome would not be denied
Lining the docks was a cheering crowd
And I heard that their cheers were very loud

She'd been launched in the pouring rain
Beautifully crafted with axe and plane
Christened with a gold loving cup
In the harbour to bring her good luck

With thousands of applicants to join her cew
The captain could only chose a few

Such a triumph for Upham's shipyard
The ship sailing on when a storm hit her hard
With English oak and canvas sail
Mr Charlton's vision would prevail

In Plymouth Massachusetts a special ship arrived
And a warm welcome would not be denied
Lining the docks was a cheering crowd
And I heard that their cheers were very loud

12th April 2020

I've just put new strings on one of my fender electric guitars. I think it's been at least a couple of years since it had new strings on it and the old ones were very rusty! It's got a Bigsby tremolo arm on it and because of that it's a little bit awkward to restring which is probably why I've not done it for sometime. I must admit I am a bit lazy when it comes to restringing my guitars. In fact I discovered today that some of my spare guitar strings are so old that they've gone rusty as well and I had to throw away a few into the bin.

I've written another new song, actually it was written before the one about the Brixham Mayflower which was mentioned in my previous blog. It's about the author Agatha Christie, who was born in Torquay, and it is set during the time just after her first husband left her and she went to the middle east. There she met her second husband via an interest in archaeology. I have only just found out that I used to walk past where she was born virtually every week when I was at Torquay Boys Grammar school in the 1970's. The site of her house is next door to where my school was located. My Dad worked at the technical college which was also located by my school. Both the college and the school buildings have been replaced by modern flats, apart from my old sixth form building which is now a residential house on the other side of the road. This is near the top end of Torre, in Barton Road, and there is a blue plaque near the site of Agatha Christie's birthplace which was called Ashfield.

'AGATHA HEADS OFF EAST'

Agatha heads of east
With hope and belief
Tomorrow where will she be

The Orient Express
Takes her from the west
Tomorrow what will she see
Dear Agatha Christie

It healed her broken heart
It healed her broken heart

A ticket for Baghdad
A new dream to be had
In the desert lands

Ancient artefacts
Amongst the ziggurats
Amidst the shifting sands
In the archaeologist's hands

It healed her broken heart
It healed her broken heart

19th April 2020

I've just found the website for the gentlemen who gave the brilliant lecture about the Torquay pageant of 1924 that I attended at Torquay museum earlier this year. So far this lecture has given me the inspiration to research the history of Torbay and write lots more songs about some of it. Hopefully there will be more songs to come. I can honestly say that this is the happiest musical period of my life and I seem to be able to compose a new song as often as I like which on average seems to be about once a week..

On Thursday I had an especially very good day when I drove my car for the first time in a couple of weeks, to go to my office in Exeter to collect a new computer monitor and my office work chair. The weather was wonderful and the roads traffic free. I decided to go via Shaldon bridge which I always enjoy and I was listening to some of my favourite music in the car. I think it was the most enjoyable journey to and from Exeter that I have ever experienced.

Despite these happy thoughts we are expriencing very difficult times due to the covid 19 virus. I worry about my sister who works at Torbay hospital. I desperately miss being able to see some of my best friends such as Jerry Brimicombe, Debby and Phil Helmore I can't visit my Mum who is in a care home and I miss Lord Zarquon coming over to help me with the problems I have understanding the music software with which I record. I miss being able to go to see Torquay Utd at Plainmoor but at least I don't have to worry about them losing at the moment! I miss being with my work colleagues at my office in Exeter but I can see them via skype and I have got used to working from home. I was terribly ill for most of February and

March with a very bad cough and then I had a cold as well. I worry that if I catch the corona virus it will kill me but I have to say that I do feel happy. I am very very lucky to work with some of the most wonderful people I have ever met in my life.

26th April 2020

My cousin Julie Levy recently sent me some old family photos and one of these was of my Grandad Gordon in his First World War army uniform. I can always remember my Dad telling me about the brother of my Grandad Gordon who was killed at the battle of Jutland on a battle cruiser that was hit by shells from a German warship. I think a shell hit one of the main gun turrets and exploded the magazine and blew the ship in half. I believe he was a stoker on the ship. His name is on the war memorials in Plymouth and Newton Abbot. When I was a child we frequently visited my Grandmother Claria Causley and Grandad Gordon Churchward who both lived in Exeter. We would have driven past the Newton Abbot war memorial and I had a spell in my teens of visiting the orthodontist which was directly opposite the memorial. When I used to visit Grandad Gordon I always enjoyed looking at his War medals which must have been from WWI.

I used to also enjoy looking out at the view of Exeter from the first floor living room window of the flat where he lived with my Uncle Eric. I would be allowed to look at the view with the binoculars that were kept in the living room. My sister Linda and my cousin Julie used to enjoy it when Uncle Eric let them make cigarettes using his cigarette making machine. Aunt Char lived in the flat immediately below and she was quite over weight. My sister remembers that Aunt Char used to do the ironing for Uncle Eric and Grandad Gordon. My sister and I also used to love it when Uncle Eric would take us to buy sweets on a Sunday morning. We would then go for a walk, often by the River Exe with our Dad and Uncle Eric and then go to a cafe where Linda and myself would have ice cream. I was always fascinated by the mustard pot in the cafe which reminded me of a Dalek. The cafe was virtually opposite Barclays Bank where I would later work in Exeter.

My Grandmother Claria Causley lived in Abbots Road in Exeter and Grandad Gordon lived with my Uncle Eric in a flat which is very close to my office in Southernhay in Exeter. I drive by it when I go to work in Exeter in the morning and again when I drive home from my office back to Torquay.

I have just started reading a new book by David Scott about Torquay in WW2 called *The Funk Hole Myth*. This has given me the inspiration for a song about Torquay during WW1 which mentions Arnold Ridley (Godfrey in Dad's Army). He had been wounded three times in 1916 and was then discharged from the army. In 1917 he was a teacher at Torquay Boys Grammar School and a suffragette gave him a white feather. Men that were not eligible for service were given silver war badges so that they could avoid being vilified but Arnold Ridley kept his badge in his pocket rather than wearing it. A Torquay musical director had the surname Hindenburg and had to change his name to Basil Cameron to avoid coming under suspicion because anti German sentiment was rife and lots of English people were paranoid about German spies.

'ARNOLD'S WHITE FEATHER'

The suffragettes are busy in the town of Torquay
Handing out white feathers to the men that they see
Yes handing out white feathers to the men that they see

Mr Hindenburg had to change his name
Anti German sentiment and spies are to blame

A local Austrian arrested on his wedding day
Such paranoia was rife all around Torbay

The suffragettes are busy in the town of Torquay
Handing out white feathers to the men that they see
Yes handing out white feathers to the men that they see

Arnold Ridley was a teacher at a Torquay school
Received a white feather which was rather cruel
Seen by a suffragette who wore a fox fur
His silver war badge he didn't show to her

Wounded three times in the First World War
Arnold fought at the Somme with great valour

The suffragettes so busy in the town of Torquay
Handing out white feathers to the men that they see
Yes handing out white feathers to the men that they see

3rd May 2020

When the Prime minister recently announced that we were only allowed out once a day for exercise, to buy essential shopping, or if we were key workers, I had a sense of what it must have felt like to have heard Neville Chamberlain announce the outbreak of war via the radio in September 1939. The current crisis caused by the Covid 19 Corona virus is surely the greatest threat that our country has faced since the Second World War. Now that I am only permitted to go out for exercise once a day I am enjoying my walks much more than I would have done before the current Corona virus epidemic, when I could go out whenever I felt like it. I think that better weather helps now that we are in Spring, especially after the long periods of heavy rain that we had virtually every day during the winter.

When I went for a recent walk with my wife we were looking at all the lovely wild flowers near Meadfoot beach. This reminded me of the wild flower school project that everyone in my class was given by the biology teacher at the end of my first year at Torquay Boys Grammar school. That summer whenever I went for a walk with my parents I would often be ble to pick a selection of wild flowers, press them, paste them into a folder and then with an ink fountain pen write the name of each flower by each pressed specimen. I was given a book written by Keeble Martin of wild flowers as a present. This was in the early 1970s. I was quite good at collecting wild flowers, and I am quite good at collecting lots of things. As well as collecting stamps here is a list of other things I have collected:-

1970s Devon Genral Bus Tickets
Coins
1970 Football World Cup Cards
Brooke Bond Tea Trade Cards
Vinyl Records
Torquay United Football Programmes
Quicksilver Messenger Service Bootleg Recordings
Scanned Photos and Posters of Quicksilver Messenger Service
Science Fiction Magazines
Books about Richard III

10th May 2020

David Scott's very excellent book about Torquay in the Second World War has now given me the inspiration for three songs. The latest one came to me after reading the end of chapter nine describing a mock invasion of Torquay in which the Home Guard of the town were the defenders and the regular English army the invaders. This took place in 1942 and honestly it sounds like it was an episode very similar to those portrayed in the brilliant Dad's Army TV comedies. Colin Ross was a school boy at St Olaves School which was closed in London during the Second World War and evacuated to Torquay. Sixty Five years later he wrote an account of his time in Torquay for the St Olaves school magazine. With several other pupils of St Olaves he watched the fake invasion taking place and apparently the civilian population of Torquay largely went about it's normal business while the battle was going on. This probably infuriated the army much more than the antics of the Home Guard. Colin and his school mates took the side of the Home Guard and kept them posted on the movements of the regular army. Colin felt that the regular army cheated quite a bit and needless to say won the battle. There was one ambush in which a platoon of the Home Guard were very successful but the referee disallowed it for some reason. Colin remembers that a biology teacher who was part of this platoon was very unhappy about it.

'THE FUNK HOLE MYTH'

There was a pretend battle in nineteen forty two
The Torquay home guard knew what they had to do
To defend their town from a mock invasion
For the regular army it was a strange occasion

A weekend long defence of the town of Torquay
Colin Ross remembers the event quite clearly
The residents of Torquay carried on regardless
The antics of the army were considered harmless

The funk hole myth you had better not believe
The national newspapers were out to deceive

The pupils of St Olaves sided with the home guard
For the regular army they had very little regard
Being quite annoying as they mingled with the troops
The schoolmates spying on the men in many groups

Amongst all the tragedy there was farce
Like a scene from Dad's Army common sense was rather sparse

Colin thought the army cheated quite a bit
He remembers how one teacher complained about it
A referee disallowed a home guard victory
It was a successful ambush in the town of Torquay

The funk hole myth you had better not believe
The national newspapers were out to deceive

17th May 2020

When I went to Denver in the USA a few years ago, I visited the Buffalo Bill museum at Lookout mountain and I was very surprised to discover that William Cody had visited Torquay with his Wild West show. When I started writing my songs about Torbay earlier this year I had forgotten about Buffalo Bill's visit until I saw some information about it at Torre Abbey. For a few weeks since then I have wanted to write about his show visiting Torquay and now I have been able to do so.

'BUFFALO BILL IN TORQUAY'

Buffalo bill in Torquay
His wild west show we must see
William Cody his real name
A living legend of great acclaim

In the year 1904
He's not been here before
To the Newton Road we must go
For great excitement at his show

Buffalo Bill in Torquay
His wild west show we must see
William Cody his real name
A living legend of great acclaim

Riders from many a nation
Bringing great acclamation
Colonel Custer's last stand
With Buffalo Bill in command

A thrilling and daring bicycle feat
Wild west stars that you can meet
Sideshows and staged races
At this pageant excited faces

Buffalo Bill in torquay
His wild west show we must see
William Cody his real name
A living legend of great acclaim

In the year 1904
He's not been here before
Of great excitement I have been told
Tickets for his show to be sold

Buffalo Bill informed the press
His liking of Torquay he would express
He loved the view from Daddyhole Plain
His delight for it he could not contain

24th May 2020

While on my way back to my house after a short walk one evening
a few days ago I bumped into Nick Pascoe and we had a long chat.
He lives just around the corner from me and his older brother Chris
was in the same year as me at Torquay Boys Grammar School. Nick
was also at the same school. This reminded me of an old photo
when Nick and myself took part in a WH Smith sponsored walk
along the Newton Road in Torquay. We walked from Torquay to
Newton Abbot and then back along the same route to Torquay. This
was probably sometime in 1979. We talked about several things,
including supporting Torquay United and I mentioned my songs
about our local football team. Nick said that he was at Plainmoor
with his brother to see the game against Cambridge when Pat Kruse
scored the record breaking own goal. Nick said that they didn't see
the first goal at the game because it happened so quickly but he does
remember the second own goal. He'd forgotten that Torquay scored
all four goals in the 2-2 draw that day.
Since talking to Nick I have remembered one funny event at a
grammar school assembly when the school governors attended. One
boy called Morris, had cellotaped down all of the keys of the piano
so that when Mr Hopkins' hands descended onto the instrument it

resulted in a most horrible cacophony ringing out. There was a huge roar of laughter from all of the school children whereas the teachers, especially the headmaster did not look amused at all! Morris' younger brother was called Kevin and he was in the same year as me at the grammar school. In fact we had attended the same junior school. Kevin died in his early thirties of lung cancer. His wife was called Joy and for a while she lived in the same road as me. She was a very talented singer and I remember hearing Kevin play rock n roll music on the grammar school piano in the assembly room at lunchtime.

I had another idea for a tune last week which turned into another song. I was plucking two strings in unison on my guitar but not using the fingers of my left hand on the fretboard. It provied me with an interesting melody in E minor. It sounded a bit medieval and I'd been waiting for something like this to come along to me so that I could write a song about Torre Abbey.

'TORRE ABBEY'

An abbot from Welbeck Abbey
Arrived on the shores of Torbay
William Briwere had gifted some land
Thanks for the safe return of his son

For the monks Torre Abbey was made
And throughout the day they prayed
Many gifts and bequests were received
And their faith in God they truly believed

On the west side a cruciform church
The buildings around a courtyard
Built on a Benedictine plan

Beer limestone used for the arcades

For the monks Torre Abbey was made
And throughout the day they prayed
Many gifts and bequests were received
And their faith in God they truly believed

The monks made sure that the poor were fed
Looked after the folk in Torbay
A genuine holy cast of mind
Destroyed by a tyrant King

Because of King Henry the abbeys dissolved
To take all their wealth he was resolved
King Henry the Eighth the great evil King
Great misery he would surely bring

31st May 2020

I have been reading Agatha Christie's autobiography and found two excellent sections about her life in Torquay at the turn of the 19th into the 20th century that gave the inspiration for two more songs. It's a really interesting read, especially when she talks about swimming from Meadfoot beach to the large rock that I can see just about every day when I take the opportunity to go for a walk near my house.

One of the songs is about the wedding of her sister at the church in Torre in which Agatha was the chief bridesmaid, There was no reception after the marriage service in the church because they were in mourning for the death of her father the previous year. Elaine wrote most of the lyrics for the second song but I did change a few words as I wanted to include the reference to how Agatha, as a child, would start saving money in May for the eagerly anticipated fair which was part of the regatta in Torquay at the end of August each year.

'THE TORQUAY REGATTA'

It's the regatta in Torquay
The thought of it brings such glee
With yacht racing in the bay
Money for the fair saved since May

On the switchback you'll lose your bearings
Come and buy some dainty fairings
Try your luck on the coconut shy
Bid for nougat please come and try

It's the regatta in Torquay
The thought of it brings such glee
With yacht racing in the bay
Money for the fair saved since May

Penny monkeys in every hue
Pin your coat with one or two
Can you pitch a ping pong ball
A goldfish prize for one and all

Out in the bay the yachts race by
From Haldon pier you can watch them fly
Brittania sighted up goes the cry
Beneath the blue August sky

It's the regatta in Torquay
The thought of it brings such glee
With yacht racing in the bay
Money for the fair saved since May

I had never heard of fairings until I read about them in Agatha Christie's book. They were given away as prizes at fairs and were very popular in the Victorian era up until the start of the First World War. There is one in my dining room that used to belong to my grandmother and I never realised it was a fairing until Elaine looked up some information about them on the internet.

7th June 2020

I am continuing to slowly read through Agatha Christie's autobiography. The first part of the book goes into lots of detail about her childhood at Ashfield which is quite fascinating and is making me think about my early years, trying to think of all the things that I can remember. Visits to the dentist is something that immediately springs to mind. Probably breaking one of my back teeth last weekend has almost certainly helped to revive those memories! Not a good time to break a tooth with dentists being closed for business due to the Covid 19 virus. Up until my early twenties I used to dread going to the dentist. I ate too many sweets as a child and always seemed to need a new filling when I went to the dentist in my teens. My first visits to the dentist were in Exeter. Although I was then living in Torquay, I think that my parents took me to the dentist in Exeter because we had previously lived in Pinhoe. I don't remember anything unpleasant about those visits, but when we started going to the dentist in Shiphay, that's when I remember the injections and the drill. The needle always hurt and despite the numbness it caused, the drill still hurt as well. I would imagine that the drill would have been even worse without the injection. Then there was the horrible numbness in the mouth which seemed to last for hours afterwards with the feeling that you were dribbling and unable to speak or eat properly.

On more than one occasion a sticky sweet such as a toffee would remove a filling and consequently result in another trip to the dentist for another injection and further drilling and filling. I think my dentist in Shiphay was a very good dentist. Whenever the school dentist checked my teeth at the Torquay Boys Grammar school I was usually informed that my fillings were extremely good. They've also lasted rather well.

As well as going to the dentist in Shiphay I also went to an orthodontist in Newton Abbot. There is still a dental practice in the same building by the war memorial in Newton Abbot. I remember coming back on the bus from one visit to the orthodontist when I saw a fire in a church in Kingskerswell.

At the orthodontist moulds were taken of my teeth, top and bottom and I have still got these somewhere in my basement. I then had to have four back teeth removed.This was not a pleasant experience and then I had to wear a brace. The brace used to make my teeth ache and when I was eventually able to dispense with it I found that I had gained a very slight speech impediment. Still the removal of the teeth ultimately proved to be a good thing. Those teeth all had fillings and after their removal the gaps between my teeth were better and made it easier for me to clean them with a tooth brush. I had a few further fillings in my early twenties but since then I have had to endure only one further filling and after that there was the replacement of an old existing one in my late thirties.

I remember being with my sister the first time that she had a filling. I saw her panic at the sight of the needle and she knocked the hand of

Mr Abrahams, the dentist, so that he accidentally pricked one of his fingers.

My fascination with the history of Torbay continues and I recently purchased a jigsaw puzzle of a map of Victorian Torquay and this gave me the idea for another song.

'THE TOWN OF TORQUAY'

Lets take a walk by the harbourside in 1893
Life would be quite different then
In the town of Torquay

Everything looks so old fashioned
The ladies' hats their shoes and dresses

Lets take a walk up Union Street in 1903
Life would be quite different then
In the town of Torquay

Gas lamps to light the street
A horse and cart but no cars seen

Soon there will be trams
With electrification
The terminus for them
Located by Torre station

Take a walk to the town hall in 1923
Life would be quite different then
In the town of Torquay

14th June 2020

I have been on holiday this week. It has been much more enjoyable than my previous week off work which was ruined by a very nasty cough. It would have been even better though if we had been able to go to Northumberland as originally planned, but this had to be cancelled due to the present restrictions caused by the very nasty virus that has caused so much misery. So instead it has been a holiday in Torquay which is a very nice place to be but I could have done with a change of scene.

I have written another song about some of the old things in Torquay that I have noticed for the first time despite having been around them for years. I have also become slightly fascinated by Torquay man hole covers.

'I SEE MUCH MORE TO MY SURPRISE'

So much I'd not noticed before
Why I hadn't I'm not sure
Now with a discerning eye
I see much more to my surprise
I can see much more than I did before

A fairing in my dining room
Surely it's a family heirloom
On a letter box George the Fifth
A red metal monolith

So much I'd not noticed before
Why I hadn't I'm not sure
Now with a discerning eye

I see much more to my surprise
I can see much more than I did before

Shackleton at the Torbay Hotel
At a dinner when he said farewell
A stone laid by Mrs Cain
So that we won't forget her name

Manhole covers that say Torquay
But some of them say Thomas Dudley

So much I'd not noticed before
Why I hadn't I'm not sure
Now with a discerning eye
I see much more to my surprise

21st June 2020

On Wednesday I was working back in my office in Exeter for the first time today since the end of March. There wasn't very much traffic on the road and I enjoyed listening to some of my favourite songs as I was driving to and from work. I hope that when this horrible virus goes away lots of people will continue to work from home so that there will be less traffic on the roads.

I have just started recording a new song about when the news arrived in Torquay that the First World War had ended. It was when I started to decide on the tempo of the song that I made some real progress with how to use the drummer programme in Logic. Suddenly I have a better understanding of it, whereas for several years I now realise I was being quite stupid! I have always struggled to know whether the time signature of a song is 3/4 or 6/8 and using the Logic drum loops for these time signatures always seemed to present problems. I thought that my new song was in 3/4 but when I set the time signature for this in Logic and tried to use the drummer programme it sounded completely wrong, I then had a thought and changed the time signature to 6/8 and the drummer programme worked for the song. Presumably the song is actually in 6/8? I do remember Bridgit England saying to me that one of my other songs was in 6/8 and not 3/4 as I had originally told her. I wonder if it was the 'Torquay Pageant Part Two' song?

'COME CELEBRATE'

Come celebrate the war is over
An armistice has been signed
It's the eleventh of November
By sea the news has arrived

From HMS Onyx
Great news was received
In Torquay's harbourside
Of the victory that was achieved

Come celebrate the war is over
An armistice has been signed
It's the eleventh of November
By sea the news has arrived

Marching from St Marychurch
The New Zealand troops in Torquay
They were singing at Castle Circus
A great joy to hear and to see

The mayor led the crowd in cheers
For Sir Douglas Haig
The prime minister, king and queen
And the national anthem was played

Crowds of joyful people
On the pavements and in the road
Applause erupted for the mayor
Later fireworks would explode

Andy and Bridgit England have been helping me quite a bit with recording my songs for the Pageant of Torbay album. They live in Madron near Penzance in Cornwall. Andy has been recording Bridgit singing lovely harmony vocals which he then sends to me as a wav file via the internet. They didn't do any recording for me last week because Andy has been busy dismantling an old shed and replacing it with a new one.

28th June 2020

Recording songs with Lord Zarquon has been a great inspiration for me. He has given me lots of new ideas. I have enjoyed listening to a few songs by the Strawbs because of him that I probably wouldn't have heard if it hadn't been for his recommendation. Phil Swann let me borrow one of his Strawbs albums called Baroque and Roll. This is an album of acoustic recordings and he suggested that perhaps I could record something similar with him. I think that Lord Zarquon thought highly of this album and so I am now recording another album although this time Lord Zarquon isn't involved with it. I hope he doesn't mind and I think he has got enough on his plate at the moment trying to finish the recordings for the Amazing Songs and Pageant of Torbay albums. Graham Moores has painted a great album cover for the acoustic album project which I have decided to call the Acoustic Almanac 2020.

5th July 2020

We have now completed 16 songs about Torbay and there are a few more unfinished ones. I have therefore decided to see if we can record 2 Torbay Pageant albums. I had originally intended that the 'Torquay Pageant Part One and Two' songs would start and end an album but I will now move the 'Torquay Pageant Part Two' song across to a second album.

I am hoping that Lord Zarquon can let me have the mastering projects for the songs on Monday so that I can create 16 bit wav files which I need for the digital distribution via CD Baby. I have completed a large part of the information that is required for this and I have obtained a bar code. Graham Moores has been in touch to let me know that he should soon be able to make a start on the Pageant of Torbay album artwork.

12th July 2020

Further progress has been made with my various music projects. Andy England has recorded Bridgit singing some lovely harmony vocals at their home in Madron, Cornwall for my song about the Brixham Mayflower. I have uploaded the Logic project of the song into drop box for Lord Zarquon. Hopefully this one can be included on the Pageant of Torbay Part Two album.

A few days ago I recorded a new vocal for the song that I composed with Ashley Mantle called 'God aid the Marshal'. This tune should be included on the Amazing Songs album. I think we are nearly there with this album and I need Lord Zarquon to let me know the order of the tracks so that I can submit it for digital distribution. I've decided not to include the song about Santa being grumpy because I don't want a one festive song on the album. I'm also not sure about the song called 'Lease on Your Heart'. This is another one that I composed with Ashley Mantle. At the moment the mastered version of the song doesn't include my best ever guitar solo and I am hoping that I can persuade Lord Zarquon to produce another version with this solo. I really feel that the guitar solo adds an extra dynamic to the song.

19th July 2020

Lord Zarquon celebrated his 60th birthday last weekend and I have written some new lyrics for him as part of the celebrations. Sing these words to the tune of 'God aid the Marshal'.

'GOD HELP LORD ZARQUON'

To Torquay he travelled
Testing his patience with Sir Ian's songs
Into a basement to be thrust
Bravely recording until dusk

Making albums was his aim
To sell for financial gain
As a musician he tried
With Sir Ian's songs he cried

On his motorbike see him ride

No more songs please you hear him cry
God help Lord Zarquon

Lord Zarquon of renowned fame
In the studio cemented his name
Hundreds of songs he's recorded
More songs from Sir Ian to be avoided

On his motorbike see him ride
No more songs please you hear him cry
God help Lord Zarquon

Under Sir Ian he served
Fame and honour he deserved
With Mellotron sounds he played about
To save a new song without a doubt

On his motorbike see him ride
No more songs please you hear him cry
God help Lord Zarquon
God help Lord Zarquon
God help Lord Zarquon

26th July 2020

I hadn't written a new song for a couple of weeks which is about
my longest barren spell since I started recording the Torbay Pageant
songs. I think it is partly due to work which is a bit tedious and
complicated at the moment. Also with the new albums nearing
completion I have been spending lots of time trying to deal with all
the things that need to be done for a new release. I have had a couple

of ideas in my head for some new songs but I couldn't seem to find the spare time or inspiration to sit down and write some lyrics. Also whenever I have picked up the guitar over the last few weeks I haven't found any new melody ideas, although I must admit I hadn't tried very hard to find them. Anyway last night I had some spare time to kill while I was trying to send a file of mp3's to Phil Swann. I tried several different methods to send the mp3s which meant that I spent lots of time waiting for the songs to be uploaded. It took me 3 attempts before I was able to complete this task. During this time, waiting for the computer to do something, I started to write some new lyrics and I think I have got the composition of the new song pretty much finished.

When I started writing songs about Torbay I made a list of as many things that I could think of that might be good ideas for songs. Something about the Spanish barn at Torre Abbey was one of those and there is a good account of the Nuestra Senora del Rosario in a book I have just finished reading about Torre Abbey which I referred to so that I could write the lyrics.

'THE NUESTRA SENORA DEL ROSARIO'

The armada was sighted from St Michaels mount
Then from Plymouth the English ships sailed out
Commanded by Lord Howard and Sir Francis Drake
The odds were stacked against them with so much at stake

During the first skirmishes in late July
Two Spanish ships would disastrously collide
One lost two sails and was crippled in the sea
And from Sir Francis Drake that vessel could not flee

Captain Whiddon on the Roebuck into Torbay to tow

The Nuestra Senora del Rosario

Drake hoped that he could loot the stricken vessel
With the ship at his mercy he was so successful
The Spanish surrendered their gold coins and their swords
Drake taking fifty nobles so history records

Captain Whiddon on the Roebuck into Torbay to tow
The Nuestra Senora del Rosario

From the revenge Don Pedro saw the campaign
The cunning English sailors against the might of Spain
At Calais the fireships burning so bright
The armada in disarray for him a painful sight

Captain Whiddon on the Roebuck into Torbay to tow
The Nuestra Senora del Rosario

Our Lady of the Rosary a flagship of the sea
Don Pedro her Captain for a ransom would be free

Back in Torbay the Rosario remained
And the hopes of the Spanish crew would surely be in vain
For they were held as prisoners in Torre Abbey's barn
For the history of Torbay this is such a thrilling yarn

2nd August 2020

I've written a song about General Herbert Plumer who lived for
a period of time at his parent's house in Haldon Road. Torquay.
After his father had squandered away the vast majority of a large

inheritance on drink and horses the family moved from London to Torquay where they purchased the villa Malpas Lodge in the Lincombes in Torquay. Having recently read a book about him I now know what a clever officer he was and it might come as a surprise to some people how well he commanded during the First World War.

'STRATEGIES WELL PLANNED'

A hero of the Boer war
His strategies well planned
He served in India
And in the Sudan

Young Herbert went to Eton
With holidays in Torquay
Cricket in the summer season
There by the sea

A general of the Great war
His strategies well planned
He served in the Flanders mud
Where he was in command

He came back from Torquay
From the Great war
Honoured with a ceremony
In the town hall

They gathered in the town hall
To honour his return
The freedom of the borough

He was given and he had earned

A general of the Great war
His strategies well planned
He served in the Flanders mud
Where he was in command

Commander of the army
That occupied the Rhine
After the armistice
That had been signed

9th August 2020

I've received a copy of a new book by David Hinchcliffe about the drinking fountains of Torquay which the author delivered to me in person at my house. My wife and I have very much enjoyed reading this book. We found it quite inspiring really and we have written a song about it.

'THE DRINKING FOUNTAINS OF TORQUAY'

Tea and coffe is too dear
Come and drink the water clear
Leave the cider leave the beer
Come and drink the water clear

If you've toiled up Meadfoot Hill
Take a rest and drink your fill
Mr Trant has built a fountain
For those who climb this seaside mountain

Tea and coffe is too dear
Come and drink the water clear
Leave the cider leave the beer
Come and drink the water clear

To Watcombe on a cycle run
To Lion Rocks you go for fun
At the fountain take a rest
Mr Bosanquet's name be blessed

But Torquay's mayor and corporation
Have caused some aggravation
Ellacombe's fountains have run dry
The public want the reason why

The drinking fountains of Torquay
Will surely quench your thirst for free

At Old Maid's Perch and Penny's hill
St Marychurch and Chapel hill
All around old Torquay town
Drinking fountains can be found

Tea and coffe is too dear
Come and drink the water clear
Leave the cider leave the beer
Come and drink the water clear

I have been visiting some of these old fountains and hope to make
a video to help to promote David's book. I don't have to go very far

to see one of them as it is virtually at the end of my road. I often wondered what the inscription WHT signified on it, and now I know.

Everything has been submitted to CD Baby in respect of the Amazing Songs album and here is some information about it and also the lyrics for one of the songs:-

'Old Family Photos' - Memories of black and white family photos.
'I can see Much More' - Noticing the large amount of local history in Torquay.
'God aid the Marshal' - A song about Sir William Marshal the First Earl of Pembroke.
'Ye Olde Bouzouki Meets ye Olde Mellotron' - Instrumental featuring a bouzouki and a mellotron.
'Love Dies' - Composed in the mid 1980's after reading a short story written by Steve Honeywill.
'The Jameson Satellite' - Based upon a 1930's science fiction story written by Neil R Jones.
'The Half Angel' - Inspired after reading an article in the March 2020 Ricardian Bulletin.
'Lease on Your Heart' - A song about a failed love affair.
'St Albans Way' - Wars of the Roses street names turned into a song.
'Driftwood' - This song started off as a simple keyboard melody played by Jeremy Brimicombe.
'Wake up' - You're dreaming again, you've been dreaming since I don't know when.
'C Scope 600' - A song about a metal detector.

Recorded by The Legendary Ten Seconds for Richard the Third Records in Torquay, Marldon, Kingsteignton and Madron. Mixed and mastered by Lord Zarquon at Rainbow Starshine Studios.

All songs composed by Ian Churchward except:-

'Old Family Photos' music composed by Graham Moores.
'God Aid the Marshal' and 'Lease to Your Heart' lyrics written by Ashley Mantle.
'Ye Olde Bouzouki Meets ye Olde Mellotron' composed by Ian Churchward and Phil Swann.
'Driftwood' lyrics written by Elaine Churchward and the music composed by Elaine Churchward, Jeremy. Brimicombe and Ian Churchward.

The minstrels of the Legendary Ten Seconds for the Amazing Songs album are:-

Ian Churchward vocals, guitars, mandola, mandolin, violin and keyboards
Graham Moores guitar on 'Old Family Photos'
Lord Zarquon keyboards, bass guitar and drums
Guy Bolt vocals, drums, bass guitar and stylophone
Bridgit England vocals
Elaine Churchward vocals
Phil Swann bouzouki and guitar
Sam Swann bass guitar
Jules Jones vocals on 'God aid the Marshal'
Rowan Curle backing vocals on 'Lease on Your Heart'

Richard the Third Records catalogue number R14, August 2020.

'SAINT ALBANS WAY'

Walking along down Woodville Road

I saw Warwick Close
In Lancaster Gardens a red rose
Taken to York Close

Percy Street who might you meet
St Alban's Way such a strange day
Clarence Street who might we greet
Then to St Alban's Way

Walking towards King Edward's Court
Can you see there's York Close
In the garden a white rose
Right there in York Close

Percy Street who might you meet
St Alban's Way such a strange day
Clarence Street who might we greet
Then to St Alban's Way

Walking down Beaufort Road
I saw Warwick Close
In the garden a Tudor rose
Right next to York Close

Percy Street who might you meet
St Alban's Way such a strange day
Clarence Street who might we greet
Then to St Alban's Way

16th August 2020

The Amazing Songs album was released on Friday and the recording of the Acoustic Almanac album has also been completed. This includes acoustic versions of songs previously recorded with electric guitars and keyboards. Here is some information about the album (please note that although I am playing the violin on one song I can't play this instrument properly and I am just using a violin bow on the open strings with very little skill):-

1) 'Billy Ruffian'
2) 'Song About me'
3) 'Gallants Bower'
4) 'James Templer's Legacy'
5) 'Mayflower'
6) 'Song of a Metal Detectorist'
7) 'St Albans Way'
8) 'Sitting in a Trench'
9) 'The Old Bouzouki'
10)'The Teign Valley'
11)'Walk of Shame'
12)'The Medieval Free Company'
13)'Tant le Desiree'
14)'Capel Celyn'

Phil Swann acoustic guitars, mandolin and bouzouki
Ian Churchward vocals, acoustic guitars, mandola, violin and percussion
Martyn Hillstead glockenspiel, drums and percussion
Tom Churchward drums, percussion, harmonica and melodeon
Sam Swann acoustic bass guitar
Ashley Dyer trumpet
Lis Durham violin
Guy Bolt vocals and drums

Bridgit England vocals
Pippa West vocals
Jules Jones vocals
Rowan Curle vocals
Elaine Churchward vocals
Bridgit England vocals

Just before I started recording my songs about Richard III, Elaine wrote a poem about a lost village in Wales called Capel Celyn. This was inspired after watching a very moving TV documentary about the flooding of the Tryweryn valley to create a dam for the city of Liverpool. I tried to compose some music to make the poem a song but couldn't find a tune for it. Then I lost the sheet of paper upon which the words were written. A few years later I found the lost piece of paper then lost it again only to stumble across it years later and then I found a tune for it in the autumn of 2017. I have also recorded another version of the song in a different key but the recording of this has not yet been completed.

'CAPEL CELYN'

The wind that ruffles these lonely waters
Ruffled the hair of our sons and daughters
Out of the schoolroom, along the stone alley
To farms on the hillside and houses in the valley

Patterns and rhythms of life handed on
The lilt of our language, a sharing of song

Liverpool city teeming with life
The sailor, the docker, the merchant his wife

All of them must be decently quartered
The masses of people provisioned and watered

The narrow necked valley just over the border
Perfect to dam up and fill up with water

They wanted more water
No permission was needed
We wanted our homes
But our needs went unheeded

So they took all our houses, they bulldozed the chapel
Drove the sheep from the hill, transported our cattle
They gave us the notice to dig up our dead
Compulsory purchase, that's what they said

The house of our forefathers forfeit and we are
Dispersed and forgotten, a lost community

They wanted more water
No permission was needed
We wanted our homes
But our needs went unheeded

The wind that ruffles these lonely waters
Ruffled the hair of our sons and daughters
Out of the schoolroom, along the stone alley
Capel Celyn in the Tryweryn Valley

23rd August 2020

The artwork and sleeve notes have been completed for the Pageant of Torbay Part One album and I have also completed the submission to CD Baby for the digital distribution. I will now be looking to arrange for the CDs to be duplicated and I have been in contact with the museum in Torwood Street to see if the CDs can be sold from their shop.

Here is some information about the album:-

1) 'The Torquay Pageant Part One' - inspired by a lecture at Torquay museum
2) 'Torre Abbey' - inspired after reading a book by Anne Born
3) 'William of Orange' - inspired after reading a book by Anne Born
4) 'The Billy Ruffian' - inspired after reading a book by David Cordingly
5) 'Riots in Torquay' - inspired after reading an article in the Beach Hut magazine
6) 'Torre Station' - inspired after reading a book by Anne Born
7) 'The Wonderful Paignton Pudding' - inspired from reading a book by Anne Born
8) 'Patent 8294' - inspired after reading a book by Anne Born
9) 'The Torquay Regatta' - inspired from reading Agatha Christie's autobiography
10) 'Buffalo Bill in Torquay' - inspired after walking passed Torre Abbey
11) 'Arnold's White Feather' - inspired from reading a book by David Scott
12) 'Agatha Heads off East' - inspired after reading an article on the internet
13) 'The Lady Cable' - inspired from reading a book by David Scott
14) 'The Funk Hole Myth' - inspired after reading a book by David Scott

15) 'The Theatre of Pain' - inspired by a comment made by my friend Chris Donovan

Produced and mixed by Lord Z at Otherworld Studios, Marldon Devon.

Recorded in Torquay, Marldon, Kingsteignton and Madron.

All songs composed by Ian Churchward except tracks 1 & 9 composed by Elaine & Ian Churchward, and track 7 composed by Ian Churchward & Bridgit England.

Album artwork Graham Moores.

Richard the Third Records catalogue number R12.

Ian Churchward vocals, guitars, Mellotron keyboard sounds and mandola

Lord Zarquon Mellotron sounds and other keyboards, bass guitar, and drums

Bridgit England vocals, keyboards and violin

Phil Swann 6 and 12 string guitars, and slide guitar

Sam Swann bass guitar on tracks 4, 5 and 15

Guy Bolt drums on track 15

Elaine Churchward vocals

'TORRE STATION'

The Opening of Torre Station
Just below Chapel Hill
An event of celebration
The first train arrives such a thrill

Applauded with due circumstance
Access to Torquay it would enhance

Though difficulties were not forseen
We celebrate the age of steam

The Opening of Torre Station
Just below Chapel Hill
An event of celebration
The first train arrives such a thrill

The Temperance Society band
Led a procession I understand
Sergeant Boyd's buglers brought up the rear
The sound of the music a joy to the ear

Sir John Yarde Buller gave an address
The whole event was a great success
Banners proclaimed Brunel's broad gauge
Locomotives in the Victorian age

The Opening of Torre Station
Just below Chapel Hill
An event of celebration
The first train arrives such a thrill

30th August 2020

Graham Moores has sent me some CDs that he has put together
with very lovely artwork. One of the CDs contains a collection of
songs of Iain Smith and this reminded me of the local music scence
in Torquay in the early 1980s.
It made me laugh when Steve Honeywill told me the story about
when he was in a band called the Walking Wounded (later called

MIA) with Steve Rawson. They paid a visit to Martin Johnson's shop called Individual Fashions in Market Street to see if he could arrange a gig for them, I think it was Steve Rawson's idea. Martin said " We want bands Rawson that are threatening the system not funky salsa crap."

I remember that Iain Smith went to Exeter University to study after our last year at school. I would see him occasionally but then in the very early eighties I didn't see him for ages until I happened to visit the rehearsal room in Swan Street. This was somewhere that most of the local bands used to rehearse. Iain was rehearsing with a new band and Richard Hele (previously in the Golgotha Boys) was playing bass. I think he had a really rubbish Satellite bass that had originally belonged to Gary Long who then gave it to me. Later possibly I had given it to Richard? The machine heads were made of plastic and one had broken off so that Richard had to tune it with a pair of pliers!

6th September 2020

I have now received the duplicated CDs of the Pageant of Torbay Part One album and it can presently be purchased via the Torquay museum shop, my wesbite or send an email to me. I will be donating money from the sale of the album to Torquay museum.

13th September 2020

Back in the late 1990s John Kelland wrote a booklet about the history of the district of Shiphay in Torquay. My parents purchased a copy and I remember reading it several years ago. Last week I had another read through of this booklet and once again found it interesting. It brought back happy memories of my childhood growing up in Shiphay in the 1960s and 1970s. Remembering the country lane which has just about disappeared, which was next to my first school for instance. I always thought it was a shame when the school lost one of it's playing fields when a new housing estate was built. We used to have our sports day on that field.

Of particular interest was the section about Cadewell House which was demolished before I was born. One of my ex Barclays Bank work colleagues called Kathy Hayes used to live in a house on the site of where the Georgian house used to be. I remember her making visits to the library in Exeter to try to find out some information about it. As a child I used to play on the green in Cadewell Park Road which was part of the extensive grounds of the estate of Cadewell House. When I first started playing in Cadewell Park Road with my friends, the green was covered in stinging nettles and we had great fun cutting pathways through those nettles. My hands had a few blisters on them after a busy day of whacking down nettles with a stick. When the stinging nettles disappeared the green was not very green and I remember it being a field of mud. We would then have mud fights! Later on there was grass and then we used to play football and cricket on it. I recall that there were a few relics such as the remains of a concrete sand bag from when it was used as an American fuel depot during the second world war.

I am currently in the process of writing a song about Cadewell House and if I finish it I will try to remember to put the lyrics onto this blog.

20th September 2020

Here are the lyrics of my new song about the Torquay fire brigade. The first two verses are about the firemen in Torquay before the First World War and the last verse is set in the 1920s.

'THE OLD TORQUAY FIRE BRIGADE'

Hooves striking the tram rails
Sparks flying up to the horses tails
The wagon of the Torquay fire brigade
It deserves a great accolade

A fire in the town
See the building burning down
Smoke up in the sky
A despairing cry

The Torquay firemen quickly on the scene
With their engine powered by steam
A fire on the Strand at Slade's
Thank heavens for the fire brigade

A fire in the town
See the building burning down
Smoke up in the sky
A despairing cry

Christened by the mayoress in may
This event such a proud day
Firefly was a motor fire engine
Because the danger of fire is never ending

A fire in the town
See the building burning down
Smoke up in the sky
A despairing cry

27th September 2020

My song about Cadewell House makes me think about all of the children that played with me on the green at Cadewell Park Road. Tony Perry, Simon French, Jonathan Gibbs, Duncan Jones, Robert Fraser, Andrew Tanner and Jethro Miles were just some of them. We had a wonderful time in the late 1960s and early 1970s. Tony Perry and his older sister Kay lived next door to me. Opposite my house was Simon and his sister Nicola. Jonathan Gibbs and his sister Caroline lived in Cadewell Park Road. I remember one winter when Caroline Gibbs got stuck in the mud in the midddle of the green and Jonathan and his father had to rescue her. They pulled her out of the mud and carried her to safety. After that they then had to go back and retrieve her wellngton boots that had been left stuck in the mud after they had her pulled out.

'CADEWELL HOUSE'

A naval man purchased Cadewell Field
Part of his land on which to build
The grandest house Shiphay has known
The admiral died far from his home
On board his ship far from his home

As children we played on the green
Near to where that house had been
Near to where Cadewell House had been

The estate passed to the eldest son
Then purchased by Horatio Carlyon
See where the town hall stands

A business man who bought that land
An architect and a business man

As children we played on the green
Near to where that house had been
Near to where Cadewell House had been

After Mr Carlyon died
Mr Chapman retired there to reside
His wife like Dresden china
Of the ladies none were finer
None were as kind as her

As children we played on the green
Near to where that house had been
Near to where Cadewell House had been

It's a shame the house was knocked down
The Yankee army came to our town
Their depot where the house had been
They built the road around the green
Cadewell Park Road around the green

4th October 2020

A few weeks ago I was interviewed on the phone by the newspaper reporter Tim Herbert about the Pageant of Torbay Part One album. When I told him how many albums about Richard III and the Wars of the Roses that I had recorded, I could hear a certain amount of disbelief and bewilderment in his voice. There is now an article about my songs in the Torbay Weekly.

11th October 2020

At the present time Lord Zarquon is very busy recording some of his Prophets of Zarquon songs for a second album. I would imagine that he is enjoying a well earned rest from my songs. I am still writing new songs. The latest one is about the explorer Percy Fawcett who was born in Torquay. I have recently finished reading a very interesting book about him called the *Lost City of Z* by David Grann, although I was a bit dissapointed that it didn't mention anything about Percy's time in Torquay.

'PERCY FAWCETT'

He was born in a house in torquay
Commissioned with the royal artillery
A novel by Sir Arthur Conan Doyle
Was inspired by Percy on the Amazon soil

El Dorado and the lost city of Z
An obsession always in his head
The amazon forest a living hell
Percy Fawcett the explorer knew it so well

In the First World War he faced danger again
He witnessed the horror of so many slain
And the horrors of the jungle were just as bad
The Amazon could drive the bravest man mad

El Dorado and the lost city of Z
An obsession always in his head

The Amazon forest a living hell
Percy Fawcett the explorer knew it so well

So strange to think he was born here
I had wondered where and it was so near
A shame that Devonia Villa has gone
The sight of Shirley Towers feels so wrong

El Dorado and the lost city of Z
An obsession always in his head
The amazon forest a living hell
Percy Fawcett the explorer knew it so well

As well as writing new songs I have also been doing some recording with Phil Swann for another album in a similar vein to the Acoustic Almanac, only this one will be a Semi Acoustic Almanac. Phil has recently purchased some new music software and has become very interested in the mastering process. He is enjoying being able to learn how to do a bit of mastering for some of our songs.

Finally I have just been advised by Apple music that the Legendary Ten Seconds had a shazam in Grand Rapids in the USA. The last time Apple music told me about a shazam for my music it was in Kazakhstan. Shazam was an album by the Move and I think that a shazam in Kazakhstan would be a great idea for a song.

18th October 2020

I have now written a song about the letter collection of Hester Pengelly who was the youngest daughter of William Pengelly. Her father is probably best known for his excavation work at Kent's cavern in Torquay. Hester was married to a prominent metallurgist called Henry Forbes Julian. He was very unfortunate to lose his life on the Titanic in 1912. He was on his way to a business meeting in San Francisco and was originally booked to sail on the Olympic. This travel arrangement was transferred to the Titanic because of a coal strike. When the Titanic was sinking, after hitting an iceberg, he gave up his place on a lifeboat. Hester had been due to travel with her husand but stayed at home because she was ill with influenza.

Hester and her husband lived in Torquay at a house called Redholme. Their house still exists and is located in Braddons Hill Road East and is being used for a bed and breakfast business. My song idea about Hester Pengelly came from reading an article about her in the Torbay Weekly. She inherited a collection of letters which included ones from such famous people as Nelson, Wellington, Keats and Byron. She added to this collection with her correspondence to important members of Society who had visited her house in Torquay.

'HESTERS LETTERS'

She invited members of society
To accompany her for afternoon tea
In Torquay a popular resort
the replies in their letters she eagerly sought

A letter from Keats to his fiancée
In Torquay museum it was hidden away
Byron's payment for his gambling debt
An autograph hunter would love to collect

She lost her husband when he went to sea
On the Titanic so tragically
Letters of condolence were received

Some from European royalty

25th October 2020

Last month two of my Torbay Agatha Christie themed songs were included in an online Agatha Christie festival. There is usually an annual Agatha Chrisite festival in Torquay but this year it was an internet only based event because of the dreaded virus that is continuing to cause world wide problems.

Another Torbay festival that was internet based for the same reason as the Agatha Christie event, is the Torbay Ageing Well Festival. I was interviewed at Torquay museum a few weeks ago by Carol Kendall about my songs, particularly the ones about Torbay. This interview and three of my songs were included in the Ageing Well festival livestream which was available to watch yesterday.

1st November 2020

At one stage last week there were 5 cruise ships in Torbay and 3 in Babbacombe Bay. I decided to compose a song about this and on Monday morning Lord Zarquon visited and we recorded him playing a Mellotron sound keyboard solo in one of the short instrumental sections of the song. He has completed the recordings of further songs for the Torbay Pageant Part Two album. These songs are, 'The Neustra Senora Del Rosario', 'Come Celebrate' and 'The Mysterious Affair at Styles'. I am particularly pleased with 'Come Celebrate' which includes some firework sounds which give the song a great sense of atmosphere. I can easily imagine the celebrations when the news of the armistice reached Torquay which included the New Zealand troops marching from St Marychurch to Castle

Circus. Then the mayor leading the crowd with cheers for the King and Queen.

Last week I also composed a comedy song called 'A Shazam in Kazakhstan'. Here are the lyrics for the chorus.

I'm plagiarising myself
And not the work of someone else
And I had a shazam in Kazazhstan
A shazam in Kazazhstan

I'm not clued up about a shazam
I was told that I had one in Kazakhstan
My songs have been heard in Australia
But not at all in Venezeula

8th November 2020

An article has been published in the Torbay Weekly about my fastest own goal song. Also a new version of the first Richard III, Legendary Ten Seconds album has just been released in digital only format which includes the narratives written by Sandra Heath Wilson. The album is called Loyalty Binds Me.

This Sunday morning I went for a walk in the direction of Hope's Nose. On the way back there was a crowd of people gathered by Meadfoot beach watching the cruise ships which sounded their horns before and after a period of silence in memory of the armistice that signalled the end of the First World War. I later found out that the trawlers in the harbour at Brixham had also sounded their horns. Apparently the idea started when a local resident, Louise Lewis, posted a message on a Brixham community facebook page asking as many boat owners in the bay to sound three horns at 11am on

Sunday, followed by two minutes silence, then a further three blasts after the silence. One of the biggest cruise ship companies, the Holland America Line, took up the idea and their four ships off Torbay - the Volendam, the Westerdam, the Zaandam and the Nieuw Statendam - all took part.

15th November 2020

I happened to see Phillip King in the shopping precinct of St Marychurch on Saturday, the previous weekend. He told me that an American lady had purchased a copy of the Torbay Pageant album from the museum shop. Mind you they won't be selling many copies for the rest of this month as the museum is closed again due to the latest covid 19 lockdown. I know Phillip from the recording sessions that I did for Renaissance Folk a few years ago. Phillip played some percussion for this folk music band. This is also how I came to know Fleur Elliott who was one of the singers. I didn't sing or play any instruments at the Renaissance Folk recording sessions, instead I was recording them in the basement of my house.

Like myself Fleur is a Torquay United supporter. I would imagine that she is also very disappointed that our team managed to give away a two goal lead twice in last Sunday's 5-6 defeat in the FA cup. It was pure agony to watch the late goals that were conceded in injury time although I have got used to watching the games live via my computer while the football is played with the terraces empty.

22nd November 2020

Lord Zarquon has now completed the recordings of nine songs for the Torbay Pageant Part Two album. The latest one is called 'Dreaming of Ashfield.' Another one that was recently completed is the 'Brixham Mayflower' but I have decided not to include this one for the album. The song feels like it is too long and boring at the moment and I may see if I can shorten it and make the song sound a bit more interesting. I think the lyrics are good but the tune hasn't got enough in it to inspire me.

29th November 2020

The journalist Guy Henderson has written an article about the Torquay drinking fountains song which has been published on a Torquay news website. In the article he states that the song is on the Acoustic Almanac album but it is actually on the Torbay Pageant Part One album.

I have recently been composing some songs with Martyn Hillstead who lives in Teignmouth, although I haven't actually seen Martyn since he played with the Estuary Buoys at Tom and Sasha's wedding last year. We have been communicating by email and Martyn has been mainly writing the lyrics for the songs while I have been composing the melodies. This leads me onto something that is a bit strange really. I am presently recording with Lord Zarquon on the Torbay Pageant Part Two project as the Legendary Ten Seconds but I am also recording as the Legendary Ten Seconds on a different music project with Phil Swann and Martyn. In an ideal world I wish that these projects could be combined but unfortunately Lord Zarquon doesn't feel that my recordings with Phil are professional enough and Phil doesn't like the drums on my recordings with Lord Zarquon. As for myself I'm somewhere in the middle of all of this! Never mind I'm having fun.

6th December 2020

Howard Jones was painting the top window frame at the front of my house last weekend. Like myself he used to live in Shiphay. This reminded me of one of my first friends called Anthony Bromell who lived next door. Anthony was about three years older than me and one of my most vivid childhood memories is walking with him up Dairy Hill when he escorted me to my first day at the junior school in Chelston. At the bottom of Dairy Hill he took me along a paved footpath to Stanbury Road. Why that moment in my life remains in my memory I do not know as I have no other memories of that day. When Anthony moved with his parents to live in Tavistock I was terribly disappointed although our parents kept in touch with each other and over the years I was very pleased to see him occasionally. Not very long after he moved from Torquay the new neighbours arrived and I can vividly recall the excitement of Tony and Kay Perry running around their new house. We soon became very good friends and had lots of happy times together as children.

13th December 2020

Lord Zarquon has now completed the recording of my song about the old Torquay fire brigade. He has recently purchased a new bass guitar which has been used for this song and his bass playing sounds very impressive on it. Towards the end of the recording he has used an effect on the bass which is very appropriately called burn!

20th December 2020

It's Chris Greenway's birthday this week. I'm not sure if he will have a happy birthday because his wife has been poorly with the covid 19 virus. I hope she is starting to feel better and Chris doesn't become ill with it. I have sent him a new version of his sixtieth birthday song with slightly different lyrics and called it the 'Sixty First Birthday Song.' If Chris is feeling a bit miserable on his birthday then I am certain that my song will cheer him up!

Lord Zarquon has finished recording my song about Claude Grahame White's pioneering flight over Torbay. I got the idea from David Scott's book about the Upton Vale Baptist Church. It contains some very interesting information about Torquay in the 19th and 20 centuries. It was a mention of the visit of the British warships to Torbay in 1910 that gave me the idea for the song.

'MR WHITE'S PIONEERING FLIGHT'

Mr Claude Grahame White
And his pioneering flight
See him fly over Torbay
From Torre Abbey meadows today

In July nineteen ten
The fleet is here again
Two hundred warships this time
The view of them is so fine

But Mr Claude Grahame White
With his pioneering flight
Above the fleet in Torbay
A warning for the admiralty today

A south westerly gale
Forced the fleet to sail
From their gathering in Mounts Bay
To a safe anchorage in Torbay

But Mr Claude Grahame White
With his pioneering flight
Above the fleet in Torbay
A warning for the admiralty today

The combined fleet is here
With King George it brings good cheer

Above the fleet he flew
To show them what he knew
For their guns could not elevate
To threaten his fragile flying crate

Mr Claude Grahame white
And his pioneering flight
In his Farman biplane
He will surely gain great fame

27th December 2020

Well I've nearly survived another year on Planet Earth. It's been a very difficult time for lots of people but I reckon I can't complain and my music has kept me happy. I will be looking forward to releasing the Torbay Pageant Part Two and the Semi Acoustic Almanac albums next year. I've got a few other musical ideas up my sleeve which should hopefully keep me busy and continue to keep me happy. Hopefully the rollout of the new vaccines will mean that it is a much happier new year for all of us.

The old drinking fountain near to my house in Torquay and which is mentioned in one of my songs.

Chapter Thirteen
Ian's Blog 2021

3rd January 2021

Several years ago Phil Swann wrote a song that was inspired from a sign which he saw when he was driving to Plymouth which said "The spirit of discovery". He wasn't very happy with the original lyrics so in recent weeks I have rewritten them. The song is about explorers like the Pilgrim Fathers from Plymouth, the Wright brothers' first aeroplane flight and the first person to climb to the summit of Everest. Phil has started recording the song using the new lyrics. On the recording Phil is playing guitars and mandolin and I have contributed the vocals, bass and keyboards. Eventually we will probably get Jules to sing it. We have also asked Martyn Hillstead to add some drums and or percussion.

'SPIRIT OF DISCOVERY'

They sailed from Plymouth's harbourside
Unchartered waters to be crossed
With prayers not to be lost
Far from the safety of the land
Of great rewards they would dream
Their eyes were all agleam

With the spirit of discovery, discovery, discovery

A few miles south of Kitty Hawk

In December 1903
To defy gravity
They launched their biplane
Nearly a minute of flight
Not reaching a great height

With the spirit of discovery, discovery, discovery

Some suceeded and I realise
Is it fair just to criticise
The mistakes of all those who have tried before

To reach out and not let go
It's in our minds because we need to know
Learning from all those who have tried before

He climbed the world's highest peak
The air so rarefied
His ambition satisfied
On the mountain high in the clouds
So many mountaineers
Have died or disappeared

With the spirit of discovery, discovery, discovery

10th January 2021

I have previously mentioned on my website about the older brother
(Christopher Churchward of my Grandad Gordon Churchward
who died at sea on the Indefatigable at the battle of Jutland. I was
told about this when I was a child by my father when I was with

him in Newton Abbot. My father showed me that the name of C M Churchward is on the war memorial in Newton Abbot. I have often thought about him, especially whenever I went past that memorial in Newton Abbot.

A few days ago I received a facebook message from Stephanie Medwell who wondered if I was related to the Christopher Churchward who was lost at sea at the battle of Jutland. She told me that she was the granddaughter of Olive Reynolds who had been engaged to be married to Christopher. I had previously had no idea that he had been engaged to be married. When I told her that I was related and knew about him she sent me some further interesting information, photos of him and postcards that he had written that I had not seen before. She told me that the last time her grandmother had seen Christopher, was after a meal at his mother's house, at the railway station in Exeter. She said that her grandmother never forgot about him and that their wedding banns had been made on the Indefatigable shortly before the ship took part in the battle of Jutland. She also sent me a photo of the wedding banns certificate signed by the chaplain of the Indefatigable.

I have shared this information with Ian Waugh who was told about Christopher by his grandmother who was a daughter of George Churchward who was the an older brother of Christopher. Ian Waugh also had no idea that Christopher had been engaged to be married shortly before he died at sea. The wedding had been planned for June 1916 with everything arranged for it such as the wedding cake and clothes.

I have now written a song about this.

'FOR CHRISTOPHER AND OLIVE'

Banns of marriage witnessed
Dated in May

On three Sundays
Before he sailed away
But for Christopher there would be no wedding day

At the station in Exeter
He said farewell
It was the last time she saw him
Such a sad tale to tell

Shells from the Von Der Tann
Screaming across the sea
Death and destruction
Created so terribly
And for Olive Reynolds bad news she would receive

At the station in Exeter
He said farewell
It was the last time she saw him
Such a sad tale to tell

She never forgot him
And her memories live on
Told to Stephanie
Now written in this song
The photographs and postcards treasured for so long

17th January 2021

I have written a comedy song about Graham Moore's tax return that has resulted in a delay in the latest album artwork. I am hopeful that when Graham has finalised his tax return he will complete the artwork for the next Legendary Ten Seconds' album.

'GRAHAM'S TAX RETURN'

Graham's completing his tax return
Dreaming of the money he could earn
Tax returns are extremely boring
With the thought of it he can't stop yawning

Tax return, tax return
Graham's completing his tax return

Graham's not completed his tax return
When will he ever learn
To get it finished straight away
Rather than leve it for another day

Tax return, tax return
Graham's not completing his tax return
Tax return, tax return
Graham's not completing his tax return

Graham's got the tax return blues
This next line will rhyme with bad news
Tax return blues, such bad news

Tax returns are a fuss and bother
He'd rather paint another album cover
Then some money he would earn
Which would then require another tax return!

24th January 2021

I had an email from Graham Moore's telling me that he laughed out loud when he listened to the demo of the tax return comedy song that I had sent to him. Lord Z has finished the recording of my song about Percy Fawcett. There are two other Torquay themed songs left for Lord Z to consider and then we can make a final decision on the track list for the Part Two Torbay Pageant album.

31st January 2021

We have finished recording the Torbay Pageant Part Two album. I have also nearly finished writing a revised version of my book about my songs. This includes information about the music that has been recorded since 2016. The new version of my book will be called Songs About Richard III Revised Edition. I have asked Lord Zarquon to design a cover for the book. I think it would be rather good if the design could be based upon one of my favourite Legendary Ten Seconds posters.

7th February 2021

I have now submitted the Pageant of Torbay Part Two album to CD Baby for the digital distribution. Here is the information for this new album:-

1) 'The Nuestra Senora Del Rosario'
2) 'John Nutt'
3) 'Cadewell House'

4) 'The Drinking Fountains of Torquay'
5) 'The Town of Torquay'
6) 'The Old Torquay Fire Brigade'
7) 'Strategies Well Planned'
8) 'Madge's Wedding'
9) 'Mr White's Pioneering Flight'
10)'Hester's Letters'
11)'Percy Fawcett'
12)'The Mysterious Affair At Styles'
13)'Come Celebrate'
14)'Dreaming of Ashfield'
15)'Torquay Museum'
16)'Cruise Ships in Torbay'
17)'The Torquay Pageant Part Two'

All songs composed by Ian Churchward except 'The Torquay Pageant Part Two' and the 'Drinking Fountains of Torquay' composed by Elaine and Ian Churchward. Musical contributions from the following:-

Ian Churchward vocals, guitar, mellotron sounds
Lord Zarquon mellotron sounds and other keyboards, bass guitar, and drums
Guy Bolt guitar solo on Strategies Well Planned
Phil Swann bouzouki and mandolin
Graham Moores guitar
Bridgit England vocals
Elaine Churchward vocals
Rowan Curle vocals

'JOHN NUTT'

John Nutt was a pirate who lived in Torbay
His crews would respect him for their regular good pay
He had an illegal business all along the coast
Of immunity from capture he could surely boast

The Lord Mayor of Dartmouth sent off an urgent plea
To the Lord Admiral of London of the danger of piracy
From John Nutt the brigand who sailed from Torbay
With sailors from the Royal Navy that he lured away

He was captured by John Eliot in sixteen twenty three
But from the secretary of state he gained his freedom successfully
This caused a scandal because the pirate was set free
And poor John Eliot was sent to prison in Marshalsea

14th February 2021

I have made a recording of my song about Christopher Marks Churchward and the battle of Jutland with Phil Swann and Martyn Hillstead. There is now a link to it on a battle of Jutland website.

21st Febraury 2021

My friend John Dike has sent me lots of images of his old Torquay postcard collection and I have written a song about them. It is my intention to make a video using my new song and the images of the old postcards.

28th February 2021

On Monday I spoke to the organiser of the annual Agatha Chrisite festival in Torquay. Apparently someone complained about the content of my song and video about Agatha Christie's house in Torquay because it didn't contain the blue prints for the plan of the property!!! The festival organiser deleted the comment on you tube which I thought was a bit of a shame.

On Tuesday morning I was interviewed via the internet by Peter Cartwright of Riviera FM and this was included in his lunchtime radio show on Friday. You can hear me about two thirds of the way into the show.

7th March 2021

I have been exchanging emails with Stephanie Medwell and I have just discovered that her grandmother's sister used to live in Shiphay. In actual fact in the same road where my sister lives, literally opposite her house. Like myself, Stephanie remembers the prefabs in Wallace Avenue in Shiphay.

14th March 2021

Last week I had a great idea for a new guitar riff and I decided to see if I could use this for a new song. I then decided to see if I could write a new one about the battle of Jutland and here are the lyrics for the new song.

'THE BATTLE OF JUTLAND'

They departed from the Firth of Forth
While the German fleet sailed North

Sailing towards that fateful day
A naval battle at the end of May

The Germans had hoped to lure and trap
A portion of the British fleet
But their signals were decrypted
And Jellicoe's larger fleet
Admiral Scheer would meet

They departed from Scapa Flow
To the south they would go
Sailing towards that fateful day
A naval battle at the end of May

The Germans had hoped to lure and trap
A portion of the British fleet
But their signals were decryted
And Jellicoe's larger fleet
Admiral Scheer would meet

In the run to the south
On the British ships was wrought
The German superb gunnery
As the battle cruisers fought

21st March 2021

Have I previously mentioned the Semi Acoustic Almanac on this blog? I can't remember if I have. This has been mainly recorded with Phil Swann and Martyn Hillstead and follows on from the Acoustic Almanac as a separate project from the recordings with Lord Z. I guess it is a bit like Lord Z's Prophet's project (although the music is completely different in style) except that I'm using the LTS brand name for both of my musical ventures. Could be a bit confusing of course.

For the time being I have decided not to get any CDs duplicated for the Pageant of Torbay Part Two album as I want to see if I can sell the Torbay Pageant Part One CDs at local lectures provided we come out of lockdown in the summer. Depending on this I will then consider duplicating CDs for the Part Two album.

28th March 2021

Having recently written a song about terrible tenants I have now written a song about a fictitious terrible landlord.

'GRAHAM THE GREEDY LANDLORD'

Graham was a greedy landlord
Who charged extortionate rent
He owned lots of properties
Throughout the county of Kent

He had a very lavish life style
And owned a fast sports car
Dining at expensive restaurants
With champagne and caviar

Graham was a greedy landlord
Who charged extortionate rent
His tenants were caught in a poverty trap
And of this they would often lament

He went on expensive holidays
Drinking coktails in the sun
Dreaming of his rents rolling in
Always looking after number one

Graham showed no mercy
If his tenants couldn't pay their rent
He'd kick them out as soon as he could
Into the street they were sent

Graham was a greedy landlord
Who charged extortionate rent
He owned lots of properties
Throughout the county of Kent

He had a clever accountant
So he never had to pay any tax
With complicated trust accounts
He would always cover his tracks

4th April 2021

Last weekend I recorded two jingles for Peter Cartwright of Riviera
FM which I think he will use for his radio show. This has given
me the idea for a new album which would start and end with the
radio jingles and would have songs all about various aspects of the
county of Devon. I have written several unreleased songs already
about this subject matter and I have started sending new recordings
to Lord Zarquon for him to consider. So far this year I have been
mainly recording with Phil Swann but now I intend to concentrate

on mainly recording with Lord Zarquon (I can hear him groan as he reads this while Phil breathes a sigh of huge relief!). I will also try to write and record some new songs with Martyn Hillstead who has written some very good lyrics which have resulted in some excellent songs over the last twelve months or so.

11th April 2021

A small section of music recorded from the Mer de Mort album has been used to introduce the recent Mortimer History Society lectures. I instantly recognised my mandola and the sound of Lord Zarquon's keyboards when I started watching the introdction to one of the lectures but I didn't recognise the tune. I then asked Lord Z to listen to it on you tube and he didn't recognise it either and we then began to wonder if perhaps it hadn't been recorded by us. I then decided to listen to the Mer de Mort album to see if I could find it on the album. I thought that perhaps it was the introduction to one of the songs but I eventually found that it is taken from the middle instrumental section of 'The Round Table' song.

18th April 2021

A few days ago I wrote a song about a smuggler who was born in Beer, South East Devon called Jack Rattenbury. I am now trying to concentrate on writing songs with a Devon theme. For the time being I have parked my comedy album idea despite having written enough songs for it. Later this year I am also hoping to release another album of songs that I have recorded with Phil Swann and Martyn Hillstead. The only thing that is left to do to complete this is the album the artwork and the addition of some vocals to a few of the songs.

'JACK RATTENBURY'

Jack Rattenbury the smuggler
Was born in the village of Beer
Where his family lived in poverty
With no comfort throughout the year
Jack Rattenbury the smuggler
Was born in the village of Beer

His father was pressganged
And was never seen again
Jack was the oldest child
And sought work with the fishermen

Jack became a smuggler
All around the coast of beer
Chased by custom officials
Of the risks he had no fear
Jack became a smuggler
All around the coast of beer

He was a local hero
Giving money to the poor
With lots of trusted friends
To protect him from the law

His memoirs were published
In eighteen thirty seven
And I wonder if Jack
Is a smuggler up in heaven

I do wonder if Jack
Is a smuggler up in heaven

Jack became a smuggler
All around the coast of beer
Chased by custom officials
Of the risks he had no fear
Jack became a smuggler
All around the coast of beer

He was a local hero
Giving money to the poor
With lots of trusted friends
To protect him from the law
Lots of trusted friends
To protect him from the law

25th April 2021

There is a song about Perkin Warbeck on one of my Ricardian albums which I wrote several years ago while on holiday in Scotland. Last Sunday I finished writing a second song about this pretender to the English throne.

'AT THE GATES OF EXETER'

A young pretender to the throne
His real name is still not known
Came to the West Country with intent
A warning to the Tudor king was sent

He raised his standard at Penzance
Towards Exeter he would advance
Gathering supporters along the way
He was Richard of York some do say

At the gates of Exeter he arrived
And to force an entrance he duly tried
Attacks on the North and East gates failed
The defence of Exeter prevailed

2nd May 2021

I received some exciting news from Dave Clifford last week. He has been able to find his friend Carl Hutson on Linkedin. Dave shared a flat in Brentford with Carl and played him the short recording that I had made of a Decontrol gig. Carl called the recording the Legendary ten Seconds! Dave had lost touch with Carl many years ago so it is great news that they have now made contact with each other.

9th May 2021

Lord Zarquon has been busy since we started the Songs About Devon music project. So far he has finished the recording of six songs for this album. I have also been in contact with Graham Moores who is in the process of creating the album cover.

16th May 2021

I received an email last Sunday to tell me about my music being played on some local radio shows. The songs Old Family Photos and Country Fayre on EVRV (Phonic FM) and Strange Daze (Soundart Radio).

23rd May 2021

There is a new article about the Torbay songs of the Legendary Ten Seconds on the People's Republic of South Devon website. Lord Zarquon has included a link to this on the blog page of our website.

30th May 2021

I have written another new song. It is the first time that I have written one about North Devon.

'THE FLOODING OF LYNMOUTH'

One night in August
There was an awful storm
A tidal wave of water
To Lynmouth it was borne

Trees, boulders and debris
Thrown so violently
The worst flood in England
That we've ever seen

The bridges collapsed
The houses were destroyed
The deadly flood water

They could not avoid

Trees, boulders and debris
Thrown so violently
The worst flood in England
That we've ever seen

Lynmouth was destroyed during that night
In the morning they surveyed an awful sight

6th June 2021

Work continues on the Songs About Devon music project. Drums and bass have now been recorded for several new songs including the ones about Plymouth in the Second World War and the terrible Lynmouth flood in the 1950s. Here are the lyrics for my latest song:-

'HAYTOR GRANITE'

This granite tramway that you see
Was built in eighteen twenty
For Haytor granite was in demand
Used in construction throughout the land

London bridge was built of it
Over the river Thames to sit
Also used at Ludgate Circus
The stone has such a fine surface

This granite tramway that you see
Was built in eighteen twenty

For Haytor granite was in demand
Used in construction throughout the land

There's Haytor stone on Cathedral green
The finest cross I've ever seen
For those lost in the First World War
To remember them for ever more

Stover house such a grand home
Is also made of Haytor stone
Throughout the country you may roam
And you might see the Haytor stone

This granite tramway that you see
Was built in eighteen twenty
For Haytor granite was in demand
Used in construction throughout the land

13th June 2021

Someone in Austin, Texas likes listening to my songs about Richard III. Last week they listened to my songs 66 times on Apple music. The week before that it was 41 times while in that week someone in Houston, Texas listened to my songs 87 times. The week before that it was 56 times. The week of the 4th June 2021 was probably my best ever week for people listening to my music on Apple music with a total of 186 plays.

20th June 2021

On Tuesday I met up with Phil Swann and Martyn Hillstead in Teignmouth on a glorious sunny evening to have some photos taken of us together. The photos will be used for publicity purposes. We did consider going to a nearby pub but we were told that it was extremely crowded so we just enjoyed the nice weather and scenery.

27th June 2021

Last Sunday afternoon I started to get a new idea for a song while I was listening to Torquay United lose the National League play off final on BBC Radio Devon. In the evening I had a reasonable idea of the chord structure for a verse but I didn't have any lyrics. I was trying to think of an idea for the lyrics based upon the mood that the chords created in my head. It made me think of Torbay on a sunny summer's afternoon and then I thought about the man that draws patterns in the sand at low tide on Torquay sea front. By Monday moring I had written a new song based upon this article

4th July 2021

A revised edition of my book about my songs has now been published in digital only format. The original version of Songs About Richard III was published in 2016 and this revised edition includes details of the songs which have been recorded up until the end of 2020.

11th July 2021

I have made a video for Lord Zarquon's birthday using the comedy song of 'God Help Lord Zarquon'. This song uses the tune of the 'God Help the Marshal' song.

18th July 2021

I am currently reading a couple of books. One of them is called Devon and Cornwall's Oddest Historical Tales by John Fisher. So far I have written three new songs after reading the first three chapters of this book. I have also written a song about when Lord Zarquon lost his Lordly status on facebook.

25th July 2021

There is a demo version of 'The Year of Three Kings' which I have just released via Amuse.

1st August 2021

Phil Swann has recorded some very nice finger picked acoustic guitar for my song about Jack Rattenbury. On Wednesday I decided to play and record a much better guitar solo for it.

8th August 2021

Graham Moores has sent me a low resolution first draft of the artwork for the Songs About Devon album. I am hoping that Lord Zarquon will finish the recordings of a couple further songs for this album. He is currently reviewing one about Perkin Warbeck's siege of Exeter during the reign of Henry VII.

15th August 2021

Phil Swann has recently recorded some guitar for my song about the Siege of Plymouth during the English civil war of the 17th century. I have written a new song about an eighty four year old lady called Mary Kelynack who walked all the way from Newlyn in Cornwall to London to see the Great Exhibition in the Crystal Palace. This was during the reign of Queen Victoria. I would like to use these songs for an album which I might call Songs of the South West. Some other songs that could be included on such an album have a Spanish theme, one about Catherine of Aragon arriving in Plymouth and another about the Spanish Armada. I recorded Ashley Dyer playing trumpet for these two songs and Martyn Hillstead has recorded some drums for the new Spanish Armada song. This is the third song that I have composed about the Spanish Armada and on Wednesday evening I really enjoyed recording myself playing bass guitar for it.

22nd August 2021

The recordings for the Songs About Devon album have been completed. I am due to see Lord Zarquon tomorrow so that I can obtain the files for two of the songs. I can then add the introductions recorded by Peter Cartwright to those two songs.

29th August 2021

Graham Moores has now sent me the completed Songs About Devon album cover. I should now be able to complete the submission to CD Baby to start the process of getting it onto Apple Music, Spotify, Youtube and Amazon etc.

5th September 2021

It was Mum's funeral on Tuesday and this is the eulogy for her:-

Molly was born on 4th July 1929 in Launceston to Clara and Stanley, younger sister to Betty. They moved to Hoopern Street in Exeter in 1939 when for her dad's work on the South Western Railway. Molly went to Episcopal School – her great claim to fame was winning an English prize – most disappointed to receive a copy of the "Vicar of Wakefield" which she never read!

Of course the family lived through the Exeter Blitz and Molly would tell the tale of coming back from the Anderson shelter to find her underwear hanging on a picture frame, always regaled with great amusement. Once the family were using a torch to sweep up some broken glass following a raid – the whole of Exeter was ablaze, but they were nevertheless asked by the air raid warden to put the light out because Jerry might see it!!

Molly left school at 14 and undertook a secretarial course, her first job was in a building society, then she worked for a firm of solicitors called Ford Simey and Ford at Cathedral Close, and at their office in Exmouth. Molly met Geoff at the Wrentham Hall in Exeter where they went to dances. After marrying in 1951 they moved to Radstock for Geoff's work as a teacher. Molly then had a number of jobs, her least favourite being Dents Gloves where she gave in her notice within the first week as she refused to co-operate with the rule of having to put your hand up to ask permission to go to the toilet! After a spell with Frys confectioners she then worked very happily for Prattens, a local building company and made many good friends. In 1960 they moved to Pinhoe for Geoff to work at Exeter college and welcomed the arrival of Ian in 1961. In 1963 they moved to Grosvenor Avenue in Torquay for Geoff to work at South Devon College and welcomed Linda in 1964. It was a happy home with lots of fun

Molly was a full time mum until Linda started at Junior school in 1971 and then began a part time job with the Torbay Holiday agency, and she worked there with them until she finally retired in 1999. Geoff sadly passed away in 1997, but Molly was a capable, resourceful independent and joyful person, and made the most of her retirement enjoying the company of good friends and family. She was a wonderful Nan to Tom, Emma and Holly – when the children went to stay everything else was put on hold to spend time with them - they were her priority. She made Gentian and Guy, Ian's step children very welcome in the family and when their children came along enjoyed family occasions with them. She was lucky to have lots of good friends, and in particular enjoyed many holidays with Maureen, she was a regular swimmer at the ERC and enjoyed meeting "the girls" for coffee. Daily walks on the seafront befriending and chatting to anyone who might be sitting next to her on a bench was common.

By late 2018 Molly needed full time care and moved into Cornerways in Paignton, here she was well looked after by a wonderful care team and her family are grateful the love and attention she received.

12th September 2021

I have now completed the submission of the Songs About Devon album to CD Baby. My wife heard me checking some of the audio for this and when she heard Peter Cartwright's spoken introductions she thought that I was listening to his radio show. This is exactly how I want it to sound to the listener. From start to finish it sounds like it is being played on Peter Cartwright's radio show on Riviera FM in Torbay! It start's with one of my jingles for his show, followed by his first introduction and at the end of the last track is my second radio jingle.

One of the songs on the album is about the Canadian Foresters who came to Stover in Devon during the First World War. Most of the lyrics for this song were written by Martyn Hillstead after he had visited Stover.

19th September 2021

I have now made a short promotional video for the next album of the Legendary Ten Seconds.

26th September 2021

Coming to terms with Mum's illness was very difficult. When she started to lose her memory it was like losing her and then when she passed away in August it felt terrible. I also felt very sad when I heard that the actor John Challis had recently died. It was only just over 2 years ago that we recorded him reading the narratives for the Mortimer History Society album and also helping with the Mortimer comedy song. Several people that I have come into contact via my Legendary Ten Seconds music project have now died over the last few years.

3rd October 2021

Last weekend I spent most of Saturday at Torquay museum and enjoyed some very interesting lectures about the local history of Torbay. The first lecture was given by Dr James Kneale, associate professor UCL, which was about the Salvation Army being persecuted by the local authorities in Torquay in 1888. One of the other lectures was given by the local historian Kevin Dixon who has an article about the Salvation Army's problems in late Victorian

Torquay on this website. The next day I decided to write a song about this. Here are the lyrics:-

'THEY KEPT ON MARCHING'

The Salvation Army was marching in Torquay
With the sound of a trumpet and a joyful tambourine
Sustaining their challenge to authority
This confrontation caused such a public scene

They'd marched through the town
Unmolested for six years
Saving many souls
Like God's new pioneers

The Salvation Army was marching in Torquay
With the sound of a trumpet and a joyful tambourine
Sustaining their challenge to authority
This confrontation caused such a public scene

The local board passed
A new harbourside act
In the thirty eighth clause
Was a little known fact

No procession was allowed
On any Sunday
Except of the military
So the act did say

To the Salvation Army many fines were handed out

Prison sentences served of that there is no doubt

The Salvation Army kept on marching in Torquay
With the sound of a trumpet and a joyful tambourine
Sustaining their challenge to authority
This confrontation caused such a public scene

10th October 2021

The Songs About Devon album is now listed on Amazon and Apple Music with a release date of 23rd October

17th October 2021

I had a very enjoyable recording session with Jay Brown and Jules Jones on Monday. Jay played guitar, keyboards and tambourine on my song about the Salvation Army and I recorded Jules Jones singing on the chorus of it. I now need to pass this one on to Lord Z. A couple of weeks ago I recorded a new song based upon some lyrics with a First World War theme written by Annie Routley. The lyrics were given to Lord Z and then passed on to me to see if I could use them for a new song. On Friday Lord Z finished mastering the recording and I am very pleased with the sound of it.

24th October 2021

Here is a list of the people that feature on the new Songs About Devon album:-

Ian Churchward vocals, guitars, mandola, mandolin and Mellotron keyboard sounds
Lord Zarquon bass guitar, drums and Mellotron keyboard sounds
Martyn Hillstead drums and percussion
Phil Swann guitars, mandolin and bouzouki
Ashley Dyer trumpet
Bridgit England vocals and violin
Elaine Churchward backing vocals
Violet Sheer backing vocals
Peter Cartwright introductions
Album artwork Graham Moores

31st October 2021

David Hinchcliffe sent me an email on Tuesday to let me know that he gave a talk in Galmpton about the 1920s Torquay Pageant on the previous Friday. He said that he played my Torquay Pageant music and video as a recap at the end of his lecture. Also on Thursday the Tudor Society added a link to my new song about Perkin Warbeck on their website.

7th November 2021

The Brixham Mayflower song has been included on the Acoutstic Routes radio show number 371. You can hear my song about 8 minutes from the beginning of the show. It's just after a song by Jim Causley which also has a Devon theme. Jim is the grandson of George Causley who was a brother of my grandad Stan. George married Phyllis and they then had a son Ross who is Jim's Dad.

14th November 2021

A new article about how Peter Cartwright of Riviera FM helped with the recording of the Songs About Devon album has just been posted onto his radio station's website. Also the song about Martyn Hillstead moving from Birmingham to live in Teignmouth (many years ago) was included rather appropriately on a Birmingham based radio show called Brum Radio. It is presented by Mike Davies for his Alternative Roots show.

21st November 2021

My Ricardian songs continue to be the most popular ones that I have written so I felt that I ought to try to compose another one. In my new song called 'John De Vere' I tell the story about the Lancastrian Earl of Oxford capturing St Michael's Mount during the reign of Edward VI.

28th November 2021

For most of this year I became so engrossed in the Songs About Devon music project, also planning an album of South West songs that I nearly forgot about several songs I had recorded with Phil Swann and Martyn Hillstead that we had originally intended for an album project that never came to fruition. A few weeks ago I gave these unfinished recordings to Lord Zarquon who has been beavering away at completing them in his recording studio. A couple of these recordings have now been completed and eventually there should be enough for another album.

One of the songs is a version of a traditional folk tune/sea shanty called 'The Wellerman'. The completon of this recording is a bit of a land mark for the Legendary Ten Seconds and is the first time that we have completed the recording of a tradional song. This won't be anything to do with the South West songs which I am also currently recording with Lord Zarquon.

5th December 2021

An article about one of my songs has been published in the Mid Devon Advertiser. It is the song which tells the story of Chris Churchward who died at the battle of Jutland.

12th December 2021

Jules and Jay came over to see me on Monday and I recorded Jay playing bass on my new songs, 'Sir Cloudsley Shovell' and 'Haytor Granite'. Another one was the recording of a traditional song called 'A Man You Don't Meet Every Day'. Lord Z finished the mastering of this traditional song on Thursday. Later in the week Rowan Curle came to stay for a few days and I recorded him singing some harmony vocals on the chorus of 'Sir Cloudsley Shovell' and my new song called 'Cornish Folklore'.

'SIR CLOUDSLEY SHOVELL'

Now gather round and hear this tale
Of Sir Cloudsley Shovell
He was a hero you should know
Who gave the French much trouble

It was a stormy autumn night
Near the Isles of Scilly
The charts were inaccurate

And this would cost him dearly

HMS Association
Sunk by the Isles of Scilly
Two thousand sailors drowned that night
A tragedy quite clearly

His flagship struck the Gilstone reef
Of the Isles of Scilly
Longitude and latitude
Were confused and queried

The Eagle and Romney lost
Sunk by the Isles of Scilly
Two thousand sailors drowned that night
A tragedy quite clearly

They found his body washed ashore
On a cove of St Mary's
Of Those deadly Western rocks
Brave sailors must be wary

And Firebrand struck the Western rocks
Of the Isles of Scilly
Two thousand sailors drowned that night
A tragedy quite clearly

19th December 2021

It's the 62nd birthday of Chris Greenway in a few days time and I have recorded a new version of his birthday song. I have also made a special CD cover for him including a photo of where he lives in Exmouth.

26th December 2021

Another Christmas day has been celebrated and another year draws to a close.

A photo of Christopher Marks Churchward with my grandfather which was sent to me by Stephanie Medwell.

Chapter Fourteen
Richard the Three

At the time of writing this book the following song remains unfinished, probably because Lord Zarquon isn't very interested in it. The words for this comedy song were mostly written by John Morey. I tweaked a few of the lines, for instance the line "Don't bury me in Leicester I'm a York City fan". I then worked out some music to go with the words and this song was included on the CD that I sent to some of my friends at Christmas. I believe that John Morey was inspired to write the lyrics after hearing me perform several of my Ricardian songs at the Red Rock near Bishopsteignton.

'RICHARD THE THREE'

This song tells a story of true history
Of a king in battle, King Richard the Three
He faced rebellion on Bosworth Field
In a fight to the death to make Henry yield
A fight to the death to make Henry yield

To make henry yield, to make Henry yield
In a fight to the death to make Henry yield

One day in August he stayed overnight
At the Blue Boar inn which was actually white
Before the name changed so it was said
After he lost his crown to the victorious reds
He lost his crown to the victorious reds

Victorious reds, victorious reds
After he lost his crown to the victorious reds

Through westgate in Leicester he made his way
With ten thousand men for a one night stay
They camped out of town upon Ambion Hill
Drank too much ale and made themselves ill
Drank too much ale and made themselves ill

Made themselves ill, made themselves ill
Drank too much ale and made themselves ill

The king never slept in any old bed
He took his own with him a flat pack instead
A right royal camp bed was his idea
Specially made there was no Ikea
Specially made there was no Ikea

Was no Ikea, was no Ikea
Specially made there was no Ikea

Against Henry's army five thousand strong
To win should be easy what could go wrong
At Bosworth Field they faced one another
Just to one side the two Stanley brothers
Just to one side the two Stanley brothers

The two Stanley brothers, the two Stanley brothers
Just to one side the two Stanley brothers

Which side would they favour, who would win

At the start of the day Richard thought it was him
The cannons roared as battle commenced
Those rats the Stanleys sitting on the fence
Those rats the Stanleys sitting on the fence

Sitting on the fence, sitting on the fence
Those rats the Stanleys sitting on the fence

Tragedy loomed to kick Richard's arse
The Stanleys decided to have the last laugh
Treason cried Richard as he heard their plan
Don't bury me in Leicester I'm a York city fan
Don't bury me in Leicester I'm a York city fan

A York city fan, a York city fan
Don't bury me in Leicester I'm a York city fan

They displayed his body I've heard it was said
At a visitors centre to prove he was dead
There's more to this tale but I've run out of time
Some say he deserved it some call it a crime
Some say he deserved it some call it a crime

Call it a crime, call it a crime
Some say he deserved it some call it a crime

In a car park you say his bones were interred
Why pick such a place it seems so absurd
Did they hide him away in a grave they'd just rented
To wait years and years till cars were invented

At the entrance to the Richard III visitor centre in Leicester.

Acknowledgements
With a Little Help From my Friends

I would like to thank the following, not necessarily in historical order:-

My Mum and Dad, because without them I wouldn't be here (Dad I am so sorry you tripped over my guitar case and hurt your ankle all those years ago).

My sister Linda Beard, for showing me the basics of how to play guitar.

Pam Benstead, for helping to spread the word about my Richard III music project.

John Bessant for playing lap steel guitar on the instrumental 'Lambeth MS474'.

Rob Blaikie, for playing the mandolin on 'York City Fair'.

Guy Bolt, for playing the snare drum on 'Fanfare for the King' tambourine on 'Jewel of Middleham' and contributing to some of my other songs.

Andy Botterill, of Pastime Records.

Susan Bounaparte, of Loyalty Binds Us for selling my CDs.

Malcom Bowen, for pointing out that I am 'Ricard Ian!'

Rob Bright, for his guitar and banjo playing on my songs.

Jeremy Brimicombe for being such a good friend.

Jay Brown for playing bass on some of my songs.

John Challis for his great comedy vocals on the song about the Mortimers.

Elaine Churchward, for being my wife, singing on my songs, writing some of the best words for my songs and putting up with my obsession with all things Richard III.

Tom Churchward, for playing the melodeon on 'Tewkesbury Tale' and 'Richard Liveth Yet' and contributing to some of my other songs.

David Clifford, for playing bass on some of the songs on the Murrey and Blue album.

Steve Collings, for singing on 'Richard the Three'.

Jackson Cooper, for playing my songs on his radio show.

Steve Dungey for buying my albums.

Ashley Dyer, for his trumpet playing.

Bridgit England for her wonderful harmony vocals.

Shirley Hall for taking a great interest in all of my songs about Richard III.

Georgie Harman for her wonderful album artwork.

Sandra Heath Wilson, for her narratives, letting me use some of her words for my songs and help with editing this book.

Debby Helmore, for arranging for me to be able to borrow a copy of the Arthur Kincaid book about Sir George Buck via Torquay library.

Phil Helmore, for singing on a couple of my songs.

Martyn Hillstead for playing drums and percussion.

Steve Honeywill, for selling me his tape recorder, without which I could not have recorded the punk rock band that gave me The Legendary Ten Seconds.

Jackie Hudson, for her pickles and singing.

Philip Hume, for all his help with the Mer de Mort album.

Carl Hutson, for calling my tape recording of the punk rock band The Legendary Ten Seconds.

Wayne Ingalls, for sharing my music on the USA Richard III society facebook page.

Judy Jacobs, for selling some of my CDs and helping to write some narratives that were read by Camilla at a gig in Guildford.

Jingle and DD from the band Gentian, for singing on 'By Hearsay'.

Camilla Joyce, for her singing.

Jules Jones for her singing.

Mary Jo Kalbfleisch, for her words of encouragement.

Susan Lamb, for giving me the inspiration for the songs 'Ambion Hill' and 'Hollow Crown'.

Joanne Larner, for mentioning The Legendary Ten Seconds in her books and her review of my gig at Stony Stratford.

Matthew Lewis, for his 'Richard III' narratives.

Ashley Mantle for his help with the songs for the Mer de Mort album.

Kathy Martin, for the wonderful Francis Cranley novels and the introduction for this book.

Adrian Maxwell for playing drums for the Legendary Ten Seconds at the Summer Moon festival.

Mike Middleton, for playing the bass guitar on 'York City Fair'.

Dick Milner for buying my albums.

Graham Moores, for his artwork.

John Morey, for 'Richard the Three'.

Richard Napier, for all his driving for The Legendary Ten Seconds in Colorado.

The NBT radio station, for playing so many of my songs.

Elke Paxson, for writing about my songs.

Frances Quinn, for letting me use some of her poetry and artwork for my songs.

Pete and Dawn Shafer, for looking after The Legendary Ten Seconds in Breckenridge.

Jeff Sleeman, for allowing me to play some of my songs about Richard III on his radio show.

Dominic Smee, for helping with a video recording for my 'Confort Liesse' instrumental at the Bosworth Heritage centre.

Phil Swann for his bouzouki, mandolin and guitar playing.

Sam Swann for his bass playing on some of my songs.

Joe Strummer, for giving me the inspiration to try to play a guitar.

Robert Temple for buying my albums.

Karla Tipton for reviewing my music.

Pippa West for her singing.

Lord Zarquon, for investing so much of his time on the recording of the songs, the website of the Legendary Ten Seconds and book cover design.

Everyone at the Red Rock, who has sung along on the chorus of 'The Year of Three Kings'!

Apologies to anyone else that I have forgotten to thank.

The Legendary Ten Seconds outside my house in Torquay in 2015.

Appendix One
A List of Mainly Ricardian Books

Here is a list of most of the Ricardian books I have read which have helped me to write my Ricardian songs but which I haven't mentioned previously. Apologies to any Ricardian authors for their books that I have not yet read or any that I have read and I have forgotten to include in this list.

Bosworth by Michael Jones
Cicely's King Richard by Sandra Heath Wilson
Cicely's Second King by Sandra Heath Wilson
Cicely's Lord Lincoln by Sandra Heath Wilson
Eleanor the Secret Queen by John Ashdown-Hill
Elizabeth Woodville by David Baldwin
Honour by Matthew Lewis
Loyalty by Matthew Lewis
On the Trail of the Mortimers by Philip Hume
Sovereign by C J Sansom
The Adventure of the Bloody Tower by Donald MacLachlan
The Art of War in the Middle Ages, Volume II, by Sir Charles Oman
The Deceivers by Geoffrey Richardson
The King's Niece by Liz Orwin
The Lordly Ones by Geoffrey Richardson
The Seventh Son by Reay Tannahill
The Wars of the Roses by Matthew Lewis
The Wars of the Roses by Trevor Royle
What Could Possibly Go Wrong by Jodi Taylor
The White Princess by Philippa Gregory
The Wrath of Kings by Philip Photiou
White Rose, Golden Sunnes by J P Reedman

Appendix Two

The Full-Length Narratives for the Loyalty Binds Me Version of the Loyaulté me Lie Album

There are no narratives on the original release of the first Richard III concept album by The Legendary Ten Seconds, but I had an idea that I suggested to my friend Sandra Heath Wilson for a new version of the Loyaulté Me Lie album. These would once again be narratives, but unlike those on Tant le Desiree and Richard III, these could be in the form of an exchange of letters between Cecily, Duchess of York, and her daughter Margaret, Duchess of Burgundy.

Sandra liked this idea and set about writing these fictional letters. When finished, they seemed to need shortening, for the listener to follow the exchanges with ease. Much like a conversation. Matt's narratives were entirely different, and benefited from being much longer.

We have reduced the length of the letter narratives for the eventual recording, but here they are as originally written.

(1)

Margaret of York to her mother . . . .

Summertime, the Year of Grace 1468. Right worshipful and entirely beloved mother, I recommend me to your heart and pray that I am in yours. Already my heart breaks of missing you, and all your smiles and kindnesses that I crave. My husband is without the charm of York, but I must also concede that he is also the hauteur and falsity of Lancaster. Which, God pray, will never return to blight England. His little daughter from his first marriage is a delight, as is his mother, even though she is Lancastrian by descent. But for that I cannot blame her.

How fares the queen? I hear whispers that she is hopeful of carrying again? Will it be a son this time? Two daughters will not do for Edward. All kings need sons. Perhaps, had he wed a princess, not a calculating Lancastrian widow who lied about being with child, fate would have favoured him more. Can he really have believed her tears on having "lost" that first babe at a mere three months . . . ? I know I did not. It was a device to get his ring on her finger. And then came the ravening hordes of her Woodville family. The Almighty preserve us all from their ambition and greed.

Oh, how I yearn to reverse time itself, and return to those happy days of childhood, when we attended the fair in York city . . .

(Song: YORK CITY FAYRE)

(2)

Cecily, Duchess of York, to her daughter . . . .

April, in the Year of Our Lord 1471. Greetings, my cherished daughter. It pleases my mother's heart to have received word from you, but it pleases me even more to confirm that which you will already know; the House of Lancaster and the weathervane Earl of Warwick have been vanquished at a place called Barnet. Warwick is dead, God destroy his treacherous soul, and *that weak-minded, monkish fellow, Henry VI, now languishes in the Tower. It is to be regretted that his whelp and vixen queen are safely in France. Oh, how iniquitous that you and Margaret of Anjou should share a name!*

Your brother Edward is secure on the throne and, and reconciled with your other brother, foolish George. Oh, so foolish, believing his father-in-law Warwick would put him on the throne in Edward's stead. Then seeing the truth when Warwick gave his younger daughter, Anne, to the Lancastrian Prince of Wales. So, back came George, to throw himself upon Edward's mercy. Which was forthcoming, of course. I pity the Lady Anne, for she did not seek the Lancastrian match, and I am told her new husband, although only a youth, is cruel and heartless.

There is still more sibling trouble ahead, I fear, for the heart of your youngest brother, my dearly beloved Richard, has been broken because Anne was wed to another. His love is deeply engaged. I do not know what will ensue from all this, daughter, but it will be stormy between your three brothers.

I must end now, for the messenger awaits, but yet must tell you that the queen has presented Edward with the desired son. A Woodville has done something useful at last! Ah, but I wrong at least one of that voracious brood, for her brother, Lord Anthony Woodville, is surely a credit to them. A learned man and talented writer, to say nothing of a dashing spectacle in the joust. And he is a Woodville? The age of miracles is surely not past.

But fate is cruel to you, my dearest daughter, deciding you shall be childless. I fear our shared consolation must be the victory at Barnet . . .

(Song: THE BATTLE OF BARNET)

(3)

Margaret, Duchess of Burgundy to her mother . . . .

The sweet month of August, the Year of Grace, 1472. Right, most beloved and honoured Mother, I greet you from the bottom of my heart, for you are surely in my thoughts at every moment. I have received your letter of 13th July and am 'twixt joy and despair at the news contained therein.

The joy, of course, is that Richard and Anne are now wed, and will soon make their home at Middleham. At least, I hope such joy is well-placed, for I have heard whispers that she was in love with her first husband. Surely an impossibility, for he was a vicious tick, but we women do not always show sense when it comes to the heart. Thanks be to God Almighty that the noxious fellow perished at the Battle of Tewkesbury. Not a moment too soon, I fancy. But, Anne is now Duchess of Gloucester, and had better be a good and loving duchess to her duke, for Richard is a prince in every meaning of the word.

George, however, can be all that is not princely. Hence my despair. How unspeakable he has been, trying to imprison Anne to prevent Richard from making her his wife. Why cannot George be satisfied with Isabel's half of the Warwick inheritance? Why must he be so selfish and grasping as to try to keep Anne's portion as well? I will warrant that Edward's good temper is shortening by the day. Where George is concerned, at least. I know mine is!

Yet Edward cannot be displeased with Sir Anthony Woodville, who decked himself with laurels at the expedition to save Brittany from the French. Would that he was not a Woodville! But if there is to be one of them eventually in charge of the little of Prince of Wales at Ludlow, I suppose he will be the best of a bad lot.

But it is of Richard and Anne that I must think now. They have gone to their new life together at Middleham, and I wish God's blessings on them both . . .

(Song: LOYALTY BINDS ME)

(4)

Cecily, Duchess of York, to her daughter . . . .

Written at the end of April in the Year of Grace 1483. Greetings and a mother's eternally loving and protective embrace to a daughter whose presence on this earth she will always treasure.

King Edward is dead. Oh, I can hardly bear to write it. He was still young, but there is no denying his licentious and self-indulgent way of life is to blame. On his deathbed he named Richard as Lord Protector, to guard both the realm and Edward's eldest son, the new boy-king. This was Edward's command, given on his deathbed, but Richard is far away in the North and must ride south to take up his role, and in the meantime it is said that the Woodville woman and her wolf pack of a family are plotting against him. Pray with me, daughter, for Richard's safety is of the utmost importance to us both. He is such a loyal and honourable man, the finest brother Edward could have had, but he is alone. My last remaining son, and the most beloved to me.

George, of course, invited his own tragic end five years ago. Why, oh why did he continue to scheme against Edward and cause such endless trouble? Edward did all he could to be lenient, but in the end had no choice but to imprison and condemn him. Richard strove with all his might to plead for clemency, but Edward's mind was set. George was under attainder at his death, and now that shadow hangs over his children. Foolish George was foolish to the end.

But I digress. Daughter, I have heard alarming whispers that the queen orders her brother, Sir Anthony Woodville, to bring the new king to London from Ludlow with all speed. They mean to see the boy crowned King Edward V before Richard can take up his responsibility as Lord Protector. I fear they mean to eliminate him from his duty . . . and from this earth. If this is true, Sir Anthony is revealed to be a treacherous Woodville after all, and totally unworthy of my good opinion. A knight without chivalry, a lord without a shred of loyalty in his Judas body!

(Song: LORD ANTHONY WOODVILLE)

(5)

Margaret, Duchess of Burgundy, to her mother.

Penned June, 1483, in the first year of England's Lord Protector, Richard, Duke of Gloucester. I greet you, honoured lady mother, and pray this finds you in good health and spirits.

How right you were concerning Sir Anthony Woodville. He well deserved to have his head separated from his body at Pontefract for having set himself on his sister's side, opposing Richard. And when her wicked, treasonous machinations failed, Sir Anthony paid the price. She, of course, languishes safely in sanctuary with her daughters, and her sons are lodged in the comfort of the royal apartments at the Tower. Poor Richard, he did not seek any of this, but his loyalty and honest conscience compelled him carry out Edward's wishes. At least he is now Lord Protector, and will prove himself to be a wise, just and good lord to the realm. And a wise, just and good uncle to the new king, Edward V.

But Mother, all manner of rumours are reaching me. Tell me truly, was my brother Edward IV really married already when he made his vows with the Woodville woman? Are all his children baseborn? Was Lady Eleanor Talbot the real and rightful Queen of England? I am so shocked and bewildered that I do not know what to think. I always feared the Woodville marriage was suspect, because it was clandestine, which is no way for a King of England to be wed. Now it seems that the woman was never more than his mistress, bearing him an illegitimate brood. Oh, how I would like to tell her so. My glee would not be concealed! Although I am sorry for the children, for this was not their fault.

Heaven alone knows how this must be affecting Richard, because if it is proved to be the truth, then—George having destroyed himself and his line—Richard is the rightful King of England? He is the only remaining son of my father, the noble Duke of York, and he is the most senior true born prince of our House. To say nothing of the truly good king he would be.

(Song: THE LORD PROTECTOR)

(6)

Cecily, Duchess of York, to her daughter . . . .

I write this letter on 7th day of July in 1483, the first Year of King Richard III, and am still overwhelmed with joy that yesterday, by the Grace of God, Richard was crowned King of England. And at his side Anne was crowned queen. The service was conducted in English*! He is the first King of England to use the language of his land. I am so proud that I fear I might burst of it.*

Of course, this means that my eldest son, Edward IV, was indeed a bigamous lord, and had indeed intended his baseborn offspring to occupy the throne. Shame stains my heart that he could have done this, but pride shines around me when I think of yesterday. It was by far the most well-attended coronation of which anyone knows, and the fanfares were surely the most splendid and inspiring. England has a strong new king.

(Song: FANFARE FOR THE KING)
(7)
From Margaret, Duchess of Burgundy, to her mother . . . .

To my most respected and loved mother, greetings. It is the first day of April in the Year of Grace, 1485, the sun shines and the spring flowers are in their glory, but there can only be great sadness in our hearts because of the tragic news. My poor, beloved brother Richard, to have first his little son taken from him, and now his wife, whom he surely loved throughout his life. Now he is a widower, beset by enemies and disloyalty. So much is expected of him, but I know he will do all he can to meet his duties. No king has ever been more dedicated to the welfare of his realm, yet I hear more and more of that maggot Henry Tudor, who calls himself Earl of Richmond, and is a Lancastrian with a presumptuous eye to the throne. He will never defeat Richard, or be worthy of challenging him. Plague take the name Tudor!

But I must write of Richard's dearest Anne. She was never strong—her sister, George's duchess Isabel was not either—and the blow dealt to Anne on the death of her only child must have been insupportable. I am not a mother, but I have yearned for that happy state. If I were to then lose my child, I do not know how I could continue to live. Anne could not continue, and went to her Maker, leaving Richard alone. Never was a king more isolated and without comfort.

(Song: THE LADY ANNE NEVILLE)
(8)
Cecily, Duchess of York, to her daughter.

August, in the Year of Ill Grace, 1485. Oh, my beloved daughter, after such terrible news, how can I possibly offer you greetings? I still cannot believe that Richard is dead. The dearest and most loving of all my boys, and set to be the greatest king England has known. Yes, I do not hesitate to make that claim, for greatness was within him. May God curse forever the name of Bosworth Field, and all those who set themselves against the true and anointed King of England.

I do not know how to tell you of my distress when I received word of the Tudor's advance from Wales, marching his foreign army, his army of French invaders, across the harvest fields of England. They trampled the good crops and cared not for the damage and harm they did to the people. And all in the cause of ridding the land of a tyrant and usurper. Richard? How can any of these evil fools believe that? No lord was more generous and fair, more informed and concerned about his people.

Henry Tudor cares for nothing and no one except himself, and we have his chienne *of a mother to thank for that. I now loathe Margaret Beaufort, who is of baseborn stock, even more than I did before, and God alone knows I have always despised her. Henry Tudor is the spawn of rape, and his father was a monstrous chimera begat in as much shame as he passed on to his only child. There is nothing trueborn on either side of Tudor's low stock, and I am told he has an evil eye, which is the Almighty's sign of his wickedness. Oh, Margaret, send a thousand and more prayers for Richard's dear soul. May he be at peace with his Maker. And may the crops in the field grow again in his memory.*

(Song: THE WHEAT IN THE FIELD)

(9)

Margaret. Duchess of Burgundy, to her mother

The first day of September, in the abominable year of 1485. My sweet and revered lady, I will not greet you with any joy, even though you are my most honoured and adored mother, because I share your grief for Richard. This will be a very short letter, because even as I write, there are minstrels playing. A pretty melody, but from this day, whenever I hear it, I will think of Richard, who loved music but will never hear this. But Tudor will. May God rot his dark, treacherous soul.

An afterthought: Pray tell me it is not true that he is to marry Edward's eldest daughter, Elizabeth. How will she be able to bear surrendering herself to the Tudor toad?

(Instrumental: TUDOR DANSE)

(10)

Cecily, Duchess of York, to her daughter . . . .

To my daughter, Margaret, a million warm words of consolation, even though they have to be hollow. Yes, it is true about my granddaughter Elizabeth, whom they call "of York". I do not speak of her, for she is willing, maybe even eager to be Queen of England. It matters not who may be the king! She protests that the marriage will unite York and Lancaster after so many years of strife, but to me she is little more than a traitress.

On to more important matters. When I thought the situation could not be worse than Richard's death, I have now learned far more of that wicked day at Bosworth. He was betrayed. Yes, his so-called allies drove knives into his back, and thus Tudor won, through infamy and shame. There was still more ignominy when Richard's naked body was displayed for all to see, and then he was hurriedly buried in Greyfriars, Leicester. A King of England in a mean, secretive grave.

The Stanleys were most to blame, and Northumberland, and others. They did it for personal gain, not because they believed Tudor was the true king. I only pray that Tudor is fearful for his future, because lords who will betray their king once, will surely do it again.

Richard stands accused of many foul deeds, including the murders of his Woodville nephews. Can you believe it? Richard? A killer of children? He was too honourable a man to even think of such a terrible recourse. Oh, there are other vile charges, and they even exaggerate his poor back, naming him hunchback! I wept when first I heard it, and now I weep again. Never has any good man been more tragically maligned. Never.

(Song: THE HOUSE OF YORK)

(11)

Margaret, Duchess of Burgundy, to her mother . . . .

The last day of October, 1485. Hallowtide. To my dear mother, greetings. How almost amusing it is that Richard is accused of murdering his nephews, when he saved them from death at the hands of others. The Woodvilles sought them, in order to rule through them, but Margaret Beaufort, her brother Sir John Welles, the unlamented Duke of Buckingham and even Henry Tudor himself have reason to want them dead.

But I can confide in you now, Richard having sworn me to the utmost secrecy. The boys live. They lead quiet, safe, comfortable lives here, and do not speak evil of their uncle. They will lack for nothing, Richard saw to that, and their futures will be well-to-do and pleasing. He treated them handsomely, and was sad for what he had to do by accepting the crown himself. Nothing he said, not one word, set their hearts against him. They knew they were baseborn, because their heartless mother told the youngest boy the truth, when she had him in sanctuary. Now both boys blame her and their father, but never Richard.

(Song: THE MYSTERY OF THE PRINCES)

(12)

Cecily, Duchess of York, to her daughter . . . .

Every greeting to you, daughter. My heart is still heavy as I write to you this Christmastide of 1485. The first Christmastide of the reign of King Henry VII, who is the most cold-hearted gargoyle it has ever been my misfortune to encounter.

However, it is not of him that I write now, but of his father-in-law, the odious Lord Stanley, who is soon to be Earl of Derby, no less. Oh, the misfortune of that poor county.

Minstrels are playing in the hall, a fashionable melody that is entitled "Sans charger". What did this exquisite music do that it should bear the motto of that felon, Stanley?

(Instrumental: SANS CHARGER)

(13)

Margaret, Duchess of Burgundy, to her mother . . . .

To my dearest, most noble mother, greetings. I feel so far away from you, but am with you in spirit. I know how it breaks your heart to know that all your dear sons have been taken from you, but especially how you suffer for losing Richard.

I know too that Tudor is busying himself with blackening not only the name of Richard, but of the House of York itself. Those who had shown support for the White Rose are punished, attainted, condemned.

At this time I know it all seems so hopeless. Everything has been lost. But one day, far in the future, maybe, the truth will out, and people will begin to think twice about Tudor . . . and thus see the true Richard. There will be folk who look beyond the lies and view Richard again, in a clear and honest light. He will garner fresh support, and be recognised for the great and honourable lord he was. When he was murdered on the field of battle, England was condemned to Tudor rule. Which God alone knows how long it will endure. The tyrant already has a son by Elizabeth, and that son will have a son, and so it will go on. But our day will come, Mother. My heart tells me so.

(Song: THE FELLOWSHIP OF THE WHYTE BOAR)
(14)

Cecily, Duchess of York, to her daughter . . . .

My agents have returned to me with word of Richard's last resting place. I dare not go there myself, for Henry Tudor is a great venomous spider with a poisonous web that covers the once glorious realm of Yorkist England. Duchess or not, I would be his prey. It would not matter to him that I am his offspring's great-granddam. See how badly he treats the Woodville woman, and she is their grandmother.

Richard's grave was the very best the good brothers of Greyfriars could provide, and they buried him with all the respect at their disposal. They dared not do more, for fear of arousing Tudor's wrath. So there my dearest son lies, and will be lost forever in the coming centuries. I know it. But it will be my prayer that Tudor's lies will one day be exposed for the foul fiction that they are – and he for the tyrannical and cruel miser that he undoubtedly is. Oh, those traitors who deserted Richard are now regretting their self-seeking decision. For that at least I thank Tudor.

One day, daughter, there will be people who will defend the name of Richard III, and fight to not only restore his stolen honour, but to find him again, and see him laid to rest as a King of England should be. This I implore of Almighty God, as I also pray that from the portals of Heaven itself, I will see the great day when right-thinking and honest people will be able to show their love and deference to Richard III, King of England and France and Lord of Ireland. My son. Your brother.

(Song: THE KING IN THE CAR PARK)

Lord Zarquon and Sandra Heath Wilson taking a break from recording the narratives for the Tant le Desiree album.

Appendix Three
A Collection of Photos

Playing guitar in Chapter 29 in the summer of 1983, probably at Torquay town hall.

Playing bass guitar for the recordings of the tunes written by Graham Moores which eventually appeared on the Wonderclock album.

A photo of four of the members of the original line up of the Phoenix ceilidah band taken at a rehearsal in Kennford village hall, from left to right, Nigel Skinner, Mary Howells, Ian Churchward and Nigel Howells.

Mike Middleton playing bass guitar on the recording of 'York City Fair' in my basement at Rock Lee in Torquay, sometime during 2013. Mike used to play bass guitar in a Torbay band called Arthur's Other Tortoise in the 1980's.

My son Tom playing melodeon on a recording of one of my songs, either 'Richard Liveth Yet' or 'Tewkesbuy Tale'.

A collage of Legendary Ten Seconds photos created by my friend
Judy Jacobs. Camilla Joyce is trying to play my mandolin. This
instrument is featured on 'The Battle of Barnet' song. I am holding
my mandola next to Camilla which I have used on quite a few of my
recordings after I recorded it for the first time on the 'Gold it Feels
so Cold'.

Rob Bright on electric lead guitar with myself playing acoustic rhythm guitar at a fund raising gig for Torquay museum on a Saturday evening, 5th March 2016. The Legendary Ten Seconds were supported by the Renaissance Folk band.

Chris Greenway wearing a Richard III t shirt.

Appendix Four
Ian's Ricardian Quiz

This a not to be taken very seriously Richard III quiz to test your knowledge after reading my book!

1) What was the name of Richard III's horse?

Is it

a) White Slurrey
b) Champion the wonder horse
c) Black Beauty
d) Muffin the mule
e) White Surrey

2) With which of these do you associate the Princes in the tower?

Is it

a) Blackpool tower
b) The tower of London
c) The Eifel tower
d) Alton towers
e) The hanging gardens of Babylon

3) Which one of these was Richard III's castle?

Is it

a) The Elephant and Castle
b) Castle Cary
c) Middleham Castle
d) Muddleham Castle
e) A sand castle

4) What was the name of Richard III's wife?

Is it

a) Queen of the South
b) Anne Neville
c) Anne of green gables
d)Annie get your gun
e) Anne Boleyn

5) Who won the battle of Bosworth?

Is it

a) No one it was a draw
b) Henry VII
c) Leicester City Football Club
d) Bosworth Cricket Club

6) What was Richard III's name?

Is it

a) Richard I

b) Richard II
c) Richard III

7) How many songs has Ian Churchward written about Richard III

Is it

a) 10
b) 20
c) 30.2
d) More than 32
e) Too many

8) Did Richard III suffer with a back problem?

Is it

a) Yes he had scoliosis
b) No but Henry VII was a pain in the neck

9) What is a Stanley knife?

Is it

a) A knife for DIY
b) You use it to stab someone in the back

10) What was Richard III's motto?

Is it

a) Loyalty binds me
b) I'm alright Jack
c) The old jokes are the best
d) See you later alligator

About the Author

Ian Churchward's main hobby is music and he has played guitar in several bands in South Devon. He started recording as the Legendary Ten Seconds when he was the lead guitar player of The Morrisons who were featured on John Peel's radio one show back in 1987. Ian lives with his wife in Torquay and is a keen supporter of his local football club

Read more at www.thelegendary10seconds.co.uk.